M000279724

Praise for *No Harmle*

"A biography that reads like a great a[...]
of freedom-fighting and myth-making in early twentieth-
century Eastern Europe is as entertaining as it is necessary."
—Stephanie Feldman, author of *Angel of Losses* and *Saturnalia*

"Charlie Allison has turned his talents to a topic that was colorful
and interesting even before recent global events gave Ukraine fresh
relevance. Allison's accessible and humorous writing saturates the
book with passages that are chock-full of the sort of informational
nuggets that readers will enjoy passing along to friends and family."
—Matt Hongoltz-Hetling, author of *A Libertarian Walks into a Bear*

"Charlie Allison's examination of Nestor Makhno's life is the most
well-researched and cool-headed assessment I have read. Makhno's
idealism was matched by his skills as a military strategist, his
growing political sophistication and his commitment to Ukrainian
independence. His revolutionary ideas were innovative and effective,
and he remains a great Ukrainian hero both for his courage and
for his intelligence. How Ukrainian history might have played out
through the twentieth century had Trotsky and his fellow Bolsheviks
not betrayed Makhno is of particular and urgent interest to today's
political students and commentators. Allison's research is both more
thorough than anything we have seen for many years and displays the
reality behind the myth of this Ukrainian hero. I cannot recommend
it more enthusiastically. To read Allison today is to understand
not only yesterday's conflicts but also tomorrow's politics."
—Michael Moorcock, author of the Pyat Quartet
and *London Peculiar and Other Nonfiction*

"*No Harmless Power* is an exhilarating ride through the revolutionary
life and times of Nestor Makhno. With wry humor, original research,
and an unforgettable cast of characters, Charles Allison gives a
vivid account of a tumultuous period in the history of Ukraine
and the Russian Revolution that ripples to the present day."
—Tauno Biltsted, author of *The Anatomist's Tale*

No Harmless Power

The Life and Times of the Ukrainian
Anarchist Nestor Makhno

Charlie Allison

With illustrations by N.O. Bonzo and Kevin Matthews

BTL

No Harmless Power: The Life and Times of the Ukrainian Anarchist Nestor Makhno
Charlie Allison
With illustrations by N.O. Bonzo and Kevin Matthews

This edition © PM Press
All rights reserved. No part of this book may be transmitted by any means without permission in writing from the publisher.

ISBN: 978–1–62963–471–5 (paperback)
ISBN: 979–8–88744–032–3 (hardcover)
ISBN: 978–1–62963–679–5 (ebook)
Library of Congress Control Number: 2022942472

Cover illustration and design by N.O. Bonzo
Interior design by briandesign

10 9 8 7 6 5 4 3 2 1

PM Press
PO Box 23912
Oakland, CA 94623
www.pmpress.org

First published in Canada in 2023 by
Between the Lines
401 Richmond Street West, Studio 281, Toronto, Ontario M5V 3A8, Canada
1-800-718-7201
www.btlbooks.com
ISBN: 978–1–77113–643–3

Printed in the USA.

Contents

"The bandit hero—the underdog rebel—so frequently becomes the political tyrant; and we are perpetually astonished! Such figures appeal to our infantile selves—what is harmful about them in real life is that they are usually immature, without self-discipline, frequently surviving on their 'charm.' Fiction lets them stay, like Zorro or Robin Hood, perpetually charming. In reality they become petulant, childish, relying on a mixture of threats and self-pitying pleading, like any baby. These are too often the revolutionary figures on whom we pin our hopes, to whom we sometimes commit our lives and whom we sometimes try to be; because we fail to distinguish fact from fiction. In reality it is too often the small, fanatical men with the faces and stance of neurotic clerks who come to power while the charismatic heroes, if they are lucky, die gloriously, leaving us to discover that while we have been following them, imitating them, a new Tsar has manipulated himself into the position of power and Terror has returned with a vengeance while we have been using all our energies living a romantic lie. *Heroes betray us. By having them, in real life, we betray ourselves.*"

—Michael Moorcock, "Starship Stormtroopers"

A Japanese Anarchist in Paris (1923)

> "Even we in our success-worshipping culture can recognize the nobility and poignancy of those eager, outrageous, uncalculating men whose purity of purpose doomed them to a hard journey leading ultimately to disaster."
>
> —Ivan Morris

Ōsugi Sakae—Japanese agitator, translator, linguist, brawler, activist, author, free-love advocate, and anarchist—could slip the traces of his secret police detail in the same way that you or I would kick off a pair of well-loved slippers before bed. This he did, stowing away to China to get a false identity and papers to let him enter France without the Japanese or French governments being any the wiser.[1]

He arrived in Paris in early 1923 and immediately charged into trouble. The picaresque adventures of Ōsugi in Paris have been covered in far more detail elsewhere, but a brief summary will do. Ōsugi stayed in brothels, hostels in filthy conditions, reading in poor light till his eyes grew red and puffy. When he wasn't reading he battled horrific French tenement plumbing (or lack thereof), faked his identification and bluffed the police when they questioned him, pickpocketed his fake ID back from police in the middle of a May Day celebration in Saint Denis (which he radicalized and went to prison for), tried to sneak across the border to Germany, and wrote bawdy postcards featuring naked ladies to his comrades in Japan.[2]

Suffice to say, Ōsugi was a very, very busy man during his unpleasant months in Paris. The only upside to France as far as Ōsugi was concerned was its prisons, which he saw the inside of fairly quickly after being arrested for incitement on May Day. Ōsugi was allowed to order food and wine from nearby restaurants to be delivered to his cell. In prison he gained a measure of privacy, a writing desk, and even an excellent blanket—all improvements over his boarding house in Belleville.[3] Ōsugi gave the impression that life in prison was far more comfortable for him than life in the French tenements. But he left prison eventually and continued the work he had set out to do.

Ōsugi was looking for Nestor Ivanovich Makhno—or more specifically, anyone who had known him, since Makhno's whereabouts were in flux after the fall of the anarchist polity unofficially called the Free Territory of Ukraine (or Makhnovia), in 1921. There was a conference scheduled for April in Berlin, where Voline, one of the higher-level survivors of the Makhnovschina (time of Makhno, roughly translated), would be in attendance.[4] Ōsugi was zealously eager to attend the Berlin conference to learn what he could from the man who had once stood very high indeed in Nestor Makhno's confidences.

Admiration for Makhno in Asia was hardly limited to Ōsugi Sakae. Hatta Shūzō, a renowned translator and formidable anarcho-communist theorist in his own right, kept a framed picture of Nestor Makhno on his writing desk.[5] Later in the 1920s, the Korean People's Association in Manchuria (KPAM), a group of Korean anarchists, would rally under the charismatic generalship of Kim Chwa-chin (dubbed "the Nestor Makhno of Korea") to resist the scourge of Japanese imperialism and create a stateless polity.[6] It lasted two years under attack on all sides by the Japanese, Stalinists, and Chinese nationalists. After Kim Chwa-chin's assassination, the anarchists went underground inside Korea to resist the Japanese till the end of the Second World War and then to fight the American-installed dictatorship in the south until its collapse in the 1970s.[7]

Ōsugi spent his free time in Paris in poverty and hounded by police. Nestor Makhno, when he arrived in Paris a few years later with his wife and daughter, would spend the remains of his life in similar circumstances. Like Makhno, Ōsugi wrote ceaselessly about matters that were important to him and his anarchist beliefs—specifically about Nestor Makhno and the anarchist movement in Ukraine.

Ōsugi was under constant scrutiny in Paris. The French culture he was told was one of the most open in the world was engulfed in post–World War I paranoia. Any sort of dissension was taken by the authorities to be proof positive that the speaker was in league with the perfidious

Germans, and seeking to undermine French morale with talk of strikes or collective action against the government repressions.[8]

In another bit of bad news for Ōsugi, the anarchist conference in Berlin had been moved from April to August. Ōsugi was already low on funds, and this didn't help matters—it made his illegal presence in France more difficult to maintain and conceal. Still, he wrote and wrote.

Ōsugi's writings on Makhno (started in Europe and finished in Japan after Ōsugi was deported there) can be seen as a time capsule of what a determined polyglot from a non-European country could have gathered about Makhno and the Makhnovschina with the information available. Considering all the obstacles and rumors in his way, while not free from errors, it is a fairly accurate document. It tells us a lot about its author, the state of

Ōsugi Sakae, 1921. Ōsugi was a tireless agitator with a theatrical flair, prominently involved in the Rice Riots of 1918. He was a moving orator, a student of languages, and an inveterate reader and writer who relished fistfights, evading the police, and free love. Had he and Makhno met in Paris, it seems rather likely that they would have gotten along, at least for a little while.

information available, and the attitudes regarding Makhno amid the wider anarchist community.

Ōsugi wrote of Nestor Makhno as the instinctive embodiment of the revolutionary power of the peasants of Ukraine: "It is not that the anarchist Makhno first created Makhnovshchina, but the revolutionary riots based on the instinctive self-defense of Ukrainian people brought Makhno forward as a hero. And his revolutionary characteristics and his anarchist ideology exactly matched the nature of these movements, making him the most prominent person in the movement." Ōsugi definitely is guilty of idealizing and heroizing Nestor Ivanovich Makhno in his work.

After all, he never met Makhno in person, nor any member of the upper levels of the Makhnovist movement. Some of the idolization of

Makhno can be attributed to Ōsugi's personality—he preferred the fiery, apostolic writings of Bakunin to the more measured and scientific style of his successor Kropotkin, though he translated both anarchists' writings into Japanese. Makhno had met the elderly Kropotkin in Moscow and been impressed by the stately "Prince of Anarchism" in his final years.

However, Ōsugi loved people of action—fitting, since he was one himself, and his ego was of a more than comfortable size. It is easy to see why the dashing portrait that Ōsugi sketched of Makhno's battle against Ukrainian nationalists, Bolsheviks, the Austro-Hungarians, and the White Army would assume more Robin Hood–like dimensions than the bitter realities of the brutal world war that became the Russian Civil War.

There was truth to some of this characterization—Makhno was a moral person, stuck in deeply immoral times, who did his best to adhere to a form of "revolutionary ethics."[9] The same could not be said for Lenin or Trotsky of the Bolsheviks, Denikin or Wrangel of the White Army, or Petliura or Grigoriev of the Nationalists and Cossacks respectively, who not only ordered purges of dissidents, but encouraged wholesale slaughter and rapine, pogrom after pogrom.

In Ōsugi's view, by leading the struggle against monarchism, imperialism, and centralized power through military means, expropriations, and education, Makhno was advancing the cause of anarchism and spreading direct democracy and socialized land throughout Ukraine.

In "Nestor Makhno: Anarchist General," Ōsugi writes:

> Makhno's propaganda was employed at every front line of his army and has grown into a great public movement by Ukrainian peasant workers. Makhno was called Bat'ko Makhno (Father Makhno) by these workers and he, himself, often used this name. Thus, this public movement started to become popular by the name of Makhnovshchina even outside of Ukraine.
>
> Wherever Makhnovshchina was adopted, first, a Soviet was freely elected and organized in each village. It made decisions on all the lives in the village. Lands were expropriated from landowners and distributed to the farmers. The farmers cultivated these lands independently or cooperatively.
>
> Whenever the Cossack soldiers around the Don River increased their forces and seemed to threaten the farmers' lives, villages of Makhnovshchina held a general meeting and mobilized several

numbers of partisans from each village. The mobilized farmers gathered under the Makhno force, but when it became free from danger, they returned to their villages to work peacefully again.[10]

Combined with several brilliant military victories over armies with superior numbers and firepower, it is hard not to view Makhno as a legendary heroic figure. He robbed the rich to feed the poor, then taught the poor to arm themselves. He dynamited prisons so they could never be rebuilt, after freeing all caged there. He liberated women and teachers, peasants, and radicals from chains and fought the forces that wanted to establish a new dictatorship or restore the old.

That is a heavy weight for any one man to bear, and Makhno, like anyone of flesh and blood, could not hold all the ideas and ideals thrown onto his shoulders. Every heroic pedestal has a weak base—in this case, the decentralized nature of the Black Army that Makhno led meant that massacres and horrors occurred as some people joined the army to settle personal scores, loot their peers, or commit pogroms. Makhno, unlike almost every other power in the Civil War, executed pogromists on sight— which didn't stop the Bolsheviks from smearing him as one after his escape from the Civil War.

Yet for all his gushing over Makhno's dash, derring-do, and principled adherence to anarchism, Ōsugi also noted that the larger anarchist movements ranged from indifferent to mildly hostile to the Makhnovschina. There was real fear among the anarchists of the Russian Civil War—and beyond—that Nestor Makhno's charismatic pull would lead to a dictatorship of personality, vanguardism, and repression based on personal power. Makhno was impulsive, brusque, and had little patience for explanations in the case of Bolshevik or White Army spies in his camp, and was willing to cut corners to make sure those so labeled were executed quickly and at times without trial. Other anarchists considered Makhno's unilateral behavior disturbingly Leninesque and as footing for a possible power grab. The anarcho-syndicalists of Russia refused to endorse Makhno or his movement in the Ukraine.

Even the Nabat Confederation of Anarchists, which had close ties to Makhno, stated, as quoted by Ōsugi: "[The] Makhnovshchina is not an anarchism movement and an anarchism movement is not equal to Makhnovshchina."[11] The anarchist's greatest enemy is the idea of coercive power itself, no matter who wields it or what they call themselves.

It is nearly impossible to read Ōsugi's account of Makhno without thinking of Ivan Morris's classic work *The Nobility of Failure*. Morris considers the role of the "tragic hero" in Japanese culture specifically—why heroes that failed in their laudable goals are especially treasured by Japanese storytellers and the public alike. The failure of the anarchist projects in Ukraine—especially the Makhnovschina—has a tragic element to it in Ōsugi's telling that persists in subsequent accounts.

For Ōsugi Sakae in 1922, the fate of the Makhnovschina was sealed—but not necessarily that of Makhno, who was in the wind (that is, on trial in Poland at the time of Ōsugi's writing). The future was undefined—the tragic hero's fate uncertain, and it wasn't impossible that the exiled Makhno could return to lead the cause of anarchism to glory. Supremely unlikely, certainly, but the promised return of tragic heroes—King Arthur, Yoshitsune, Saigō Takamori, Makhno—is key to their appeal and immortality.

Ōsugi's study of Makhno and the Makhnovschina had far-reaching effects on Japanese anarchism and communism. It further cemented Ōsugi's distrust of the Japanese Bolsheviks—the authoritarian left, a hierarchical and dogmatic graft from the tree of Lenin, Trotsky, and Stalin. Such people, Ōsugi concluded, correctly, could never be trusted with the task of social revolution or building a stateless society: "The Moscow government could never approve this self-government or autonomy by the people. The statement by Marx 'the emancipation of the working class must be conquered by the working class themselves,' and the statement by Lenin 'All Power to the Soviets' were downright lies of Marxism which was originally nationalism. Marxism never permitted people to create their own destiny by themselves."

Alliances of convenience with the Bolsheviks were far too costly to be justified in any anarchist or socialist social revolution—as Makhno's experience, twice betrayed by the Bolsheviks—had clearly shown. Makhno's deepening suspicion and continued railing against the perfidy of the Bolsheviks made the anarchist-Bolshevik split—already widening in Japan—an uncrossable chasm. The Japanese government took brutally repressive steps against any left-wing philosophy and certainly wasn't above murder and intimidation. Right-wing terrorism was A-OK by them, but any sort of activism to better the conditions of non-elites, whether that be syndicalism, communism, socialism, or anarchism—was ruthlessly crushed under the imperial jackboot.

Ōsugi, his long-time partner Ito Noe, and their nephew were strangled in cold blood by the Japanese police forces mere months after his return to

Japan from Europe in the hellish aftermath of the Great Kanto Earthquake in September 1923.[12]

Ōsugi Sakae became a martyr for Japanese anarchism and joined the ranks of fallen heroes—remembered, memorialized, written about, dramatized, mythologized, misunderstood, ignored, and appropriated by the peoples of the earth to suit their various needs. It is the nature of heroes to be everything to everyone.[13] The generation before Ōsugi Sakae's had the legendary Saigō Takamori (who is discussed at length in Ivan Morris's aforementioned work)—savior of the ancient way of the samurai class in a modernizing age to some, a modernizer and pacifist to others, one of the only people to rise against the new Meiji government and die in combat— and then be canonized for it by the state that desperately sought legitimacy and a popular expression of patriotic passion. Even today, Saigō is loved by both the far right (for his alleged patriotism) and the far left (for his somewhat paternalistic brand of "proto-socialism").

Nestor Ivanovich Makhno died in 1934 in Paris, exhausted and covered in scars of all kinds. But the stories of him as a hero, revolutionary, small god of anarchism, demonic force inflamed by the fires of burning mansions and prisons, bandit, liberator, drunk, and idealist—those live on. Those myriad phantoms of history overshadow the man they sprang from while the man himself is forgotten. Makhno's mythology has consumed him after his death, reducing him to a catchphrase and proto-meme. In 2013, Ukraine issued a commemorative coin bearing Nestor Makhno's face on it—that same face is found, without a shred of irony, on memorials commemorating nationalist causes. Fascists and nationalists try to brand themselves as Makhnovists to capture popular support even as Bolshevik and Marxist diehards busy themselves with labeling Makhno a kulak and bandit at once.

Makhno dead is everyone's saint and everyone's boogeyman.

That sounds far too serious, far too mythical, far too full of straw and not enough of heart and bone and veins for my taste, so let us go and explore the world of Nestor Makhno, the slight fellow from Huliaipole. Let us start with one of the myths that made him and shaped him.

Pugachev's Uprising and Beyond: Setting the Stage for Makhno's Ukraine (1772–1861)

> "The passive fruition of heroic deeds always produces myths, tales for adults that the frustrating conditions of life demand nonstop, prostheses that help one to carry on living in just the same way as alcohol or sleeping pills do."
>
> —Alfredo M. Bonanno

Catherine the Great had plenty of trouble running the rapidly expanding Russian Empire in 1773 without her ex-husband, Czar Peter III, coming back from the dead. She had enough on her plate as an enlightened despot. An enlightened despot is a ruler who makes protestations of individual human rights and liberty, but mostly values the unimpeachable privilege of the absolute monarch to rule over those self-same people with an iron fist and conquer bits of what is now Poland—enslaving people in the name of freedom. Joining Catherine in the "enlightened monarch club" were such luminaries as Frederick of Prussia and Joseph II of Austria.[1]

Enlightened or not, Catherine the Great was in a delicate situation: she was in her fifth year of a war with the Ottomans, a long-running hot-and-cold war with the Cossack Hetmanate in modern-day Ukraine, and there were intriguing calls for even further expansion coming from the far east in what was being called "Unalaska." The Russian Empire under Catherine the Great was expanding in every possible direction.

October 1773 brought more headaches to Catherine in the form of reports from the hinterlands. A man claiming to be her dead ex-husband Peter III was leading a host of Cossacks and serfs across the land and laying waste to noble estates, boasting that he would overthrow Catherine the Great's reign and put everything to rights. The rebellions that followed would be a serious challenge to her rule over the Russian Empire, and took advantage of her lack of popular legitimacy.

The 1773 rebellions were led by an illiterate Cossack named Emelian Pugachev. He claimed to be Catherine's husband, miraculously escaped from her coup, and the rightful czar of all Russia. Of course, Emelian Pugachev didn't just sidle up to everyone he met and remark casually: "I know I look rough, like a Cossack, got a few teeth missing, but I'm really Charles Peter Ulrich of Schleswig-Holstein-Gottorp, or Czar Peter III for short, the rightful czar."

There is no way of confirming whether, like the original Czar Peter, Pugachev also wore boots to bed and played with his collection of dolls before going to sleep—just two of the habits that had doubtless made it easier for Catherine to have her one-time husband killed with a clear conscience.[2]

Before we continue with this tale, it's worth noting that during Catherine the Great's rule, no less than twenty or so people claimed to be her ex-husband the czar and led rebellions against her.[3] This also means that Catherine the Great could add to her list of titles "most amount of ex-husbands"—even if she never met most of them, almost all met with tragic deaths.

Pugachev had been a Cossack under contract to the Russian Empire during one of their countless wars before deciding he had better things to do and deserting. A Don Cossack by birth and marriage, he for reasons that are unclear, did not choose to return to his wife and three daughters. This did not endear him to the Don Cossacks, who took a dim view of a man who would abandon his family.

But Emelian Pugachev was a charismatic sort, and as he wandered down the lower Volga River, he got a good sense of the popular mood.

It was a distinctly anti-Catherine mood.

The stocky, muscular Pugachev couldn't be mistaken for the tall gangly and German-speaking Czar Peter III. But Russia was large and the official portraits hadn't had much time to spread Peter's likeness through the empire thanks to his short rule, so most people went along with Pugachev's claim to czardom.

And besides, people *wanted* to believe. Peter III hadn't ruled for a long time, but during that brief period he'd abolished the salt tax, liquidated the secret police, and forbid merchants from selling serfs into factory labor. He was remembered as a good czar.

So the ground was well prepared for Pugachev's announcement that he was in fact the czar—the second time around anyway. The first announcement of his czardom—in the Urals, pitched to the Yaik Cossacks who resented the Russians for conscripting them—didn't go over well. Disguised as a fish merchant, Pugachev revealed himself as the one true czar before the Cossacks—-and was promptly arrested by the Russians and jailed in Kazan. Undeterred, he befriended a guard, escaped, and got right back to what he had been doing.[4]

For real this time, Pugachev declared himself Peter III! By gum, he was going to set things right! Despite being illiterate, he had someone write down an imperial manifesto in September 1773 that made the following points:

- Serfdom? Abolished!
- The pretender to the throne, Catherine? Thrown in a convent!
- All nobles? Cast down and all peasants freed!
- Persecution of Cossack Old Believers? That'd be stopped sharpish when Czar Peter III got the throne! Again!
- And amnesty for any crimes undertaken to place him on the throne as well![5]

Pugachev even promised a generous arms package to every Cossack that joined his mission to save Russia—salt, weapons, lead balls, and twelve rubles a year.

The Cossacks of the region, the Yaik Cossacks, already pretty cheesed off at Catherine's generals who'd kept them under their heel for some time now, thought this sounded like a pretty good idea and joined with Pugachev. They were then followed by seminomadic tribes from the area—Bashkirs, Kalmyks, Kirghiz—and local peasants with scavenged weaponry and farm tools.

Pugachev now had a small army, and he used it to attack a minor fort at Yaitsk, defying conventional strategy and attacking uphill with three hundred men against a garrison of about a thousand or so. This handicap/blunder scarcely mattered because the Cossack garrison either deserted their commander or joined Pugachev's side.[6]

By the time Pugachev reached the nearby city of Orenburg and its walls, he was commander of a force three thousand strong, lacking only artillery to break the fortress. So he elected to starve the garrison out, while sending out recruiters as far as their horses could carry them. Pugachev found a Russian Empire positively swollen with people eager to change Catherine the Great's feudal policies with the swing of a pick or pike. Miners, serfs, Cossacks, woodsmen, and steppe tribes. By the time Pugachev took Berda, he had a very strong regional army made up of many different groups. Only the Don Cossacks, who remembered Emelian Pugachev and were none too impressed with him for abandoning his wife and children to go adventuring, were unrepresented in this force.

Catherine treated this uprising as a joke at first and viewed Pugachev as a common outlaw. After all, he was leading a rabble of adventurers and serfs—how bad could it be? Besides, the serfs loved her! Catherine had made a few attempts to reform the Russian feudal system that kept thousands of serfs bound to the land. Catherine suggested more humane treatment for Russian serfs, but the nobles did not care for this one jot.

The Russian nobility clammed up at the first hint of infringement of what they saw as their ancestral rights to keep people as property. They refused to let the institution that was the basis of their wealth be altered in any meaningful way. Serfs came with the lands they were worked to death on, they were property not people. The nobility liked it that way. Feudalism was great for them.

To the nobles, Pugachev's uprising was proof of the validity of their outrage at Catherine's meddling: See what you get when you treat the serfs with anything less than an iron fist, they might have said. You get uprisings!

Given how much the very-much-German Catherine leaned on the nobility for both real power and to legitimate her coup-acquired reign, the result of this conflict was perfectly predictable.[7]

Catherine not only tolerated serfdom, but actively spread it through the expanding Russian Empire. Pugachev's rebellion only hardened the Russian upper classes' resistance to reforming or abolishing feudalism—the serfs' only opportunity to liberate themselves lay in the outlaw Pugachev's push against the empire.

Outlaw or not, Pugachev handily crushed the initial small forces that the Russian Empire mustered against him to lift the siege of Orenburg. General after general came up short against Pugachev's army and were either killed or forced to resign in shame when they were dismissed by a wave of the royal hand.

While promising to abolish the nobility, Pugachev wore the ornaments of monarchy well, issuing edicts with the aid of a secretary who wrote them down and distributed them. For Pugachev, each day during the siege of Orenburg was an opportunity to get drunk and sing Cossack songs, as well as to expand his wardrobe. He assembled a council of Cossack friends and gave them the names of the people whose lands they would take when they swept to victory. For example, if Catherine the Great had a noble in her entourage named, say, Count Orlov or Count Vorontsov—then one of Pugachev's Cossack advisors would take the name to save time. Pugachev would christen the man who would get that noble's land by the same name to avoid confusion—often to memorialize the occasion, gifts were given, including serfs.

This system and its often alcoholic inspiration was doubtless easier to remember than writing down who got what, and doubtless it made for a few good belly laughs between bawdy songs. On a related note, Pugachev also chose to get married to another Cossack woman (Ustinya Kuznetsova), since he was never going to return to the Don and his first wife and three daughters willingly.

Serfs flocked to join Pugachev's army—killing their landlords and overlords en masse. Gone in this moment was the traditional long-suffering serf, subservient to the Orthodox Church and the czar, as farmsteads and manors burned. The Pugachevshchina (time of Pugachev) had begun.

Pugachev's army and recruiters continued the push across the Russian Empire and towns that were in their way suffered as much as the landlords. Catherine's armies trying to break Pugachev's hold on the region viewed brutality as a first resort: the result was that both sides racked up atrocity after atrocity, rape after rape, and hanging after hanging. In such an environment of terror and smoke, the safe answer to the common question—"Who's side are you on?"—became "Whatever side you're on of course!"

Catherine's general du jour, Bibikov, arrived to break the two-month-long siege of Orenburg in late winter. Pugachev decided to fight the professional artillery of the Russian army head-on with an ad hoc army and paid for it with four thousand casualties and chaos. Faced with defeat, Pugachev and his inner circle got on their horses and fled over the Ural Mountains—leaving the peasants who had put their faith in him to be butchered like sheep by the Russian army.

Pugachev's concern for the peasants wasn't a deep well—it might barely have been a puddle. General Bibikov didn't survive long enough to savor his victory over Pugachev—he died of a fever at Orenburg.

Catherine breathed a sigh of relief—Pugachev's rebellion appeared to be over. She offered an amnesty for anyone who simply returned to life as before and turned her attention to other matters. For three months, that seemed to be correct, until Pugachev came storming back over the Urals in July 1774 with reinforcements—some twenty thousand men. And he said that he was coming to Moscow for the summer. Catherine's response can be imagined.

Pugachev's forces fell upon the critical city of Kazan and burned more than half of the city's buildings to the ground. The predictable actions of a sack—rapes, murders, robbery, and other horrors—followed at a massive scale. What nobles could escape fled to Moscow.

Pugachev's high point was in the ashes of Kazan. A Russian army—meant to support Kazan, but late—caught Pugachev unprepared outside the city and dealt him a stinging defeat, forcing him to flee down the Volga River. If this had not happened, it is very likely that Pugachev could have pushed his way through to Moscow, with serfs joining him along the way, and taken the capital, ending Catherine's reign.

Unfortunately, the land along the Volga had few serf-owning families, and so this natural source of reinforcement was denied to Pugachev. He was forced by circumstance to try and recruit from the people he had come from—the Don Cossacks.

The Don Cossacks largely ignored his pleas for men, horses, and guns. He was forced to content himself with hanging or shooting every nobleman his army could get its hands on, even as more and more of its members deserted.

Catherine the Great sent the eccentric but largely competent general, Panin, to deal with Pugachev. Even for Russian nobility, famous for its kookiness and idiosyncrasies, General Panin was something. He would wear his satin grey nightgown during the day in his headquarters, complete with a pink-ribboned nightcap floating around his head, for starters. No word on whether or not the good general wore that same getup to the battlefield or not. Panin got the support he needed to defeat Pugachev from the local nobles by pinky-swearing that they could keep all their privileges if only they gave him guns and money to stop this troublemaking Cossack. Unlike Bibikov, Panin was as brutal as Pugachev toward the peasants his army came across—threatening to quarter any peasant who had taken part in the revolts.

And of course, Pugachev knew General Panin a little—having previously served with him at the Siege of Bender back when Pugachev had fought for the Russian Empire.[8]

Pugachev's luck had finally run its course. The Don Cossacks publicly denounced him as a liar, deserter, and imposter, he was defeated in battle at Sarepta and his own lieutenants turned him in to General Panin for the reward money. Pugachev, to put it mildly, wasn't pleased to see his former commander in the least. Pugachev's suffering wasn't over. In late 1774, he arrived in Moscow. He had six weeks of interrogation, waiting in prison, and repeating himself ahead of him.

Voltaire, who was flitting about the court of Catherine the Great like some incredibly verbally ornate butterfly, suggested asking the distraught and exhausted Pugachev: "Sir, are you master or servant? I do not ask who employs you but simply whether you are employed."[9] Voltaire lingered under the impression that other people thought he was funny. He was so hilarious that he had to flee the court of Frederick the Great after he made one sidesplitter too many.

Pugachev immediately saw which way the wind was blowing and confessed in public that he was not in fact the true czar of Russia, to the surprise of nobody in Moscow.

Catherine the Great rather ostentatiously forbade the use of traditional torture on Pugachev during captivity, save for conversations with him. Their little chats—conducted through intermediaries on behalf of Catherine—quickly became rather repetitive. Catherine the Great would not stray from the subject of who was paying Pugachev to incite trouble in her kingdom. Was it Frederick the Great? The Ottomans? Who could possibly want Russia destabilized and its people out of their place?

Pugachev—who was having a really rotten couple of months—told the truth: nobody paid him to rabble-rouse. He barely had to do anything, really, just claim to be the true czar and people started cutting in line to join him. The peasants in particular didn't like being bound to the land and were happy for any promises to change their situation, to say nothing of the enterprising Cossacks.

Catherine the Great wasn't happy to hear this, as it reflected badly on her enlightened rule. She feared that executing Pugachev in the traditional manner, despite his public confession of nonczardom—might reignite the revolutionary tendencies of the peasants of Russia and spur new rebellions. Even in chains, Pugachev remained a source of trepidation for the empress. So Catherine resolved that he be treated gently: in the early days of 1775, Pugachev was beheaded before a cheering crowd, and then his hands were cut off. Small mercies. The Cossacks who betrayed their commander to Catherine were set free and pardoned.

With Pugachev very messily dead, Catherine and her government set about the intimidating task of covering up all memory of the largest peasant uprising against the Russian Empire to date. Catherine and the vast administrative apparatus of Imperial Russia did their utmost to utterly erase Pugachev's name and the memory of freed serfs. While Catherine declared a general amnesty and commuted future death sentences for involvement in the uprising, her generals (and the returning landlords) ignored that noble-intentioned order and brutalized what serfs they could find or coax back onto their estates.

The Yaik River was renamed the Ural River, and the Yaik Cossack Host was renamed the Ural Cossack Host. Pugachev's wife and children—who he had abandoned to chase dreams of personal glory with the happy after-effect of being perceived as a populist revolutionary—were imprisoned for the rest of their lives in Finland. Also exiled was the Cossack woman Pugachev had married during his rebellion. The winter nights must have just flown by.

The very name "Pugachev" was forbidden to be spoken aloud.[10] But even all this effort wasn't enough to erase the memory of rebellion, that orgasm of spontaneous revolt against the state. The name of Pugachev was still whispered by the peasants as a folk hero, like Robin Hood in Europe or the Cossack Stenka Razin before him in Ukraine.

Seen from a distance, the rebellion led by Pugachev gained a romantic quality it hadn't possessed in reality, along with a veneer of idealism. Pugachev dead was closer to a saint of the serfs and Cossacks than he had ever been in life. Rebellion en masse against the nobility—with tastes of success—would live in folktale and legend for over a century. Makhno was explicitly compared to Pugachev in a positive manner—leading the toilers, peasants, and oppressed against the rich and powerful and giving the land-hungry Ukrainians socialized soil.

But that intervening time—between Pugachev and Makhno—was marked by repression, not revolution. Catherine's next problem was filling all the land she had forcibly depopulated, especially in what is now Ukraine. Some of the territory could be filled with compliant Cossacks or lords and their households from the center of Russia transplanted to Ukraine.

The Hetmanate—rule of Ukraine by a confederation of Cossack hosts—was dissolved like a sugar cube through years of steady imperial pressures. Cossack poet and statesman Vasili Kapnist summarized Catherine the Great's policy in the Ukraine in 1782 in "An Ode to Slavery": "You burden them, you put chains on those who praise you."

Catherine the Great bought the services and loyalty of the Cossack hosts that could be won that way, ostracized those who could not, and sent the rest to fight the empire's enemies in the Ottoman Empire or Siberia. Many Cossack hosts went from acknowledging no authority but their own democratic forms to slowly turning into the attack dogs of the czars over several centuries.

Catherine the Great also took some time aside to deport/massacre the Crimean Tartar population of what is now Ukraine. Busy busy.

But that wouldn't be nearly enough to keep feudal policies—and finances—afloat. Russia under Catherine couldn't survive without serfdom, not if she wanted the support of the nobles. So Catherine and her son, Paul, began advertising for people outside of Russia to come settle it.

They found a receptive audience in the Germanic Mennonites, a religious minority seeking freedom from persecution. The empire was willing to do whatever it could to entice people to settle in Ukraine. Czar Paul's 1789–90 invitation to the Mennonites can be summarized as follows:

1. They would be free to practice their pacifist religion (as opposed to being forced to convert to Russian Orthodoxy).
2. Guaranteed land for each family that settled inside the empire.
3. Freedom to engage in trade.
4. They would have the right to make beer, vinegar, and brandy (privileges usually reserved for the Russian state).
5. Nobody could use Mennonite land unless the Mennonites said so.
6. They were exempt from compulsory military or civil service.
7. While they could not be compelled to billet troops or perform forced labor for the Crown, they were obligated to build roads and bridges.[11]

The vast majority of Ukrainian Mennonites were culturally German and wealthy or at least well-off landowners, a fact that remained true during Makhno's childhood. The lands that Mennonites, Russians, and wealthy Ukrainians owned were sold to them with serfs included. While serfdom was technically abolished in 1861, the Ukrainians were simply hired back for pennies to work the land of their bosses, a situation not entirely dissimilar to the failures of American Reconstruction after the Civil War.

The Russian Empire doubled down on serfdom during and after Catherine. Her protestations of enlightenment and universal human dignity were no match for her own love for power, which could only be assured with the support of the conservative nobles, military, and Orthodox Church. All of those institutions were in some way deeply invested in serfdom as a fact of Russian life—and even when it was abolished, the situation for the average Ukrainian peasant improved only marginally. It was this environment—of land-hungry peasants, folklore of heroic rebellions, incredible privation, and desperation that Nestor Makhno was born into.

CHAPTER 2

Makhno's Childhood (1888–1904)

> "Man is no exception in nature. He also is subject to the great principle of mutual aid which grants the best chances to those who support each other in the struggle for life."
>
> —Pyotr Kropotkin

Nestor Makhno was born so poor he couldn't afford a birthday. Even Nestor's birth year is a matter of debate. Various sources record his birth year as 1884, 1888, or 1889. The local church register places his birth as October 26–November 8, 1888.[1] This would have been news to Nestor—to the end of his life, he was ignorant as to his actual day of birth. He was born the youngest of five brothers, and you can be sure they never let him forget it.

Nestor Makhno's father's original surname was Mikhnenko, but Nestor shortened it to "Makhno" later in life.[2] In the course of the later revolution, Nestor would run into and nearly execute an official named Mikhno in neighboring Alexandrovsk.[3] Later still, in exile, Nestor would revert to his original surname, Mikhnenko.

Aren't names fun?

Nestor grew up in poverty, in a shack outside of the ten-thousand-strong Ukrainian city of Huliaipole, a major trading center in Ukraine. It sat close to (but not on) a major rail line that connected the cities of Alexandrovsk and Mariupol on the coast of the Sea of Azov and Ekaterinoslav near the Dnieper River. The land was rich, even if the famously land-poor Ukrainian peasant families were not.

The Makhno family couldn't even afford a pig, a staple of peasant life. If you didn't have a pig, to say nothing of chickens, you were truly in a bad way in Ukrainian farming society. The family would shiver in the winter and boil in the summers.

Nestor's father and mother had been serfs up until their liberation in the reforms of 1861. Eleven months after Nestor was born, his father perished. Makhno's mother, Evdokia Matveevna had been in the process of collecting bricks for a house during the preceding few years, and according to Makhno's diaries, "[She had] managed to put up some walls ... when my father died."[4] Bad luck turned to worse luck.

Things became so desperate for the widowed Evdokia Matveevna that she gave Nestor up for adoption to a childless (and significantly better off) neighboring family for a time. She only took him back when her other sons told her that Nestor was obviously miserable in his new home.[5] Her youngest was released back into her care.

Nestor's education began at around age eight. During winters he went to the local school, where he excelled at math and reading. It was at school that Nestor first was exposed to the theater. He had a gift for the dramatic. Later, he joined the actors' troupe and was apparently quite fond of performing—indeed the anarchist group, the Poor Peasants Union of Huliaipole would also put on productions in the town later in Nestor's life. Nestor would sometimes play the roles of female characters, complete with dressing in their clothes and makeup.

He would reprise this trick many years down the road during the Russian Civil War, in a military context, to conduct reconnaissance.[6] That old woman cracking sunflower seeds by the Mennonite self-defense force mustering in the town square?

Nestor Makhno in disguise!

The young woman out for a stroll with a bright shawl over her shoulders, surveying Red Army supply lines or artillery positions outside of a Ukrainian town?

Also Nestor Makhno!

Sometimes Nestor would dress as a "lost" member of the enemy forces—a White Army officer or a Red infantryman trying to get directions back to his unit—and collect information on his foes that way.

This just goes to show you—never underestimate theater kids. They'll fool you every time.

SKATING ON THE FROZEN HAICHUR RIVER

Little Nestor was an energetic child, and this energy swiftly got him into trouble on several occasions. He was scrawny, so he was picked on by larger boys. To retaliate, Nestor hid in the tree where the bullies liked to go and pelted them with rocks from above.[7] A nice little foretaste of the ambush tactics he would later master in life, perhaps they had their origins in outwitting bigger foes.

But the most notable of scrapes was an incident when he was eight years old and playing hooky from school during the winter. Skating on the frozen Haichur River, Nestor broke through the ice and nearly drowned. Ukrainian winters being what they are (which is to say, cold and severe), he was lucky to make it to his uncle's nearby home to recover from his unexpected hypothermic dip.

Of course, his mother, Evdokia Matveevna, was very understanding in the aftermath of her youngest son's falling-through-the-ice incident in her own way, with a severe beating being the medium of understanding. Her preferred tool for this was a knotted rope.[8] This fall into freezing water certainly did Nestor's lungs no favors, and combined with various maladies picked up in prison, was likely a factor in Makhno's death at age forty-five from tuberculosis, a respiratory disease.

Despite the beatings, Nestor was devoted to his mother and would remain so for as long as she was alive. In his memoirs, Makhno claims he remembered the name and face of a policeman who slapped his mother across the face for years, and once came within a whisker of shooting the man dead in the street.[9]

Makhno, unlike some historical figures I could mention (Lenin, Trotsky, Stalin), would later try to distinguish between people he personally hated and those who were threats to general social revolution or oppressors of the people. Often they were the same, but not always, and he personally strove to avoid confusing vengeance with justice.

For entertainment, Makhno's mother delighted in telling her youngest how much worse than awful things had been when she was a girl. She had been beaten twice by her master—"fifteen strokes with a whip."[10] To inform their offspring of how much worse things used to be is the prerogative of parents the world over, and a tradition unlikely to be interrupted as long as the human race exists. It was justified in Mama Makhno's case, as she grew up as a serf.

Then, for variety she would tell him stories of their Zaporozhian Cossack ancestors, of big men with bigger mustaches, on horses, being dashing, holding votes, and hitting people with their sabers. These semi-mythic stories constitute some of the few happy recollections of Makhno's early childhood in his autobiography.

However, being talented and energetic didn't necessarily mean that young Makhno stayed in school for long. He only got about four years of formal education, leaving to work full-time at age twelve. Nestor Makhno had many jobs in his childhood. An idle life wasn't on the table for Nestor or his brothers. His elder brothers labored at neighboring farms as hired hands, and, even with Nestor joining in, the family remained desperately poor. As he grew older and stronger, in addition to paid work, Nestor worked the family's four hectares plot (just short of ten acres) with a lone bedraggled horse.[11]

Ukrainian Mennonites, the major landowners in the area, were culturally German, having been granted lands in Ukraine by Catherine the Great and her son. Behold the power of tax breaks, the ability to brew your own alcohol (normally a state monopoly), and free land, among other things, to get people to move to a place like Ukraine. The Mennonites tended to view themselves as a people apart—colonists in a strange land. Makhno frequently found himself working on Mennonite estates, which could as large as hundreds of acres.

Nestor labored as a stable hand on Mennonite farms—grueling, brutal work. There was no shortage of dangers in this work. One could be kicked or bitten by an animal, faint from the summer heat and exertions of work, or be set upon by an overseer if one was thought to be slacking (or the overseer was bored). Nestor learned early on to avert his eyes when the overseers beat other workers and resigned himself to this simply being the way the world turned.

How could it ever be otherwise?

Consider this excerpt from a Mennonite landowner from this era, Toews, talking about his relationship with his "Southern Russian" (Ukrainian) farmhands: "If once in a while I'd hit an innocent one [farm worker] he didn't seem to mind much. All said I could do with my Russian personnel very much as I pleased. They loved me in spite of it all. Probably because they knew I meant them well. They wouldn't bear you a grudge because of one beating. This was their way of life."[12] Toews remained convinced that he "treated his workers humanely" and excoriated those damn Russian and Swiss landlords as treating their laborers worse than the Mennonites, which may very well have been true but is hardly the point.

At any rate, Toews's nickname in the Russian army, where he served as a medic, was "Dobriy Kulak" (the good kulak) so it appears that at least some people found him reasonable by the standards of the time.[13]

It would be more remarkable if Nestor *didn't* grow up hating authority and resenting the rich. It was not just that the rich were rich, but that their wealth kept the Ukrainian peasants poor, especially in terms of land, and by every other measure as well. As Makhno writes in his memoirs: "I recall my anger towards the pomeschchik's sons and the pomeschchik himself, when they passed by—sleek, well dressed, and scented, while I was filthy, clad in rags, barefoot, and stinking of manure from cleaning the calves' barn. The injustice of this state of affairs was staring me in the face. My only consolation was then my childish reasoning that this was the natural order of things: they were the 'masters' and I was a worker whom they paid so they wouldn't have to handle manure themselves."[14]

However, Makhno's blinders to the reality of his situation couldn't stay on forever. Sure, he'd nearly quit a job when an overseer (one he nicknamed "Flycatcher" for how often his mouth hung open) struck him twice with a whip while working. He nearly quit on the spot—but was deterred by the fact that if he quit, he wouldn't be paid. Nestor Makhno wrote in his autobiography that bringing back those scant wages to his mother was one of his few joys at that time in his life. It would be tested through the course of Nestor's childhood.

In the summer of 1902 the sons of the landowner Nestor worked for unleashed a particularly brutal beating on one of Makhno's fellow hired hands. The beating was evidently bad enough that Nestor ran to get the senior farmhand, Vania, who came running. A brief fistfight ensued, with the landlord's sons fleeing through the kitchen doors and windows.

It didn't end there, either. Vania gathered all the farmhands together and they marched on the estate. The estate owner, seeing all his laborers lined up with various pointy implements, was apologetic and apoplectic by turns. His sons were hapless idiots and would be punished, of course, he told the day laborers, and nothing similar would ever happen again. The brief strike was resolved.

Vania gave Nestor some advice: if anyone dared to try and beat him, Nestor should pick up the first sharp thing to hand and let him have it.[15] This advice would stick with Nestor for the rest of his time as a hired hand, though he would not always be able to act on it. He did always try to keep some sharp object by him when working from that point forward, in case he had to put theory into practice. The brawl and reconciliation was Nestor's first experience of collective direct action. It would not be the last.

On a fine Sunday in 1902, Nestor Makhno was beaten bloody in public by a wealthy landowner for the prank of harnessing some pigs to a carriage. According to the oral account of Kornei Kolesnik, a peasant youth, the whipping was interrupted by an Old Lady Kolesnik, who came flying down the stairs from her quarters above the farmhouse and punched the landowner square in the face. One can imagine she gave him a piece of her mind, as well as her fist. Old Lady Kolesnik did more than just stick it to the rich landowner—she helped Makhno recover from the lashing. It took two months for him to heal from the beating the landowner gave him, during which time, it is said, Old Lady Kolesnik put Makhno up at her place to recuperate.[16]

This sort of violence—arbitrary, unpredictable, and (from young Nestor's perspective) worse because it was public—was common, and it hardened young Nestor and thousands of other poor children throughout Ukraine. Despite the troubles and tribulations of work (and his prodigious temper), Makhno made friends at his labors—sometimes other workers. Surprisingly, according to a Mennonite oral account, nine-year-old Nestor once befriended the heir of a Mennonite estate, Abram Janzen. Abram, then thirteen, and Nestor spent many evenings playing together.[17] Nestor comes across in sources as a nervous, frenetic, and creative child, though with a temper that could run away with him at times. Nestor and Abram presumably bonded over the shared experience of losing a father at a young age, as well as the time-honored habits of little boys the world over: running around, screaming, and throwing stuff at other stuff.

Like many things in childhood, this friendship would matter down the line—years later, in 1918, when leading expropriations through his old neighborhood, Nestor Makhno came across Abram's widow and children. When he realized who they were, Makhno immediately halted the expropriation, ordered his men to return all the things they had already taken from the Janzen estate and to leave the Mennonite colony alone from this point forward. Nestor's childhood friendship with Abram had saved Abram's wife and children from robbery at least.[18]

In 1903, Nestor Makhno quit his stable job and briefly joined a local foundry as an apprentice. There he learned how to cast harvest wheels and wasn't half bad at it. The ironworkers were rather politically active in favor of unions, and this likely extended to Makhno as well. Makhno also worked as a dyer, an assistant to a wine seller (a job he loathed and quit after three months—Makhno hated the sales part of the job), and once joined a painting and decorating firm just long enough to pay for a new hay cart. He also worked for some time in vineyards owned by ethnic Bulgarians in the region of Tavria near the Sea of Azov. He grew familiar enough with the Bulgarian language that he was able to give incendiary speeches in it during the Russian Civil War some years later.[19]

In the meantime, three of Makhno's brothers, Yemelyan, Savva, and Karp had married and started households of their own. This left Nestor and his elder brother Grigori to look after their childhood home and their mother. It couldn't have been easy for anyone involved. And, as things often do in Ukrainian history, things got worse.

In 1904, Savva Makhno was conscripted into the Russian army, and sent to Siberia.[20] The Russo-Japanese War broke out soon after. The Russians anticipated a quick victory over Japan, and instead got a quick defeat. Savva Makhno survived the war, but (at a low estimate) 43,300 of his fellow Imperial Russian soldiers did not.

Nobody saw the Russo-Japanese War coming. Well, technically the Japanese did. The Japanese attacked the Russian fleet at Port Arthur one fine day in January 1905 without warning, following that up with a formal declaration of war shortly afterward, a strategy that would become something of a habit for them in the twentieth century.

This was the latest of the upheavals that would send the tottering Russian Empire down the road to revolution, and lead the unrest that was simmering inside its borders to boil over in the 1905–7 revolts. The years 1905 through 1910 would be Nestor Makhno's formal entrance into direct action, politics, and the inner workings of the Russian imperial penal system. These turbulent years would help shape the anxious, creative, young Nestor into a dedicated partisan. The anger inside Nestor that came from being poor and Ukrainian, built up over years of beatings, hard work, and cruelty—always present—would find more coherent expression in these years.

In a very real sense, Nestor Makhno's childhood ended in 1905, at the age of sixteen. That was the last "normal" year of his life, before he entered a life of activism and discovered others like him willing to push back against the state, landlords, and the power of the nobility.

CHAPTER 3

Makhno's Political Awakening (1905–9)

> "A state, coldest of all cold monsters. Coldly lieth it also; and this lie creepeth from its mouth: 'I, the state, am the people.'"
>
> —Friedrich Nietzsche

In 1906 Nestor Makhno found Jesus. And Zarathustra.[1]

Both "Jesus" and "Zarathustra," in this case, were nicknames of Czech-born Voldemar Antoni, the founder of the Union of Poor Peasants (UPP) in Huliaipole. Nestor Makhno joined the union in 1906, as the Stolypin repressions against peasants and political dissidents began.

But some context first:

A year earlier in 1905, the long-simmering pot that was the Russian Empire boiled over into widespread rebellion and slaughter. Russia had taken quite a beating against Japan in the Russo-Japanese War. This was the same war that Savva Makhno has been called away for in 1904, and from which he was lucky enough to return alive.

The people of the Russian Empire largely blamed this awkward military loss to an Asian power on a bumbling and incompetent government. Combined with less than idyllic conditions in the countryside and the heavy hand of the secret police, is it any wonder that there were rebellions? The first spark, though, came from an unlikely quarter.

In Moscow, even the Orthodox priests, long the lapdogs of the czar, led protests against the czar with workers and the poor in January 1905. The guards opened fire on them, creating Russia's very own "Bloody Sunday." According to historian Paul Avrich, one of the clerics in the crowd, Father

Gapon, would write: "The bond between tsar and people is now separated by a river of blood."[2]

Even if this link between church and state had largely been mythological or figurative, the fact was that the czar and the country had always been portrayed as synonymous by the Orthodox Church. But the people shot in Moscow were carrying Russian flags and Orthodox icons—they were people who otherwise would have feverishly supported the state and all its brutality. They were the first open, but certainly not the last, victims of czarist repression in this era.

The anarchists, socialists, and other revolutionaries were far from blind to the opportunities presented during this year. Anarcho-communist organizations spread propaganda, expropriations, and assassinations through the hinterlands of the empire, targeting the moneyed classes. They were divided in methods though not in aim: the destruction of the state and private property. Expropriations—seizure and redistribution of the land of the wealthy to the peasantry, often just shortened to "exes"—were common. Some groups relied on "motiveless terror"—that is, indiscriminate bombing of upper-class establishments, while others specialized in bank robberies, assassinations, and protests.[3]

Anarcho-communist groups were particularly well supported in rural areas like Ekaterinoslav, near Makhno's home of Huliaipole, where the lack of access to land was the major issue.

Olga Taratuta, future founder of the Anarchist Black Cross, which an older Nestor Makhno would make use of in the Civil War, and a still older Makhno would rely on in exile, was part of one of these groups. She was arrested, escaped from jail to Switzerland but grew bored. She returned to Ukraine to continue the struggle and was promptly jailed in 1908.[4]

It wasn't just the anarcho-communists, acting against the Russian Empire. Anarcho-syndicalists and socialists supported massive strikes that shut down factories and rail lines en masse, paralyzing the country. This decentralized, wide-spread, and spontaneous rebellion against authority was a true danger to both the czar's legitimacy and the foundations of empire.

The 1905 rebellion didn't fizzle out. It was murdered. A nearly solid year of rebellion, strikes, and defiance was brutally put down by the czar's military, despite the military being of uncertain loyalty at first. According to historian Paul Avrich: "The Petersburg strike movement frightened [Czar] Nicholas into signing the Manifesto of 17 October, which guaranteed full civil liberties to the population and pledged that no law would become effective without the consent of the State Duma."[5]

However, the czar pointedly ignored the economic and social demands of the citizenry and called it a day. This should surprise nobody. Nicholas II of Russia personally sympathized with the Black Hundreds (gangs of state-sponsored pogromists)—to the point of supporting them financially. He wrote (in a letter to his mother, no less!), about a series of pogroms against Jews in the western part of the empire during 1903–6, saying: "The people became enraged by the insolence and audacity of the revolutionaries and socialists; and because nine-tenths of them are Yids, the people's whole wrath was turned against them."[6]

It is also worth noting that the Russian Empire's czarist government was quick to promote divisions among its citizens—particularly antisemitism. Indeed, two years before the 1905 rebellion, the secret police, the Okhrana, wrote and distributed a pamphlet titled *The Protocols of the Elders of Zion*—a tract beloved by Nazis, nationalists, antisemites, and conspiracy theorists to this day—which purported to record the secret meetings of the Jewish cabal that ran the world. Antisemitism was Russian imperial policy, plain and simple. The repression of the 1905 rebellions, strikes and attempted social revolution began in earnest in 1906 under that bastard Pyotr Stolypin, but more on him later.

Back to Makhno.

Nestor Makhno lived through tumultuous times. Most people do, whether they acknowledge it or not. He already had plenty of experience of humiliation and exploitation under the czarist state and the near-feudal conditions. Nestor lived with his mother and brother, Grigoriy, at this time.

At the end of 1905, near the end of the rebellion, Makhno became associated with the social democrats. He writes in his memoirs that he still handed out their pamphlets and supported their end goal of the formation of a Russian republic, rather than the present monarchy.

The end of the rebellions—achieved by brute force and sustained repression by czarist forces under Pyotr Stolypin—had the effect of driving resistance to it to greatest extremes. If martial law was going to be declared—and it was—why bother getting arrested or shot for a middle-of-the-road political stance if that was equally likely to earn you a noose or bullet as, say, anarcho-communism or socialism? People left moderate, state-based parties like the social democrats across Russia, including young Nestor.

Nestor Makhno left the social democrats and found the anarchists in the UPP. The speed at which the union was formed was breathtaking. Antoni writes in his autobiography that it took a mere two months of solid agitation and propaganda to form a strong group that was self-perpetuating, and he felt secure enough in its capability to leave for Moscow to agitate there.[7]

Teenage Nestor looked up to Voldemar Antoni as a mentor. Makhno called him "an honorable and sincere revolutionary." Makhno also claimed, writing later: "He[Antoni] was the one who exerted a decisive influence on me, cleansing my mind once and for all of the slightest trace of the slave mentality and the desire to submit to any authority whatsoever."[8]

The structure of the Union of Poor Peasants bears some examination before we can look at Makhno's role with the group. The majority of the members were involved in reading and study groups—salons, in effect, discussing anarchist theory and printing and distributing propaganda. They would, according to Nestor Makhno's autobiography, meet anywhere they could gather without fear: in fields, by lakes, in the houses of trusted comrades. Night was the preferred time for such meetings, and Makhno made it a point to attend as many as possible. In short, he was an eager student of the revolutionary doctrines and so were many of the young people of Huliaipole.

Then there was the subgroup that Makhno was a part of that committed robbery, expropriations, and assassinations, which according to historian Colin Darch was most active between 1906 and 1908. Nestor Makhno was admitted to this group with some reservations, to hear Antoni and a few of Nestor's former comrades tell it.

Nestor's commitment to the anarcho-communist cause was unquestionable. However, he was still a teenager, and like many teenagers, was not without his goofy or awkward moments. It can be a bit of a drag to have goofy or awkward moments around explosives and firearms. This meant that his quick temper often got him into trouble, along with his impulsiveness. A former comrade relates one incident where Nestor Makhno nearly blew up his mother's stove in his attempt to make homemade explosives in a pan.[9]

Even in adulthood, Nestor retained a nerve-racking habit of spinning his revolver around his finger like a cowboy in a Hollywood Western when bored, which is rather far from all tenets of basic gun safety but does look cool, or so he thought.

In addition, Antoni—writing, to be fair, years after the fact and for the purposes of repatriation to the Soviet Union, so with every reason to want to paint Nestor with a less than clean brush—notes that Nestor was fond of drink, and fonder of fighting in public, especially with the police. Young Nestor Makhno, according to Antoni, was a bit of a loudmouth and loose cannon—a major liability, in theory, for a group that depended on secrecy to survive.

In October of 1906, while Antoni was still in Moscow, he was horrified to hear that Makhno had been initiated into the expropriations group. His first mission with comrades wasn't exactly a rousing success: they held up Isaak Bruk, a local Jewish businessman, at gunpoint demanding 500 rubles, but only coming away with 151, presumably all that Bruk had on him at the time. Antoni claimed in his writings that he left *explicit* instructions to keep that "that pugnacious and hard-drinking fellow" Makhno far away from any sort of direct action.[10] Too late. Makhno was now in the activist division of the UPP and it was there that he would do the most work for the next few years.

There was a lot of work to do. Pyotr Stolypin, the czarist minister put in charge of "land reform" across the empire, which really amounted to a dedicated reign of terror and counterinsurgency policies, had a statesman's prose and a butcher's sense of ethics. In a 1907 address to the Duma ("We Need a Great Russia"), in response to widespread demands for the nationalization of land and the abolition of private property, the policies pursued by the left-wing Kadet party, Stolypin sneered: "In the Government's opinion, it is not necessary to do away with anything." He then had the nerve to claim to abhor violence (unless the state was doing it, but that was implied). Even a hundred years ago, declining empires surely knew how to ignore the core sources of unrest just as ably as they do today, didn't they?

Instead, Stolypin sought to put the kibosh on any and all questions of land reform that would benefit the peasants or workers of the empire, and instead focused on an economic alliance with the relatively narrow, middle class of the empire—*pomeshchiks* (large-scale landowners) and *kulaks* (rich peasant farmers). This would be accomplished by breaking up the peasant communes that held land collectively, rather than as individual private property. In exchange for access to land, this favored class would be unfailingly loyal to the czar and help put down any future revolts. This was also meant to atomize and contain peasant resistance.

In the meantime, Stolypin eagerly used martial law, public beatings, executions without trial, and that favorite weapon of secret police forces everywhere, the agent provocateur to try to destroy any sort of resistance to these policies. Surveillance was ubiquitous, informers common, and infiltration of radical circles a matter of course. In short, Stolypin's policies enabled the czarist police—especially the secret police, the Okhrana—to conduct a reign of terror to attempt to prevent any sort of betterment of the lot of the majority of citizens of the Russian empire.

The Russian Empire had quite a few laws on the books that aided in the repression of the peasants, anarchists, and social reformers in the empire even before Stolypin got his grubby little mitts on them. Some of these ordinances were older than Nestor Makhno himself. Czar Alexander II, for example passed the Addenda of August 14, 1881, which granted police, secret or otherwise, "the right to arrest any person without any evidence of guilt at all for an act not recognized by law as a crime, based on information not subject to verification."[11]

It was from these policies and the piggish refusal to grant land rights that Stolypin gained a sinister reputation. The phrase "Stolypin necktie" was popularized by the official's fondness for hanging dissidents.

Nestor Makhno and the UPP responded to Stolypin's terror with their own "Black Terror." Makhno was a man of conscience and this comes through in his writings on the time. Makhno notes that the anarchists of the union first attempted to respond to kulak and pomeshchik media blitzes and buyouts of communal farmland with their own leaflets and lectures. This met without success, and so the union decided collectively to torch the fields and properties of the pomeshchiks wherever and whenever possible. This they did, and since none of the pomeshchiks paid workers or servants to put out the flames—their lands burned for weeks at a time. In response, the pomeshchiks often hired Cossack bands to terrorize local communes or villages, laying about with swords and whips seemingly at random.

When drawn out into direct confrontation with pomeshchiks and kulaks, Makhno again makes a distinction: if the agitators for Stolypin's privatization of the country had not resorted to violence in their adver-tisements, they would be allowed to live—but their lands would still be burned in response. Makhno notes in disgust that some social democrats even sided with the kulaks and, more unforgivably, aided the police in putting out the fires so as to "preserve capital" as Makhno puts it.[12] This pro–status quo stance backfired on the social democrats, as it prompted a wave of peasant desertions from their platform—they had sided with the landlords and capitalists in public, and not the peasants.

Things continued to escalate into 1907—Nestor Makhno and several others from the UPP were forced to go underground inside Huliaipole due to increased police pressure. Joining him in hiding was Prokop Semenyuta, the youngest of the Semenyuta brothers. His elder brother, Aleksander, was a recent deserter from the Russian army—and another influence on Nestor. Aleksander would become legendary for his talent at disguise and surprising raids and rescues, skills that Nestor admired and would learn well. It was in 1907 that Nestor was arrested and held for a serious length of time by local police. The incident went something like this:

> **Nestor Makhno:** Hello Socialist-Revolutionary Mickey Makovsky! You look down.
> **Makovsky:** Hiya Nestor. I'm fed up with being beaten by the pigs. Lend me your revolver, I'm gonna go shoot one of those bastards in the head.
> **Makhno:** Good for you buddy. Here you go (hands over his revolver). Glad to see you sticking up for yourself, they really gave you the third degree earlier, didn't they?
> **Makovsky:** Thanks. (Takes revolver.)

Makovsky then went on to shoot not a police officer but rather his fiancée in broad daylight, twice, and then himself in the head. Amazingly, all three wounds were nonfatal. Nestor Makhno felt it would be wrong to abandon his wounded friends in the street and attempted to give first aid then and there—and was still at the scene when the police arrived.[13]

He was promptly arrested. Makhno had been arrested before, but the police had never had enough evidence to hold him for anything, even though they suspected that he'd been the one who took a shot at a police officer earlier that year. "Three or four days later," Makhno recalls in his autobiography, "Voldemar Antoni was arrested for trying to arrange a meeting with me with the help of a guard."

Surprisingly, given what Antoni might have expected, Nestor refused to ever give anyone up under questioning and remained defiant during beatings and interrogation sessions. He stuck by his alibis and so did the witnesses he named.[14]

This time, while Makhno's stories checked out, he was still held in jail for months at a time. When he was released after four months, he was promptly rearrested and questioned by the chief of police, Karachentsev, who claimed to have new, damning evidence on Nestor. Nestor didn't budge and was thrown back in prison until a factory owner named Vichlinsky put up the two thousand ruble bail for him. Antoni was also ultimately released, though not before telling the cops that he'd never talk, even after being beaten with a rubber truncheon.[15]

Nestor was forced to go underground inside Huliaipole—according to him, none of the activist members of the UPP dared live openly under their own names. He got a job at a dye works—a condition of his parole—and kept his head down for a few months. But things didn't cool down.

Indeed the Huliaipole police got a funding increase and could afford to hire a squad of "two-legged curs," to use Makhno's phrase for the secret police.[16] This substantially upped the danger of infiltration for the UPP. This was a common problem in radical circles—between infiltrations by secret police and *shpiks* (radicals turned informers) operational security was at times precarious at best for anarchists at this time.

Shpiks in particular were loathed with a special intensity, as they represented an existential threat not just to current revolutionaries, but to future ones as well if left undetected. Historian Malcolm Archibald recounts incidents in prison where political prisoners would break out of their cells, and instead of escaping over the walls, would head to the shpik wing of the prison, exact a bloody and fatal revenge, and then wait to be locked up again. That was the extent of passionate hatred inspired by those who would rat out their comrades to the police. Their death was, broadly, considered more valuable than freedom for revolutionaries.[17]

While shpiks were former comrades turned informers, the secret police were generally professional thugs from outside the regions they were assigned to. We will deal with them at length in Makhno's life, but two particular things spring to mind. First, in 1911 Stolypin would be assassinated by the secret police he set loose on the country. In fact, Stolypin's assassin, Dmitry Bogrov, had spent years infiltrating socialist and anarchist circles and apparently had enough of Stolypin (at this point, who hadn't had enough of poor Pyotr Stolypin?), so Bogrov shot him to death while Stolypin was vacationing in Kiev.[18]

The second point involves a work of fiction from the same time period as Makhno's activities: G.K. Chesterton's *The Man Who Was Thursday*. It is admittedly a surreal novel that functions as much on dream logic as anything else and has an anti-anarchist moral framework. However, it's impossible not to think of Chesterton's 1908 novel in this context of constant suspicion, fear, and paranoia. For those of you unfamiliar with the work, its basic conception is that every member, save one, of a small, dangerous anarchist cell (including the protagonist) is an undercover police officer. This would not be an unfamiliar joke to anarchists like Voldemar Antoni or Nestor Makhno as they entered 1908.

CHAPTER 4

Capture and Imprisonment (1908–10)

> "Laws: We know what they are, and what they are worth! They are spider webs for the rich and mighty, steel chains for the poor and weak, fishing nets in the hands of government."
>
> —Pierre-Joseph Proudhon

Living in Huliaipole was becoming more dangerous for Nestor Makhno. In 1907, according to his memoirs, he formed a small anarchist study group in Bochansk on the outskirts of Huliaipole. It was a symptom of the increasing pressure in Makhno's hometown and the increasing suspicion of "two legged lice" as Makhno calls infiltrators or former comrades turned informers.

This tension went on for more than a year as the pressure on Huliaipole anarchists was steadily turned up. In June 1908 things came to a head: two shpiks in Makhno's group were exposed within days of each other. Both were killed. Each execution featured one of Semenyuta's siblings prominently—the first killing involved using disguise (specifically, dressing as a woman) to take the target off-guard.[1] This is not the first or last time that dressing in unexpected disguises would be used by Makhno or people associated with him to conduct scouting or assassination missions—and looking fabulous while doing so!

The second unmasking, the following day, involved Nestor Makhno and the Semenyuta brothers. A comrade who Makhno and Antoni had long suspected of snitching was implicated. This man, Levadny, begged for a chance to prove himself by committing an act of the group's choosing—and when the anarchists met to discuss this deed, surprise! By some wacky and completely unrelated coincidence, the police and their Cossack chums just happened to be outside the meeting place and surrounded it. Life's funny that way.

The shpik Levadny suggested that the group surrender to the police—and outed himself by virtue of this absurd suggestion, which was roundly mocked by Makhno and the rest of the group. A full-fledged gun battle followed. As such, it was necessarily chaotic, loud, disorienting, and eardrum damaging. Prokop Semenyuta was killed, and the Cossacks and police officers took casualties. Makhno and the others managed to escape the trap in the chaos.[2]

The Huliaipole anarchists were gaining a formidable reputation—formidable enough that the vice-governor of the region came personally to see that the group was exterminated. He took what could generously be called *stringent* security precautions.[3]

Planning the security arrangements for the vice-governor, I like to imagine, went something like this:

> **Police officer:** Sir, what about your travel arrangements to Huliaipole?
> **Vice-governor:** The anarchists are out to get me! How do I stay unshot and unexploded?
> **Police officer:** Many of the anarchists are young people, sir, especially in Huliaipole.
> **Vice-governor:** Well, naturally, all young people must be banned from seeing me while in Huliaipole! All of them, you hear me!
> **Police officer:** Of course sir. Nobody who doesn't complain of lower back pain, their aching knees, or gout, or how much better things were when they were a kid will be allowed to see you sir, or indeed, to be within a mile of you.
> **Vice-governor:** Well, that's a relief! Let's go and wipe out these young anarchists.

The policy of keeping young people away from the governor's proposed route and accommodations while in Huliaipole succeeded in preserving his life from bombs and bullets. The UPP couldn't breach that layer of security, and were forced to pick another target. It's not wise to leave perfectly good explosives lying around. Unused explosives are almost as much trouble as explosives put to their proper use. On a side note, one type of the homemade bombs used in this era were called "infernal machines," which I think we can all agree is a much cooler name for explosives that should be brought back into common parlance.

Makhno had an idea for a substitute bombing target—the secret police station, with which he was quite familiar, given that he'd been called in there frequently in the last few months. That could use a good bombing. There was no love for the secret police among the anarchists (or anyone else, for that matter) and so the plan went ahead. It was nearly blown when a detachment of Cossacks ambushed Makhno and some of the others coming out of the final planning meeting, but the anarchists managed to slip through the horsemen's fingers. That was fortunate. What was unfortunate was that the authorities managed to track down and arrest Makhno and his collaborator Onishchenko mere hours before he was set to bomb the station.

August 26, 1908, was Makhno's last day of freedom for nine years.[4]

The secret police station remained regrettably unexploded.

Informers from other regions like the neighboring Amur branch, who had been in touch with the UPP had been arrested. One of them, Althauzen, singled out Makhno as a particularly dangerous fellow, just behind the Semenyuta siblings. This, combined with some loose lips inside the UPP, helped to more or less completely round up the more dangerous members of the anarchist cell.[5]

The authorities threw the book at Nestor Makhno—every crime that even smelled of anarchists sympathies was laid at his doorstep—some of which he may have actually done. Makhno's arrest was part of a general sweep of anarchists and anarchist sympathizers that had been rather effective. Of the UPP's militant arm, only Voldemar Antoni and Aleksander Semenyuta remained free in August 1908.

It is worth taking a brief side note here to observe the fate of another anarchist who would cross Makhno's path later in life, who was also arrested, jailed, and sentenced in 1908. I am of course referring to the legendary anarchist, Maria "Marusya" Nikiforova, a bottle washer at a vodka distillery and anarcho-communist.[6] Makhno's brand of anarcho-communist activism had a moral dimension, which focused on breaking the levers of repression (the police, Cossacks, government officials) and distributing propaganda to the oppressed and teaching them practical anarchism based upon the socialization of land. To quote from historian Sean Patterson's book, *Makhno and Memory*, on Makhno's later methods and ideology: "Makhno's language suggests that he did not consider class as a fixed attribute and that former enemies could be redeemed through a conscious renunciation of wealth."

Marusya's methodology was a bit starker: The upper class itself was guilty of oppressing everyone else, and thus motiveless terror and the bombings of cafes they frequented or the factories they owned was entirely justified because they created terror among the oppressors.

Makhno never drew quite as broad a line as Marusya did in these matters—he had befriended children of the upper classes as a child, and as we saw in the previous chapter, was largely judicious in his use of force at this period in his life. The upper classes were people, in Makhno's eyes— some good who might even support the revolution, some indifferent, and some truly bad. Some had even paid bail for Makhno when he'd been arrested.

Marusya didn't make this sort of distinction: if you were not a peasant or a worker, you were a potentially valid target for a bomb—an attitude that would cause some strain between her and Makhno down the line. Marusya's early career culminated in the blowing up of a business office of a machine plant, killing the manager and a guard. She also had been a rather proficient expropriator of funds by the time she was captured—rather than surrender, she tried to take her attackers with her. Her bomb failed to detonate, and she was taken alive.[7] Marusya was sentenced to death, but ultimately spared the hangman's drop due to her youth. She engineered a jailbreak a year later and ultimately escaped to Europe, specifically to Paris, France. We'll be seeing more of her later.

Anyway, back to Makhno, in August 1908 the Huliaipole anarchists were held separately from other prisoners in Alexandrovsk prison. They awaited trial for a year, in none-too-friendly conditions. When the time came for the trial, Levadny and Althausen were moved from general population to "the bitches cages"—the wing of every Russian prison reserved for informers.[8]

The anarchist prisoners were able to coordinate an escape attempt during their transfer from Alexandrovsk prison to Ekaterinoslav. The key figure in their first attempt was their free comrade, Aleksander Semenyuta. During that year that Makhno and the other anarchists were in jail in Alexandrovsk, Aleksander Semenyuta hadn't been idle. He was constantly on the move, and just before his attempted rescue of Makhno and the others, managed to execute a remarkable feat. Semenyuta assassinated the head of the Huliaipole police, Karachentsev. This was managed by

CAPTURE AND IMPRISONMENT (1908–10)

writing an insulting letter to the police chief, who more than once had interrogated and imprisoned both Makhno and Semenyuta. According to Alexandre Skirda's biography *Nestor Makhno, Anarchy's Cossack*, the letter from Semenyuta read: "Mr. Superintendent. I have heard it said that you have been searching for me high and low and dearly wish to meet with me. If this be the case, I then beseech you to come to Belgium. Here, freedom of speech is unrestricted, and we will be able to chat at leisure."

Karachentsev let his guard down a bit thinking Semenyuta had fled the country. He and his wife took a show at the local theater—and unbeknownst to him, so did Aleksandr Semenyuta and his best friends, revolver one and revolver two! Semenyuta cut down Karachentsev outside the theater. A crueler person than me might have asked Mrs. Karachentsev, in an echo of an old joke about the Lincoln assassination at Ford's Theatre: "All in all, Mrs. Karachentsev, how was the show other than the unpleasantness?"

Makhno and the other captured anarchists managed to coordinate a rescue attempt with Semenyuta.[9] The best opportunity would be when the anarchists were due to be transferred to another prison by train. The transfer would be under armed guard, of course, and conducted early in the morning to avoid attention. The plan was set, and Makhno, in chains, was close enough as the guards pushed the prisoners into the train station, to hear Semenyuta's distinctive drawl. But the train was delayed by a significant amount, which unfortunately screwed with the timing of the rescue.

Doubly unfortunately for the prisoners, Althauzen the shpik recognized Semenyuta (the two had once been roommates), even in his peasant disguise. Which, according to Makhno's memoirs, included a big sheepskin coat and a tall furry hat to keep warm and obscure his features.[10] Althauzen shrieked his head off and set up quite a ruckus, screaming to the guards that Semenyuta, Semenyuta was here! Perhaps he had an inkling of what Makhno confirmed in his memoirs: in the event of a rescue, Makhno was tasked with killing Althauzen no matter what happened.[11] Makhno didn't get the chance to carry out this task.

Another shoot-out followed, after which Semenyuta and his revolvers were forced to flee and the prisoners beaten savagely before being boarded on the train to Yekaterinoslav prison.[12] The escape attempt had been foiled before the trial.

Semenyuta's daring attempt spooked the authorities. From then on, when the anarchists were moved in any capacity—to court for their trial, for example—they were surrounded by a ring of armed guards. In the event of a rescue attempt, the prisoners were to be executed immediately.[13]

So there was more than a little bit of tension when, during the trial of the anarchists, gunshots were heard outside the courtroom. One name was on everyone's mind: "Semenyuta, Semenyuta!" The prisoners feared they'd be shot on the spot, but the incident passed—the courtroom wasn't dynamited and the prisoners were guarded even more closely.

It wasn't, in fact, as Makhno discovered later, Semenyuta, but someone in a nearby park who happened to look like Semenyuta. The person in question was a comrade of Makhno's, as a matter of fact, and shot back at the police with a revolver before making his escape.[14] The real Semenyuta died on May 1, 1910, after a nine-hour shoot-out with the police that ended with many dead or wounded, including Semenyuta's girlfriend, Marfa Piven. Semenyuta denied the police the pleasure of killing him, and used his last bullet on himself.[15]

It wasn't much of a trial—its conclusion wasn't much in doubt by anyone in attendance. Judge Batog pronounced the death sentence on Nestor Ivanovich Makhno. His other companions were given lesser sentences—hard labor (*katorga*), but the ones that had been convicted of expropriations were given the death sentence. Makhno would later make efforts to reintroduce himself to this judge after being released from prison years later, but was unable to catch him before Judge Batog was exiled from the country.[16]

Makhno languished under this sentence for nearly two months—aware that any given day could be his last, and struggling with various diseases. Several of his comrades were taken from their shared cell in the night and hanged. Nevertheless, the anarchists kept themselves occupied as best they could, given the circumstances. Escape from Russian imperial prisons was not uncommon in this era, and so the anarchists set to work. Unfortunately, this hard work was somewhat foiled by the bong incident.[17]

Well, more accurately the *use* of a bong is what tipped the guards off that Makhno and his comrades were working on an escape attempt. The anarchists managed to get nail files smuggled in and were able to work for about fifteen minutes a day on the bars. Everything was going so swimmingly that the anarchists began to relax a bit. Escape was all but assured and they began to enjoy themselves when they could—laughing and smiling openly. And of course, making a bong and enjoying themselves in their cell. If you can't take the edge off in a terrible place like Ukrainian prison, where can you take the edge off? Unfortunately, they indulged in this when a guard was passing. The anarchist's cell was searched.

As Makhno noted in his memoirs, the prisoners couldn't explain away the files or hacksaws—the definition of contraband. The bong, maybe they could have gotten away with, but not the files and the partially sawed-through bars. Like that, their escape attempt was foiled. Beatings, isolation, and threats followed.

Somehow, things managed to get worse. One of Makhno's close comrades, Bondarenko, was executed, though not before expressing his faith that Makhno would somehow reach freedom eventually.[18] Other anarchists in similar situations—too wounded to be moved to the gallows, or to spite the hangman, took poison smuggled into their cells, while others chose to spite the hangmen by burning themselves alive in their cells.[19] Each day could have been Makhno's last, every time the cell door opened, his heart jumped in his chest.

But, in 1910, Nestor Makhno received a reprieve. His death sentence had been commuted to merely a lifetime of hard labor, *katorga*. This meant a lifetime in chains and backbreaking labor, but it was life, at least. This reversal of fortune was due to Makhno's youth—he discovered this during his time in the infirmary, in correspondence with his mother who had visited the local governor in charge of giving final approval to all death sentences.[20]

Immediately after this welcome bit of news, Makhno fell gravely ill with respiratory typhus and had to be pushed to the hospice ward. This disease did a major number on Makhno—so bad that his shackles were removed for the two months he was under treatment. Upon his improvement, the shackles were slapped back on as if they'd never been taken off. Things didn't improve—the head of the prison guards separated the prisoners by type of crime: political and everything else. The political prisoners were all confined to one cell, all the anarchists, socialists, the Left Socialist Revolutionaries were stuck together like sardines. Beatings were common, and the routine set for the prisoners was Kafkaesque in its cruelty and arbitrariness.[21]

Makhno and the others wrote a secret letter of protest to the Ministry of Internal Affairs in Petersburg, chronicling these conditions. Meanwhile the brutality continued unabated.[22] The letter from the anarchists paid off—the political prisoners were transferred to another prison, far from Ukraine.[23]

It was the beginning of Makhno's hardest stretch of prison time in the Butyrka prison in Moscow. The czarist government had learned to take its prisoners more seriously—Makhno and the others, according to his memoirs, had entertained thoughts of abducting the paddy wagon (nicknamed "Stolypin's wagons") they were being transported in. They discovered that the czarist officers had installed a grate between prisoners and guards, and were far more alert than previously.[24] It is on this uncomfortable road trip north that Makhno first met Olga Taratuta, who would become an important figure later on in Makhno's life and in the history of Russian anarchism.

Makhno's formal education—in life, in suffering, in the deeper tenets of revolutionary ethics and anarchism—was just beginning.

CHAPTER 5

The Modest One's Life in Prison (1911–17)

> "Yes, our first ancestors, our Adams and our Eves, were, if not gorillas, very near relatives of gorillas, omnivorous, intelligent and ferocious beasts, endowed in a higher degree than the animals of any other species with two precious faculties—*the power to think and the desire to rebel.*"
>
> —Mikhail Bakunin

In August 1911 Makhno arrived in Moscow's Butyrka prison. Butyrka prison was a pair of square great stone walls set inside each other, with guard towers poking ominously above the sooty stone. It held about three thousand prisoners, most of them jailed for political beliefs. With its high walls and cold halls, Butyrka was a sight to make anyone feel small and weak.

Makhno had just come from Ekaterinoslav prison, where he and his comrades had been caged for twenty-two weeks and their underwear and socks stripped from them and discarded out of spite.[1] They were then transferred to Butyrka, where they spent a dank and dire two weeks in quarantine cells before being moved to more permanent lodgings.

Nestor Makhno had an excellent view from his cell (number four, cellblock number seven) of the tower that had once held the Cossack Emelian Pugachev.[2] You remember him, don't you? He's the one all the way back at the prologue who led the last great peasant uprising against czarist power and met with a rather uncomfortable fate at the hands of Catherine the Great— her most famous ex-husband that was never married to her in the first place, and the last leader of a large-scale uprising against the Russian government.

As the saying goes, history doesn't repeat, but it often rhymes.

Existence at Butyrka was not an easy sentence, especially for a lifer like Nestor Makhno. It may have been particularly bad for Makhno in fact. He was sentenced to *katorga*—forced labor, which meant that except for when he was in the infirmary, he was in heavy chains doing hard work. The chains a prisoner sentenced to katorga wore were meant to last for eight years at a stretch, the wrist restraints weighed four pounds, the ankle 'bracelets' eight pounds.[3] This is to say nothing of solitary confinement, which Makhno was frequently thrown into for his love of insulting remarks. Solitary confinement remains, then as now, a crime against humanity.

All this is without the factors of the cold, sickness (Russian prisons, then as now, are famous for being uniquely virulent petri dishes of disease), terrible-at-best food, and beatings on the least pretext. The knout was also used in the context of beatings—a short, heavy, and sometimes weighted bit of braided leather.

Makhno was not a large or strong man, his health was not helped by such treatment, and so he spent a few months out of each year in the infirmary of the prison. Makhno's manacles were unlocked and removed during these stretches—lose consciousness, lose your manacles![4] Better yet, he was given better food than he would ordinarily get as a political prisoner until he recovered.[5] Makhno's suffering can be imagined on the day he had to leave the infirmary—being strapped back into chains, knowing he was once again at the whim of the screws and the warden must have been agonizing for reasons of both anticipation and contrast.

Makhno earned a sardonic prison nickname that he leaned into later: "the Modest One."[6] Even with being constantly in and out of the hospital wing, he remained combative and direct even when feigning passivity would have been easier. He notes in his diaries that he received "countless" one- or two-week stints in the punishment cells or solitary confinement cells—he even brags of a sentence of a month in solitary for his daring and quick tongue.[7] Makhno was never one to buckle under a challenge. This wasn't a good trait, especially in a Russian prison. It just meant that he suffered more than he needed to.

Punishment was frequent and arbitrary even without the help of a mouth as well-tuned for defiance and sarcasm as Makhno's. Canings were common and dreaded, as were whippings. Food and water could be restricted, and there were even punishments for pacing in one's cell, so there were precious few ways to work off the nervous energy that must have seized the prisoners during the dark Moscow nights.[8]

Up until the outbreak of the First World War, even something as simple as reading a newspaper had to be done in secret. A prisoner could be whipped for something like that. When the war began, the prisons began distributing newspapers documenting the war to the prisoners, including pamphlets from religious organizations, instructing the prisoners to pray to God for the czar to triumph in this holy war.[9] It was a kind gesture, the prisoners doubtless were running low on toilet paper.

Many nationalists wrote to the czar, begging for their sentences to be commuted to military service in the Russian army. Makhno made no secret of his biting contempt for people who would buy their freedom by fighting for the state, or offering to, since nobody was taken from Butyrka to the front lines. He saw how the nationalism of the Polish prisoners, for example, made them hostile to the Russians and vice versa. Makhno was quick to note how quickly people tribalized themselves, when in reality, to survive Butyrka, solidarity and unity were essential. This was made more difficult through the policy of splitting up the political prisoners, thus isolating and atomizing them.

The "Southerners" (Ukrainians) according to Makhno, were dispersed throughout the prison and not allowed to be in the same cell. The possibility of coordination among robbers and revolutionaries who knew each other well wasn't to be permitted by the jailers. Makhno was set aside with other political prisoners, chiefly anarchists, social democrats, and Socialist-Revolutionaries. There was friction between the groups on matters of correct revolutionary action, politics, and ideas. Makhno, later in his sentence, roundly mocked the social democrats' pronouncements that Russia would of course become a republic after the First World War ended and their party took power.[10]

Makhno and the anarchists jeered that the social democrats weren't revolutionaries—wouldn't a republic need prisons to feed its courts? The prisoners—particularly political prisoners—would be absolutely unaffected by this shift of governmental structure.[11] The Socialist-Revolutionaries were a bit better in their policies—swearing that when they led the social revolution, all prisons would be emptied as matter of course. Makhno believed that the prisons ultimately served the interests of the state and had little, if anything, to do with the administration of justice.

Nestor Makhno would make a point of emptying, then dynamiting, any prison he came across after he was freed, when feasible—and sometimes even if it wasn't. This even caused some friction when timetables with his comrades were concerned—Makhno could get tunnel vision about destroying prisons versus, say, escaping pursuit, or meeting up with allies at a pre-arranged time.

Makhno's rebellious spirit found opportunities for more defiance, even joining in an elaborate attempt to escape Butyrka in 1912. The plan was to continue tunneling outside the walls of Butyrka—pulverizing the earth and stone moved and dissolving it into the drainage system. Everything was going fairly well, Makhno believed, until a late arrival to the plot wrote to a friend trying to encourage him to get himself transferred to the would-be escapees' cells. As often happens with conspiracies, the letter was delivered not to the other prisoner as intended, but fell into the hands of—who else?—a guard. This proved to be a bit of a problem and the administration of the prison spent weeks trying to discover the secret escape tunnel.

The escape plot was eventually untangled, the tunnel found, and the prisoners detained. The prisoners were lucky in several respects. For one thing, this was done in the ancient and time honored tradition of CYA—cover your ass. So the prison administrators chose to believe—or be convinced by Makhno and the others, that this great tunnel was actually not a new one made by a bunch of political dissidents—but was a preexisting one from nearly two years ago, before the present administration took over running the prison. Therefore, blame couldn't possibly be assigned to them, the diligent and vigilant safe-keepers of the prison.[12] This may be one of the best examples of a successful use of the "It was like that when we found it" defense ever recorded in history, beloved by teenagers and desperate folk the world over. However, this is still a Russian prison, so let's not give the impression that everything ended well—just relatively well—for the prisoners of Butyrka. The prison administrators put Makhno and the others on bread and water as a punishment rather than cane them. At Butyrka Prison, the maximum number of strokes that could be applied to a prisoner for an offense was capped at ninety-nine, which is about ninety-nine too many for anyone really.[13]

This punishment cell contained cots, but no mattresses. It was an uncomfortable, cold, and ugly experience made better only by other prisoners lowering cigarettes and kielbasa on strings down to the would-be escapees to help them survive the punishment with at least a few small comforts.[14] Through all this, Makhno's distrust of "big shots" and "intellectual types" only grew. He saw that they railed against the cruelties of prison, but would not stand in solidarity with peasant or toiling prisoners. Class war, Makhno saw, was alive and well in prison—but the wrong side was winning.

Social class influenced who could afford to flatter or pay off the guards, for one thing. In a particularly vexing incident, the "big shots," the better-off political prisoners, paid the guards to remove their katorga chains and let them work on the prison factory floor with the nonpolitical prisoners. Makhno describes his reaction to this in his account of his prison time: "I finally understood that this was a normal manifestation of the thought-processes of intellectuals, for whom the resources of socialism were only a means to install themselves as bosses and rulers. These gentlemen had ceased to understand that it is not permissible to shake hands with or give presents to butchers who immediately afterwards are going to beat their ideological comrades. This negative moral image was imprinted in my memory, and in the memories of many of the comrades among the Moscow political prisoners where it remained for the rest of our lives."[15]

This passage foreshadows Makhno's later deep distrust of Bolsheviks, who believed that a revolution was desirable but that people must be "guided" to a stateless world through a temporary government headed, of course, by the Bolshevik vanguard intelligentsia. Makhno concludes, presciently, in his memoirs: "I came to the conclusion that in practice—in real life—all people are the same and those who consider themselves on a higher level do not deserve the attention paid them."[16] For Makhno, any system that privileged one group over another for any reason was intolerable and not in keeping with the anarchist critique of (coercive) power as a reality and as a means for organizing the world.

The famed anarchist Pyotr Kropotkin, who we will discuss at some length in the next chapter, was actually in favor of the First World War, on the Allied side (history fans may recall that the war broke out in 1914, three years into Makhno's sentence).[17] Kropotkin's logic was that while the war was awful and shouldn't be happening, it *was* happening and the Allied powers were at least preferable to the overt authoritarianism of the Central Powers. To support them would be to help governments in Europe—and indeed, world-wide—rollback what few freedoms had been won over the last fifty years. Harm reduction, in essence. Supporting the war in any regard was not a popular position among anarchists the world over, and in this regard Makhno was no exception. Regardless, Makhno takes pains to point out in his memoirs covering this time period (published in 1925) that while he strongly disagreed with Kropotkin's stance on the war, he didn't respect him or his hard work any less for it.

It is now time we turned to the core of Makhno's time in prison—agitation and further education as an anarchist.

CHAPTER 6

Makhno's Education in Prison (1910–17)

> "Lastly, all of you who possess knowledge, talent, capacity, industry, if you have a spark of sympathy in your nature, come, you and your companions, come and place your services at the disposal of those who most need them."
>
> —Pyotr Kropotkin

"Why is courage a good thing?" Tolstoy asked in one of his earliest essays, "The Raid." Tolstoy became a committed pacifist later in life (indeed laying the foundations for many of the core tenets of anarcho-pacifism whose influence would be felt even in the upcoming Russian Civil War) and much respected even by those who believed his pacifist stance to be unworkable in the face of repression.

But back to the initial question Tolstoy asks: "Why is courage a good thing?" He was not being rhetorical—Tolstoy had a true talent for asking questions that most simply let pass by as self-evident, and for getting on people's nerves. Like many pacifists, Tolstoy came by his beliefs after a stint in the military (the Czarist Russian forces in the Caucasus, to be specific) persuaded him of the futility of violence and his later meditations that convinced him that violence was the backbone of state power. It is from these experiences that the events in "The Raid" were formed firsthand. In "The Raid," Tolstoy witheringly describes young officers with stars in their eyes and a romantic view of their role in the military: "He was one of those dashing, wild young officers who attempt to model themselves on the heroes of Lermontov and Marlinsky. These officers saw the Caucasus only through such romantic prisms, and in everything they were guided solely by the instincts and tastes of their models."

Nestor Makhno, in his prison diary, specifically mentioned enjoying the works of Mikhail Lermontov in particular.[1] Those romantic novels must have been a break from Makhno's more academic readings. Lermontov's works are chock-full of tragic romances, antiheroes, and duels. Consider this passage from Lermontov's *A Hero of Our Time*, in which the hero spends a sleepless night before a duel worrying, which seems prescient and one might suppose resonated with young Makhno: "And tomorrow, it may be, I shall die! ... And there will not be left on earth one being who has understood me completely. Some will consider me worse, others, better, than I have been in reality.... Some will say: 'he was a good fellow'; others: 'a villain.' And both epithets will be false. After all this, is life worth the trouble? And yet we live—out of curiosity! We expect something new."[2]

Makhno must have read through Lermontov's work like a firestorm. He also admitted to being a big fan of *Taras Bulba* by Nikolai Gogol, a romantic novel about the life of and drama in a Cossack family. For Nestor, who was raised on stories of Zaporozhian Cossacks, it was an exciting read—a chance to feel something besides cold and hunger and momentarily escape. Nestor Makhno was a lifer in a brutal prison—barring a fight or a beating or illness striking him low, he had nothing but time to read.

There is a keen irony here: during his time in prison, Nestor Makhno experienced far more of the scope of the world as it was than he likely would have had he remained free. While Nestor had read and distributed anarcho-communist and social democratic texts as part of the Poor Peasant's Union, this was likely the most time he ever had in his young life for the serious study of theory and academics. Butyrka prison, as at least partly a political prison, had a first-rate library ("These books were found in the prison thanks to the efforts of a long succession of political prisoners [who] had served time there ... the library [of the prison] was better-stocked than the libraries of many provincial cities"), particularly in the sciences and political literature.[3]

One of the major mechanisms for spreading anarchist ideals abroad and worldwide was through scientific theories and texts. In contrast to the social-Darwinist texts of the day, anarchist thinkers like Kropotkin, Metchnikoff, and later Ōsugi Sakae would note examples of mutual aid, spontaneous cooperation, and affinity groups in the natural world and extrapolate them to the human world. In a daily life that includes beatings and brutal isolation, a book can be seen as even more of a method of escape than it otherwise might.

When Nestor wasn't reading about dashing feats of martial valor and melodrama, he busied himself discovering what he could about the empire that imprisoned him. He read Vasily Klychevsky's sprawling five-volume *History of Russia*. This is notable, as Malcolm Archibald mentioned, for its focus on the geographical and economic causes of historical events—a valuable perspective for a future maestro of guerrilla warfare.

Nestor also read a good deal of world history, claiming that Russian history, then world history, then geography and mathematics were his favorite things to study. But all these books, while valuable, paled in influence compared to one volume Makhno happened across in prison: Kropotkin's *Mutual Aid* may have been the most important book that Makhno ever read. Kropotkin's work was comprehensive and focused on the central premise that cooperation was the critical force for a species to thrive. One of Kropotkin's influences and peers, Élie Metchnikoff, summed it up in a pithy phrase: "Nature places before her inhabitants: death or solidarity. There are no other paths for humanity."[4] Words perhaps more pertinent now than even in the trying times they were written. Mutual aid inside of a species, a communal instinct to help one's fellows through solidarity and to living in a world of peers instead of masters and servants— that was the essence of Kropotkin's great work.

Kropotkin argued that not only were states unnatural but also that they frequently faltered and had to be reimposed on a public that resented top-down authority at some fundamental level. The formation of the state was not inevitable, nor was it desirable. Indeed, it is difficult to read Kropotkin's masterwork even today and not be moved by his eloquence, his focus, and his boundless empathy.

Kropotkin's perspective was especially relevant at the time where empires and governments deliberately misunderstood Darwin's theory of natural selection and spread the doctrine of social Darwinism around the world. In essence: the strong ruled because they had "evolved" over the "lesser races" and therefore exploitation was not in fact exploitation, but simply a natural law like gravity.

Makhno was almost physically struck by Kropotkin's arguments. He carried a copy of *Mutual Aid* with him wherever he could, in hopes of discussing it with whomever else had read it.[5] The new world could be built now, by organizing autonomous communes and liberating the oppressed as much as by shooting the police dead in the street.

A prince of some status, Pyotr Kropotkin left it all behind, serving multiple prison sentences in prisons from France to Russia. Looking at him in his later years, it is almost impossible not to imagine Kropotkin as the jolly, Santa-like figure of anarcho-communism. Other men and women who knew him well half-jokingly called Kropotkin a secular saint, or a saint without a god. His long white beard and eyes that almost always seem to be crinkled in anticipation of a smile helped with this impression.

This is not to say that Makhno or other anarchists didn't take issue with some of Kropotkin's stances (his support of the Allied Powers, and the First World War in general was a sour note between him and the world anarchist scene). However, Makhno made the distinction between "the great teacher's" body of work and one unfortunate point of difference.[6]

Makhno did make one close friend and comrade in prison: Peter Arshinov, an old anarcho-communist organizer. Nestor was likely predisposed to like Arshinov because Arshinov, while educated, favored practical measures in prison over flowery rhetoric without follow-up action, as was common among the "big shots" in prison. Arshinov had his feet firmly on the ground, as far as Nestor was concerned—someone as willing to organize prisoners as preach the value of mutual aid to the already converted.

Arshinov and Makhno had a tight but fractious relationship from prison to the end of Makhno's life. It wasn't a bromance, but it was close. The word "bromance" is inexact, but there were all the hallmarks of it in Arshinov and Makhno's turbulent relationship: bonding over a common cause, tensions over interpreting that cause, and ultimately betrayal.

Makhno at first looked to Arshinov as a mentor figure. In his prison diary, he noted that Arshinov was reclusive and not an extrovert. Nevertheless he was always patient when Nestor would ask him repeated questions on a point of theory or praxis.[7] Their relationship would span decades, several revolutions, multiple countries, and the founding of Makhno's Platform-style of anarchism in Paris, and end when Arshinov abandoned that project and applied for Soviet citizenship in the 1930s.[8] Arshinov, by the way, is also one of our best sources (despite his defection to the Soviets later in life) for understanding Makhno's actions and ideology in Ukraine during the Civil War. A future member of Makhno's command staff, he stood high in Makhno's esteem.

With anarchist sources on the Russian Civil War, nobody is really spoiled for choice—playing ball with the Cheka was often the only way to survive after the war had been lost (as Victor Belash, another Makhnovist-turned-historian did). Makhno's own writings have only partially survived.

The Bolsheviks, like the Russian Empire they replaced, were uncomfortable with anarchist narratives and did their level best to characterize them as a kulak-bandit movement in their official history. Nevertheless, despite all the troubles in the present moment in prison and the future ones to come—Arshinov and Makhno faced their difficulties with courage, buoyed by each other's belief and friendship.

Why is courage a good thing? Nestor Makhno might have answered that question with a tilt of his head and a puzzled smile. For someone as impetuous and bold as Makhno, the value of courage was self-evident: to build a better world and hasten social revolution. How could one do that without courageous (some would say reckless) action?

Tolstoy gives an example of true courage and false courage in "The Raid." To Tolstoy, the old soldier stationed in the Caucasus (for the double pay given to same for a dangerous assignment, to send home to his family) who refused to be rattled under fire and simply wanted to do his job as best he could, was brave. The youths who charged out ahead of the military column on horseback, hoping to impress each other with daring feats and ending up in coffins, by contrast, were simply vain.

Courage was a quality that was best understood as stemming from motivations, not outward deeds, according to Tolstoy's definition. Intention determined whether an act was brave or a reflection of vanity. By this rubric—and a bit of guesswork—we could say that Makhno met Tolstoy's more stolid, workmanlike definitions of courage in his actions after Butyrka in 1917. He would learn the value of restraint, and do his best to check his ego in pursuit of one goal: establishing anarcho-communism in his world and spreading it without coercion, but neither would he allow himself to be prevented by the police, the military, or politics.

Of course, there was more than a touch of vanity to Nestor Ivanovich Makhno—without it, and the charisma that so often accompanies it, it is doubtful he could have rallied such numbers to him in such a short time. Little did Makhno know, as 1917 dawned, that he would have not just one chance, but many, to test all kinds of courage. The courage to step away from the known world of the empire into a world with no masters or slaves, and to resist the urge to slide back into political apathy. Inertia and habit are powerful forces, and that, as much as armies or enemies, was what the anarchists of the upcoming Russian Civil War, were fighting against.

Nestor Makhno and the anarchists of the Russian Civil War would attempt, with some success, to find new ways to ford the rivers of history and habit. But that would come later. For now, Makhno was a shivering prisoner in a particularly nasty jail. Frequently sick, often combative, it was not an easy seven years. The future must have seemed an endless plain without affect or hope of deliverance to Makhno, except in the pages of Kropotkin, conversations with Arshinov, and his own mental landscape.

Then the year 1917 came, and everything changed at once.

CHAPTER 7

The Kerensky Jailbirds (1917)

"What do you see when you hear the word *volya* [Freedom, will]?
An unbroken horizon. Someone striding along, sure-footed but not
thinking about tracks or paths, not going anywhere in particular.
Bareheaded. The wind ruffles his hair and blows it over his eyes—
since for his kind, every wind is a tailwind.
A bird flies by, spreading its wings wide, and this man waves both
arms high in the air, calls out to the bird in a wild voice, then bursts
into laughter.
Freedom is a matter of law.
Volya takes no account of anything.
Freedom is an individual's civil status.
Volya is a feeling."

—Teffi

On March 2, 1917, Nestor Makhno was released from Butyrka prison in
Moscow. He had been imprisoned there for eight years by his reckoning.[1]
He was freed into a world without a czar—Nicholas II had abdicated the
throne due to Russia's disastrous performance in the First World War,
among other things. In place of the czar, an interim government was formed,
the core of which was an alliance between the Socialist Revolutionaries
and the liberals.

Liberals in the classical sense: in this context, they would be people for
reform rather than revolution, slight tweaks to the state rather than abolition of it, and in general landed in favor of overwhelming state power, but

with some nice ribbons and bows attached to it like "free speech" and "right of assembly," which of course, are only guaranteed by that same government's whims. So not really free at all.

This liberal provisional governing body was known as the Kerensky government, at least by later historians, after the most notable figure in it, Alexander Kerensky. Kerensky was not well-liked. He was called "an incorrigible chatterbox" and "a cardboard Robespierre" by his many and varied detractors. To make matters worse, this incarnation of (at best, in a bad light) reformist government dedicated to preventing further (and badly needed) social revolutions called himself the "revolutionary generalissimo."[2]

Kerensky wasn't above some czar-like bloodshed—as would be evidenced by his brutal repression of the July Days in Petrograd where anarchists, socialists, and communists rose against the interim government in the streets and were shot down. Such revolutionary integrity on display by Kerensky, by making the streets run red with revolutionary's blood.

Kerensky compounded his mistakes by continuing Russia's involvement in the First World War, which continued to spread dissent and uprising through the empire until the boiling point came again in October. Former Russian provinces like Finland, Poland, and Ukraine declared their independence from the empire and split away, much to the consternation of the interim government. Kerensky's time at the top would come to less than a year, but not to worry! He fled to a profitable exile in America, ultimately settling at Stanford University in California, which of course has no questionable history whatsoever regarding the mass killings of indigenous people, why do you ask?

Kerensky was at least nominally a Socialist Revolutionary and the minister of justice when Makhno was released. The people of the empire demanded the freeing of political prisoners. This Kerensky gladly did—it cost him nothing politically and released some of the pressure within an empire that seemed likely to explode any day—but he was only rearranging deck chairs on a sinking ship, metaphorically speaking. Nestor Makhno and Arshinov—and countless other anarchists, socialists, and communists—were freed from prison at a stroke of a pen.

Makhno was ecstatic at this unlooked for amnesty—and even considered staying in Moscow to further revolutionary work in the city instead of returning to his countryside origins. Makhno stayed in Moscow a few weeks, getting used to movement without chains and observing the local anarchist activities. Eight years of katorga and sickness had taken a fearsome toll on his body, and it was with difficulty that he regained (or began to regain) his usual strength and gait.

But Makhno returned to Huliaipole after receiving telegrams from his mother and comrades, imploring him to return to Ukraine.[3] Makhno boarded a train headed south and by late March was back in his hometown.[4] He promised to keep in touch with Arshinov, who elected to remain behind in Moscow to organize. Makhno would return to Moscow, about a year later, under desperate circumstances, in a much different world. But for now there was work to do in his homeland—to build anarcho-communism along Kropotkin's lines.

Nestor Makhno was like a man back from the dead—a prisoner given a life sentence now happily walking the streets of his hometown. While his memoirs claim that he plunged directly into revolutionary work, the truth is a bit more complicated. Nestor returned to Huliaipole to find his mother much aged and his brother Savva, a veteran of the Russo-Japanese War, heavily involved in local anarchist causes. For his part, Nestor got a job at a factory and started working, though he didn't stay there terribly long. Later in the year of his release, in November, Makhno took up with Anastasia Vasetskaia (who had been a pen pal with Makhno while he was in Butyrka prison) and the couple had a child together.[5] Sadly, the child didn't live more than a few days, and the couple went their separate ways.[6]

But before and during that, Makhno bounced between factory work, desk jobs coordinating troop movements and maps for the First World War, and local activism for anarchist causes. Even at a desk job, Makhno was a micromanager—a trait that might not have endeared him to his comrades, but the conviction that he should see to the little details of things personally would save his life several times over.

Makhno plunged into the thick of revolutionary organization, an operation with a surprising amount of physical and emotional Sturm und Drang in unexpected ways. One policeman, Nazar Onishchenko, who had beaten Nestor when he was younger and harassed Mrs. Makhno, passed him on the street in plainclothes. Former officer Onishchenko nervously doffed his hat and said an overly cheery "Nestor Ivanovich! How do you do!" Nestor Makhno lost his mind for a moment and shrieked back as most of us would do in that situation: "Get away from me, scoundrel, or I'll put a bullet in you!"[7]

Nestor did, in fact, have a revolver on him. He was seldom unarmed after being released from prison, as matter of fact. He almost ventilated Onishchenko there and then in the street, but he instead dashed off, collapsing at a nearby cafe and sobbing. If it wasn't a nervous breakdown, then it certainly was a close cousin to one.

This wasn't the only time the emotional weight of revolution—specifically around executions—got to Makhno. His high-strung nature simply wouldn't allow him to be indifferent about nearly anything. He eventually pulled himself together, and came up with several good reasons why he spared Onishchenko. While Nestor would absolutely have loved to shoot him down, doing so wouldn't have helped further the social revolution, Makhno would later argue to his comrades in a meeting meant to decide the former policeman's fate. Onischenko was actually one of the least dangerous former police at large—killing him out of hand might spook his other, more dangerous colleagues.[8]

Makhno returned to a Huliaipole in disarray—the regional government had fled or was impotent, and the few surviving anarchists of the rebellions of 1905–9 had banded together. Nestor Makhno and the local anarcho-communists had been through the mostly abandoned Huliaipole police station, you see, specifically the files they had kept on anarchist and revolutionary socialist groups. Makhno had seen to this personally, especially the files the police kept on shpiks or informers. Quite a few close friends had been police informants, which explained why they hadn't returned to Huliaipole or congratulated Makhno on his good fortune. It was a sobering bit of information, to know how thoroughly their movement had been infiltrated, indeed the fatal tip that had killed the legendary Semenyuta and his partner had come from one of the anarchist's own friends years earlier.[9]

Commissars from the Provisional Revolutionary Government would try to inveigle support from the peasants with grand speeches about motherland and rights that would be granted to them using jingoistic language. They also sent "Land Committees" to the villages to collect rent and taxes, something the Ukrainian peasants weren't terribly keen on. In June, representatives of the Provisional Government visited Huliaipole. Political power from a distant government of reactionaries and collaborators was not to the taste of the farmers, peasants, and artisans of Huliaipole, not when they could and did arrange their own affairs regarding the land. The script might be simplified to something like this:

Provisional Government representative (to a crowd of restless peasants): So it is imperative that you keep calm and go about your business just like you did when the czar was in power. Pay your rent to your landlords—or the people we've brought in to replace your landlords, don't make a fuss and we super-promise to hold a meeting and tell you what your rights are! Sounds, good, right? Trust the process! We'll build back better—while still keeping and in some cases expanding the overall social structure that makes sure that you are poor and desperate while preserving our political power!
Crowd: How about no. (A savage beating of representative emissaries ensues as they are pulled off the platform.)[10]

The anarchists, Makhno and his comrades made clear—did not seek to rule the peasants of Ukraine, only to advise them to rule themselves, to take all land in common and to despise both government and political parties as power-hungry parasites interested only in domination. However, there was no exact blueprint for how to build an anarchist utopia in rural Ukraine. According to Makhno, the anarchists scoured the works of Mikhail Bakunin, Kropotkin, and even the tireless Italian Malatesta for specific advice on their situation as anarchists.[11] Not that there was nothing useful in those texts as general precepts—local control, democratic councils, etc.—but there were no specific action points contained in the works of these writers of anarchism that applied specifically to the Huliaipole anarchists.

The methods of the city didn't translate into the countryside so they couldn't do as the city anarchists had done and were doing. Nobody was coming to help them build the new world—they would have to build it themselves, together.[12] To do this, Makhno and the anarchists ceaselessly labored to educate the peasants of Ukraine—who desperately wanted simply to control their own lands. To help with this, in this phase of history, the anarchist councils recruited heavily from the local teachers. Teachers were especially respected by the anarchists as they turned schools meant to produce factory workers and farmers into schools based on the models of Francisco Ferrer—a Spanish anarchist and educator who had the wacky idea that a child's interests should determine what they learned about or pursued. This actually leads to a brief encounter between Makhno and his future girlfriend, Halyna Kuzmenko—who was a teacher in Huliaipole at the time.[13]

THE PEOPLE'S COMMITTEE FOR THE DEFENSE OF THE REVOLUTION
ON THEIR WAY TO AN EXPROPRIATION

Makhno and his comrades kept busy—organizing local councils, leading fights and protests against rent collection, and forming committees,
most notably the People's Committee for the Defense of the Revolution. It
was this committee that Makhno headed and that was in charge of expro-
priating the property, land, and tools of the upper classes.[14] The anarchists
had learned the lessons from the Stolypin repression well. They especially
looked to prevent another alliance between wealthy landowners and
government to quash social revolution by disarming the upper classes.

The expropriations, marvelously, according to Makhno's account, were
bloodless. They may have been *less* bloody than expected, but they were
certainly not bloodless events. Five or ten peasants (with certificates from
the People's Committee for the Defense of the Revolution) per wagon
would be sent in waves out to the large manors and estates to evenly divide
the land among the people who worked it, take any and all weapons in
the houses of the wealthy, and divide the tools and livestock evenly. The
landlords and wealthy would get the exact same—enough to live on--as
the people they had formerly employed.[15] This was direct action and in
keeping with anarchist principles and initiatives, as was the formation of
communes, the holding of public votes on courses of action, and the reconstruction of schools.

One memorable incident in Huliaipole in early fall involved a member
of the Rada, one Mikhno, being sent to Huliaipole in September of 1917
to ask why they hadn't been complying with commands from the central
government. Yes, the Rada sent someone named Mikhno specifically to
treat with Nestor Makhno from neighboring Alexandrovsk. Like most
government officials, any instances of humor are at best entirely accidental.

Specifically, the Rada (basically Congress, but also used as a shorthand term for "the government" itself) was very upset at the Ukrainian
anarchists for disarming the rich and seizing their land. The Rada needed
the rich to survive—and were not terribly pleased with Huliaipole's independence. Other cities and provinces might get ideas! Already, there was
tension between Huliaipole and neighboring cities like Alexandrovsk,
which had more government forces in it and feared the spread of anarchist
ideas—mostly the socialization and commoning of land.

Makhno had terse private meeting with Mikhno. It was rather
one-sided. Mikhno sat and sputtered and blushed and asked a bunch of
questions about the disarming of the bourgeoisie, the arming of the peasants, and the expropriations earlier in the year, which boiled down to: How

dare Makhno do this! Makhno took some time to get Mikhno to be able to express all of his consternation, eventually asking him to please write his complaints down. This Mikhno did.

Makhno then told Mikhno that he had twenty minutes to get clear of Huliaipole before something tragic happened to him. The man from the Central Rada then demonstrated a remarkable alacrity and fled the city, not to return. Makhno would meet Mikhno again sometime later, in different circumstances, in neighboring Alexandrovsk.[16]

Nestor Makhno and the anarchists were busy making Huliaipole into an anarchist polity with some success and some setbacks. Ukrainian anarchist movements often were relatively small. Unlike the Shinmin Prefecture in Korea or the Confederation of Labor–Iberian Anarchist Federation in Catalonia, the active propaganda and generations of institutional knowledge required to bring forth a large number of ideological anarchists didn't exist in rural Ukraine at this time. This was a source of constant frustration for Makhno and other anarchist organizers in the countryside, along with the perceived lack of support from "city anarchists" in form of material aid, propaganda, or educators.[17]

It is in this period that Maria Nikiforova reenters our story, as a visitor to Huliaipole. She arrived as a guest speaker at a meeting that Makhno was in charge of chairing.[18] Makhno interrupted one of her speeches to a packed audience with news of a right-wing coup attempt in Petrograd with troops led by General Kornilov. Kornilov's failed putsch was the first domino to tip over in the fall of the Kerensky government and the Bolshevik seizure of power under Lenin, though this was impossible to know at the time.

The mood in the crowd switched to murderous rather swiftly. Ire was focused in particular on a former policeman, Ivanov, in the crowd. Maria Nikiforova seemed to be OK with letting the crowd lynch Ivanov then and there. This was not to be. Makhno left the dais and rushed to Ivanov's defense. He personally assured Ivanov that no harm would come to him— Ivanov hadn't opposed the anarchists when they'd taken over, and had surrendered his weapons in good faith. It would be wrong to kill him. The crowd relented in the face of Makhno's defense of the former policeman.[19]

It was the beginning of a long and uneasy association between Makhno and Nikiforova. Makhno would often travel to Nikiforova's hometown of Alexandrovsk as a representative of Huliaipole—Alexandrovsk was located directly on a rail line, whereas Huliaipole was not. This made Alexandrovsk a valuable and critical city to control southeastern Ukraine.

In 1917, Makhno entered into a guarded alliance with the Left Bloc government of Alexandrovsk against the Austro-Hungarian forces backed by the Central Rada. Ukrainian nationalists were perfectly happy to take foreign guns, money, equipment, and troops for their own ends—especially from the Austro-Hungarians, but had no patience for people who didn't match their definition of "Ukrainian" who were minding their own business, not hurting anyone.

Makhno was too keen an observer to fail to notice that the Socialist Revolutionaries and Bolsheviks, while pretending unity for the moment, would absolutely not share power once the threat was past. Betrayal was coming, if not today, than as soon as one side was willing to risk it.

Makhno's duties in Alexandrovsk ranged from helping negotiate successful strikes to reviewing the files of people accused of crimes against the revolution. In this, at least according to Makhno, most of the accused, while opposed to revolution, were not guilty of what they were accused of. Most of them, he noted in his memoirs, had been swept up by denunciations: unarmed, in their homes, and trotted out to likely execution: "The majority of them were innocent of the crime they were accused of . . . they were arrested because of the denunciations of evil people. I mean people, who in order to conceal their own dirty past record vis-à-vis the revolutionaries, had become even more odious by reversing themselves and hypocritically supporting the Revolutions."[20] Makhno was frequently at loggerheads with the other members of the tribunal in calling for leniency. Even at this early stage, he disliked the Bolshevik's methods and after-the-fact rationalizations. It was in his position as a judge, as a matter of fact, that Makhno encountered the bossy government functionary, Mikhno, yet again! Makhno didn't like Mikhno—the man had tried to brandish his authority in his face and threatened Makhno with reprisals and doubtless the dislike went both ways. Makhno writes that he wasn't sure he could judge Mikhno fairly due to these factors—but relented that Mikhno shouldn't be executed for simply doing his job under the government. Likely what landed hardest to tilt Makhno's decision to spare Mikhno was that he had a reputation for honesty in his hometown and had a reputation as a good liberal before the revolution—Makhno always admired honest people. Besides, Makhno concluded, Huliaipole and the anarchists had never followed Mikhno's strident and toothless orders nor did they intend to. He was powerless to make them do anything by force. Mikhno was not executed and allowed to go free.

This mercy and understanding was not applied by the committee (or Makhno and his comrades) in the cases of shpiks. One in particular (identified both by police records the anarchists had acquired, and by an eyewitness, Marfa Piven—Semenyuta's girlfriend who survived her partner's fatal shootout, though she nearly died from a bullet to the forehead years earlier) was a former comrade named Vasyl Sharovsky. Sharovsky was caught and made a series of excuses—but Makhno and the remaining Huliaipole anarchists weren't inclined to be merciful. The brothers Makhno and several others spent a lot of time interrogating Sharovsky and then shot him dead in January 1918.[21] Not everything was conflict though, when the chips were down, Makhno would work with the Left Bloc of Alexandrovsk—with his teeth clenched.

Maria Nikiforova and Makhno even set out into battle together in early 1918 against a trainload of White Cossacks at the Kitchkass Bridge. Makhno notes that it went better than expected (even though he complained that the Left Bloc troops arranged their heavy machine guns wastefully at the front of the line) and the majority of Cossacks surrendered to Makhno and Nikiforova.[22] They were disarmed and taken back to Alexandrovsk, where Nikiforova read them the riot act about their behavior in fighting for the czar and oppressing the peasantry. Apparently, this is the way to talk to Cossacks—the anarchists let the Cossacks go, but many of them donated money and left their addresses for anarchist publications to be sent to them.[23] Outreach!

Not that Makhno had everything his own way. He had to be prevented from acquiring sufficient explosives in Alexandrovsk, for example, to level the prison he'd once been locked into, by none other than Maria Nikiforova and the Left Bloc government.[24] Makhno became more and more disillusioned with the Left Bloc government—wondering why he was working with people determined to *stop* a revolution when he could simply go back to the countryside and make his own anarchist polity instead of being dragged through the mud of politics and compromising with counterrevolutionaries in an alliance of convenience.

Toward the end of 1917, the people of Huliaipole arranged a direct exchange of crops for textiles with workers in Moscow. They sent the food to the starving city of the north but found, to their frustration (and Makhno's), that their return shipment of cloth had been forcibly delayed by the Bolsheviks at Alexandrovsk. The idea of people dealing directly with each other, Makhno explained, made the Bolsheviks quite nervous indeed. Other cities and people might start getting *ideas*. Can't have that. Makhno was immediately on the phone to Alexandrovsk, and the people of Huliaipole immediately demanded an explanation.

The Alexandrovsk Left Bloc government made excuses, but ultimately promised to send the textile train on its way. The peasants of Huliaipole counted this as good news, but also resolved to arm themselves. If the shipment wasn't received in two days, they would march on Alexandrovsk and damn the consequences. To fail to provide consequences would be tacit permission for Alexandrovsk to jerk them around whenever they were bored. Makhno agreed, and armed himself. The march on Alexandrovsk wasn't ultimately necessary. The textile train arrived on time in Huliaipole. Kropotkin's system of exchange, so vividly imagined in *The Conquest of Bread* and *Mutual Aid*, worked despite interference from politicos and state officials.[25]

Early in 1918, Huliaipole was taken by the Austro-Hungarians with the connivance of the Central Rada—the exact circumstances of which we will examine in the next chapter. The communes and mutual aid work that Makhno and his comrades had worked so hard to establish and encourage were destroyed or disbanded. The year of stability—that had started with Makhno's chains being struck off—looked as if it would end with them being put back on.

CHAPTER 8

Makhno Returns to Moscow (1918)

> "Force is as pitiless to the man who possesses it, or thinks he does, as it is to its victims; the second it crushes, the first it intoxicates."
> —Simone Weil

Nestor Makhno had the distressing habit of wanting to get everything done himself. In short, he didn't like to delegate. This micromanaging tendency meant he was always on the go, and it was this same tendency that quite possibly saved his life when the Austro-Hungarians and their allies (the Central Ukrainian Rada) took his hometown of Huliaipole in April. Makhno got wind of this while he was with the Red Guards at Tsarevokonstantinovka (bless you) and immediately sank into a spasm of anxiety and depression.

Makhno's attack was so severe that he lost most of his memory of it. He spent a long time sobbing into the lap of a sympathetic Red Guard before he was able to compose himself. After the attack passed, Makhno excused himself and found that his brother, Savva, and several other anarchists had managed to escape Huliaipole and make their way to Tsarevokonstantinovka. They filled Nestor in on how things stood—not great, the Austro-Hungarians and nationalists were spreading and encouraging antisemitism in Huliaipole to divide the population against itself, and severe reprisals were being dealt to any remaining anarchists. The city had been surrendered without a shot due to nationalist infiltration, to hear them tell it.[1]

After prolonged discussion, the anarchists split up. Nestor Makhno and his comrades made their way to Taganrog, the temporary headquarters of the Left Socialist Revolutionary–Bolshevik government. Their plan was to organize a resistance against the Austro-Hungarians and the Ukrainian puppet government, the Rada, they had put in place. This meant that the invading forces brought back the landlords and local gentry that many Ukrainian villages had forced to flee or had exiled.

As one can imagine, neither the landlords nor their former tenants were terribly happy to see each other. Terrible reprisals against the Ukrainian peasants followed. Makhno speculated in his memoirs—and based his whole strategy around the idea—that the military progress of the Rada and the Germans was "built on sand."[2] Having had a taste of freedom—and revolutionary organization and unity—Makhno had no doubt that the peasants of Ukraine could drive out the invaders, given time, instruction on the grassroots level, and guns.

Life continued to pour salt and lemon juice on Makhno's emotional wounds. In the city of Taganrog, his fellow anarchist and revolutionary Maria Nikiforova (who you may remember from chapter 4) had been seized by the local Socialist Revolutionaries and Bolsheviks. It was almost a certain death sentence, cooked up by the Bolsheviks to remove anarchists once they were off the front lines. Makhno and the other anarchists, even at this early stage in the wars, knew that the Bolsheviks were happy to use anarchists as cannon fodder, then execute or imprison the survivors once they were no longer of use fighting the counterrevolution. It was as plain as the nose on Makhno's face. Nikiforova's troops steadfastly refused to integrate into the Red Army as ordered, and demanded the release of their commander or else.

Makhno wrote a telegram to the commander of the Red Ukrainian front, Vladimir Antonov-Ovseyenko, begging him to intercede. Antonov-Ovseyenko wrote to the judges, saying: "The detachment of the anarchist Maria Nikiforova, as well as comrade Nikiforova herself, are well known to me. Instead of concerning yourself with disarming such units, I would advise you to concern yourself with creating them."[3] Antonov-Ovseyenko would go from a rather broad "Bolsheviks and anarchists can get along" policy to being in charge of repression against anarchist movements both in this Civil War, and in the Spanish Civil war under Stalin—not that it saved him from being purged in 1938.[4]

Combined with an outpouring of support from locals and other prominent leaders of the revolution (an armored train of anarchists didn't hurt matters), the tribunal of Nikiforova found her innocent. Nikiforova rearmed herself and returned her to her combat unit, her *druzhina*. Though Nikiforova was to survive the next trial by Bolsheviks, sometime later in similar circumstance (with some of the same charges recycled), this was a small miracle. The tactic of arresting anarchist or Left Socialist Revolutionary leaders and forcibly integrating their troops into the newly formed Red Army under Bolshevik commissars was common in the Civil War. It was intended to prevent the anarchists from gaining critical mass and appeal among the peoples of the former Russian Empire, and it partially succeeded.

As he was leaving Taganrog and looking for his wife among the flood of refugees, Makhno came upon one Mikhail Polonsky, an acquaintance and head of the Huliaipole Free Battalion. Polonsky complained mightily that he was sick of anarchism and the Left Socialist Revolutionaries, and was going to try and learn how to be a Bolshevik. If that didn't work, he was just going to sit on the sidelines—trying any harder might result in hazards to his health. Makhno had a good laugh at this comment, gave him some funds from the common chest and sent Polonsky on his way.[5] Polonsky would succeed in his quest to become a Bolshevik, and a little more than a year later would try to assassinate Makhno personally. The theme of Makhno meeting people who will try to assassinate him later is at this point firmly established in the narrative, and we've barely even started.

Makhno left Taganrog, and traveled north, toward Moscow. He would see Bolshevik duplicity up close, far closer than he would like as he traveled. In the city of Tikhoretskaya, Makhno and his traveling companion were arrested on the way to buy food at the bazaar and informed they would be shot "under martial law." Makhno didn't take the threat seriously at first and joked "It's nice to be shot under martial law, instead of the normal way."[6] The Bolsheviks didn't appreciate Makhno's sense of humor and beat him with whips and rifle butts until Makhno managed to get a copy of his papers to the head of the local Revolutionary Committee, who freed him while apologizing profusely.

The former Russian Empire was dissolving like a sugar cube in water. This was not lost on the inhabitants of the former empire and there were a number of people and groups who tried to get out while the getting was good and form independent polities. Some, like Finland and Poland, succeeded to varying degrees. Others, like most of modern-day Ukraine, ultimately did not. This is to say nothing of the Islamic Basmachi, White Ruthenia, the United Duchy, Karelia, Crimea, the Mountain Republic, the Nargen Republic of Sailors and Builders, Tannu Tuva, the Far Eastern Republic, Green Ukraine, the Altai, Siberia, Idel-Ural, the Don Republic, the Kuban Republic, and the North Caucasian Emirate.

Makhno was aware of the dissolution of the Kuban Republic during his travels north. The republic only lasted from May 30 to July 7, 1918.[7] Makhno was part of an echelon that saw the sack of the revolutionary city of Rostov by White forces on his way to Tsaritsyn. He was shocked by the brutality of it all—recall his nervous breakdown when facing the police officer in Huliaipole—and wondered if there was a way to escape the cycle of reprisal and counterreprisal.

The forces of counterrevolution were many and well-funded, by France and England and even the United States. They were a real and critical threat to any sort of social revolution. Watching pillagers take advantage of the chaos and the refugees streaming out of Rostov, he despaired.

Makhno concluded that a life without a separate political class and true freedom was the only chance. "For our social life, in order to concretize real freedom, requires direct and genuine cooperation from all the people who only through their own efforts can develop and defend such freedom for themselves and for their society."[8]

As Makhno traveled, he learned again and again that the revolution itself was not simply imperiled by the upper classes and foreign powers. Other revolutionaries—Bolsheviks—were taking advantage of the chaos of a war to purge their one-time allies, anarchists and Left Social Revolutionaries.

Makhno was a keen observer—and believed that the revolutionary governments were strangling the spirit of revolution, or as he put it "maintaining themselves with whips and rifle butts."[9] He was nearly executed several times in the course of his travels—by Bolsheviks, Left Socialist Revolutionaries, and White Army men.

Makhno came upon Petr Petrenko, a man he admired, defeating a superior Bolshevik force at the city of Tsaritsyn. Seeking to avert bloodshed, Petrenko didn't follow up on his victory and offered clemency to his former allies. Petrenko consequently was caught off guard and arrested by Bolshevik forces in a moment of inattention. The Bolsheviks seized the governance of Tsaritsyn as well but were deeply unpopular with the citizens. Makhno didn't linger long in Tsaritsyn but did give some advice to a few of Petrenko's followers: if you're going to free your leader, you should do it sooner rather than later (he specifically said he thought the job could be done with a dozen men with pistols and grenades) before the Bolsheviks consolidated power.[10]

It was at Tsaritsyn that Makhno remade his acquaintance on the train with the Red Guard who had comforted him at the beginning of this chapter (who filled him in on that period of lost time and the present situation in Tsaritsyn), as well as brushed up against a future Bolshevik would-be assassin, Kliment Voroshilov.[11] Makhno then left Tsaritsyn, despondent.

Petrenko's trial, it might interest you to know, was delayed and delayed, until one fine day he was taken from his cell and executed by the Cheka when the public had other things on its mind.[12] Standard Bolshevik procedure.

Makhno continued his picaresque journey north to Moscow. The Cheka's repression against anarchists and non-Bolsheviks was intensifying, with Lenin railing against anarchists in *Pravda*. Makhno observed the widening rift between the Left Socialist Revolutionaries and the Bolsheviks—in fact, in July 1918, in an attempt to restart a war with Germany (and thus make the Bolsheviks even more unpopular, a hefty feat indeed), the Left Socialist Revolutionaries assassinated the German ambassador in Moscow, Wilhelm von Mirbach. Or at least, were accused of doing so by the Bolsheviks as a pretense to purge them.

Makhno realized the value of discretion and disguise, rarely disclosing that he was an anarchist to anyone. In true Makhno style, he secretly got in touch with the local anarchists and even submitted a poem to one of their broadsheets under his old prison nickname—his first published work! Nobody took much notice, but those who had known him in prison could have identified the author.

Makhno got into Moscow via Astrakhan disguised as a Bolshevik agitator, completely unnoticed.

Makhno wasn't a fan of most Russian cities, Moscow in particular—complaining that the anarchists he found there weren't doing much by his estimation, and that one could hardly find bread unless one went into a back alley and paid an exorbitant fee. He called Moscow "the capital of the paper revolutionaries."[13] This cemented his already dim view of city life and people who chose to live there, generally speaking.

Makhno made some exceptions to this general rule. One such exception was Alexei Borovoi, at this time an individualist anarchist and university lecturer. Borovoi once wrote, on his coming to anarchism in a quite instinctual way despite his later intellectual career: "No one taught anarchism to me, didn't persuade me, didn't infect me.... Suddenly, out of some unknown depths a great, well-formed, enlightening, united thought was born in me. With unusual clarity, with victorious cogency a feeling of an attitude that was new to me was born in me.... I stood up from the bench in the Luxembourg Garden as an enlightened, passionate, uncompromising anarchist, and I still remain one."[14]

Makhno was so swept away by Borovoi's lecture titled "Tolstoy and His Creative Work" that Makhno embraced Borovoi after he had concluded and talked his ear off.[15] Perhaps, Makhno thought, there were some intellectuals with spines as well as poetical sentiments in the face of revolution and repression.

Makhno managed to snag a meeting with Kropotkin himself. It was a short meeting, only a couple of hours, but apparently the two men were much impressed by each other. After two months of heartbreak and betrayal, of being driven from his family, and seeing his erstwhile allies turn on the revolution even in its infancy, combined with the lack of sleep, the fear, the piss-poor food and drink, and the sweltering heat and powder burns on his hands, it must have been a rare moment of complete inner peace to meet the man who wrote the words of the book that Makhno kept under his pillow.

Those same words—with their message of cooperation, solidarity, and human equality had helped keep Makhno not only sane, but something of an idealist in the best sense of the word during his prison sentence. For his part, Kropotkin, who had met more than his fair share of anarchist revolutionaries in his time, was impressed by Makhno and offered the young man words of encouragement. Sadly, no records other than Makhno's brief account of their meeting exist, so it is not possible to know exactly who said what and in what order, but fortunately, Makhno was a prolific letter writer and kept up a correspondence. Evidence of the obvious affection between the two men can be found in a 1919 letter from Makhno to Kropotkin. I've reproduced it here, complete with typos:

Dear Petr Alekseyevich!!!,,

Knowing the food supply in Russia and considering how this might affect your old bones, I talked things over with some of my comrades and we decided to send you a few pounds of victuals which we think you should have. Along with this I'm sending you several issues of our insurgent newspaper, "The Road to Freedom" and leaflets published by us. And I ask of you as a comrade who is close and dear to us southerners to write us a letter about the insurgency of our region which is accurately described in our newspaper.

Besides this it would be very important to the peasants if you could write an article for our newspaper about social construction in villages which have not yet succumbed to the world of violence. Stay healthy,
Firmly I press your hand,
Respectfully yours
"Batko" N. Makhno
Gulai Polye
30th May
1919[16]

Makhno was a functional vagrant in Moscow, moving from comrade to comrade, staying where he could go unnoticed. The Cheka were still doing their bloody work, and the anarchist counterstroke had yet to arrive. However, in this rootless time in his life, Makhno managed to secure an audience with Yakov Sverdlov and Lenin. While no corroborating documentation from Lenin or Sverdlov exists to confirm this meeting, Makhno records it. This has led some to doubt the veracity of the report, but I'm inclined to believe Makhno. Makhno might be reasonably called a sometimes-drunk, hot-headed, and brusque, but it is generally agreed that he was not a liar. Furthermore, there was no reason for him to fib about meeting Lenin and Sverdlov in Moscow. Vladimir "The Truth Is Whatever Is Politically Expedient for Me at the Moment" Lenin had every reason not to popularize or announce a meeting with an exponent of an ideology he was at that very moment trying to quash with the Cheka. Makhno saw everything through a revolutionary lens, and had little reason to lie about something like this—whereas Lenin and Sverdlov would have ample reason to conceal negotiations with a known anarchist at this fragile time in Bolshevik power. Even at this early time, both men had hands with plenty of blood under their fingernails—war communism and the purges of political dissidents were just some of the crimes they'd already committed.

Lenin was the archetypal "paper revolutionary." According to his one of his biographers: "Lenin never watched an execution squad at work, never

MAKHNO AND KROPOTKIN MEET IN 1918

saw the effects of the terror he created. He rarely traveled outside Moscow; for weeks on end he remained within the walls of Kremlin, spending all the available time in his study, poring over documents, sending out telegrams."[17] Not that this stopped Vladimir "Right-Wing Autocrat in a Thin Paper Leftist Suit" Lenin from ordering mass executions of everyone from "kulaks" (in his now infamous 'Hanging Telegram') to sex workers in Nizhny Novgorod from the safety of his office in 1918.[18]

A really subtle way to tell whether Nestor Makhno thinks someone is an asshole when you read his memoirs is as follows: If a person uses the phrase "South Russia" instead of "Ukraine" when talking with Makhno, that person is an asshole. Both Sverdlov and Lenin make this mistake. Makhno corrected them without getting outwardly angry, but it was a tense conversation—Makhno was reluctant to out himself as an anarchist (though he did), given the Bolshevik track record with them.[19]

Makhno convinced the two Bolshevik leaders to give him false papers to get back into Ukraine, with the aim of furthering revolution there. Ukraine was technically under the auspices of Austro-Hungary, so anything that the Bolsheviks could do to destabilize it (and from their point of view, eventually reabsorb it into the Russian empire with the Bolsheviks at the helm) with minimal risk to themselves was something they'd happily sponsor.[20] Makhno left Moscow having unwittingly met another man who would order his death in the future.

Makhno survived both Sverdlov and Lenin. Sverdlov died in 1919 of typhus, and in August of 1918, just after Makhno left, Lenin was nearly assassinated by Fanny Kaplan after Lenin banned (and purged) the Socialist Revolutionary Party, of which she was a member. Sadly, Ms. Kaplan's aim was not as true as it could have been—she was practically blind from previous mishandling of an IED by her partner.[21] She knew she was likely doomed in any case, whether Lenin lived or died. She was correct, and was killed by the Cheka shortly after. Her bullets failed to kill him outright—but they did incapacitate Lenin and severely compromise his subsequent health.[22]

Makhno was ultimately outfitted with papers by Volodymyr Zatonsky, who held leadership in the Ukrainian People's Republic (under Lenin's orders), to return to Ukraine. The aid included a false passport and transport to the Ukrainian border. This would be unremarkable in and of itself if it wasn't for the fact that Zatonsky would show up like a bad penny in Nestor's life nearly a year later, in yet another assassination attempt on Makhno.

The list of later Bolshevik/Soviet luminaries who tried to have Makhno assassinated could fill a bus. From Zatonsky to Polonsky (who didn't survive his own laughably overplanned attempt), to the murderously spiteful Voroshilov (who Nikita Khrushchev in the 1950s would consider something of a living fossil of the Civil War), and the ever-preening and dreadfully dull Trotsky. That is, to name but a few. To a man every one of them thought that surely they would be the one to claim Makhno's head, and to a man they were wrong. Zatonsky later barely escaped Makhno's wrath, but he didn't escape Stalin's Great Purge and was executed by firing squad in 1938.

Makhno made it over the border to Ukraine with relative ease. He was briefly arrested by the Austrians but managed to escape them and enter Ukraine. He made his way to Huliaipole through roundabout means, walking the last few miles on foot, seeing signs that read in German "Die Vaterland" around his old hometown.[23] Makhno liked what he found when he returned even less than the annoying signage. The Austro-Hungarians had shot Nestor's brother Yemelyan, burned down the family home, and abused Makhno's mother.[24] The stage was set for a very personal war for Makhno.

CHAPTER 9

Makhno Returns to Huliaipole (1918)

> "I don't remember the exact date in July when I went into the railway station to buy a newspaper and ran into Makhno, who was traveling to Ukraine to start a revolt against the government of Hetman Skoropadsky. He told me 'nothing' was going on in Moscow—there was a complete split between the Communists and the Anarchists and 'in general, the only thing being created in Moscow is rubbish.'"
>
> —Aleksei Chubenko

It's always hard to make a compelling case for the worst year of Nestor Ivanovich's life, but certainly the most rapid change of circumstances occurred in the second half of 1918. During this brief period (in no particular order) he

- adopted a pseudonym;
- was suspected of espionage and nearly murdered at a hoedown by people convinced he was a progovernment spy;
- averted a vicious pogrom in his hometown;
- helped create a resistance movement of Ukrainian toilers against the Austro-Hungarians, the Ukrainian Rada, and then the Ukrainian Directory under Petliura;
- formed the core of the Makhnovist command staff;
- narrowly escaped being captured several times by his enemies;
- was shot at in many varied and interesting locations;

- met a cute anarchist lass who then became his girlfriend (more on her later);
- got shot at some more (this would become something of a theme in Makhno's life);
- dressed as a woman for reconnaissance several times;
- personally led expropriations of the land and wealth of the rich and powerful;
- managed to retake his hometown of Huliaipole from the kulaks and Austro-Hungarians;
- met a weirdo in a sailor suit who would prove to be oddly important and a liability all at once;
- and, of course, was declared dead by his many enemies (falsely), having finally succeeded in creating an autonomous zone in southern Ukraine completely devoid of conventional political power.

But let us start at the beginning of this period, just after his return from Moscow. Makhno was back in Ukraine, and he was pissed. He made a wide circuit around Huliaipole, staying in outlying towns and keeping a low profile—from the start, the Austro-Hungarians were hunting for the elusive Makhno. This meant sleeping in haylofts, roughing it, and generally taking the pulse of the peasantry while moving from place to place. Random raids and searches were the order of the day, and Makhno managed to slip through them through luck and skill.

Nestor kept up a healthy correspondence with the anarchists in Huliaipole. The Austro-Hungarians had taken Huliaipole and, with the help of the richer members of the community, launched a vicious purge of the anarchists and other revolutionary forces. Makhno discovered this through his letter writing—and the fact that this repression was chiefly blamed on the Jews of Huliaipole (with the help of the kulaks and Austro-Hungarian agents). The surviving anarchists of Huliaipole wrote to Makhno, asking for advice: What to do? Were they to take revenge?[1]

Makhno was horrified. He wrote back immediately pleading caution and discretion and to on no account engage in reprisals now. He wrote in his memoirs:

> I did not answer the gist of their letter but only urged them not to touch any of the traitors or provocateurs for the time being; and

in particular not to lay a finger on any of the Jews and stir up the population against them because this could sow the seeds for the emergence of anti-semitism. Anti-semitism could prevent us from creating the vital preconditions for the Revolution and fulfilling the hope of the peasants—the hope of liberating themselves from reaction and expelling the Hetman with all his clique of pomeshchiks, of not allowing other authorities and tyrants to strangle them, and of getting on with living their lives according to the principles of independence from all authorities of whatever hue in a free, self-determined and self-managed society.

Makhno, as a survivor of the 1905 uprising and an active militant until 1908, claims that antisemitism was a relatively new presence in the Huliaipole revolutionary scene, though not at all new to the Russian Empire as a whole.[2] Makhno's desire to avert a pogrom and follow the mandates of revolutionary justice and morality speaks well of him in this case. The peasants ultimately agreed with Makhno's points against a pogrom.

Makhno kept busy by gathering as much information on the fate of his family and comrades as he could while staying out of the center of Huliaipole. In some cases, the rumors of Makhno's return had saved lives— an hour before he was due to be shot, Nestor's cousin Mikhail was set free by nervous landowners when they heard that Nestor was back in town.

Others weren't so lucky. Countless friends of Makhno had been executed or betrayed, including his brother Emelian, executed in front of his family by the Austro-Hungarians, who made sure to do it where his children could see it after burning nearly everything the family possessed.[3]

However, Makhno's private letters to comrades, especially ones focused on the essential nature of resisting the Austro-Hungarians and nationalists, were being widely distributed among the peasantry. Peasants from the nearby village of Voskresenka took Makhno's words of resistance to heart, formed a "Makhnovist" battalion, and attacked an Austro-Hungarian punitive division, killing several soldiers and the commander.[4] While Makhno applauded the initiative—which was spreading to Huliaipole—of the Voskresenka peasants, the wide distribution of his letters also meant that the Austro-Hungarians knew he was in the area. Makhno had no choice but to leave the area around Huliaipole, it was simply too dangerous for him.

Nestor Makhno changed his name as well as his appearance to survive. Now he was Ivan Yakovlevich, if anyone asked.[5] He frequently dressed as a woman (sometimes with a male escort and sometimes solo) to investigate more densely populated towns and cities where the Austro-Hungarian troops were thickest.[6] Makhno was constantly on the move, one step ahead of informers, random patrols and people looking to cash in on the bounty on his head. Even when he was not actively pursued, Ukraine under the Hetmanate government could be a dangerous place for the wrong reasons. Consider the following incident at the city of Ternovka.

The conversation among the youths of the village of Ternovka, in broad strokes, went something like this:

> **Youth One**: Hey guys, you know that weird guy who only comes out at odd times and goes out into the woods and fields?
> **Youth Two**: Yeah, I know him. That does strike me as odd. And his "family" won't answer any questions about him up-front and act all sketchy when we ask questions?
> **Youth Three**: Yeah, I know the guy. Short, wiry, nervous looking? So we all agree he's clearly a Hetmanate spy, right?
> **All**: We gotta kill him.

So the youths, who were actually sympathetic to Makhno's mission (preparing the toilers of Ukraine to rise against the landlords and the Austro-Hungarians) planned to assassinate him at the soonest possible pretext. Their choice of excuse and event? Functionally a Ukrainian hoedown.

Makhno was invited to the hoedown, and found an event populated by the very young and the very old. He turned down the offer of a beer (something was very wrong here, he felt, but couldn't put his finger on it) and walked the barn, trying to gauge the mood. The oldsters played hand after hand of cards and the youngsters drank themselves silly.

Makhno felt ill at ease. He stalked the barn further, and then, unable to contain himself, mounted the makeshift stage and really let them have it. Why, Makhno demanded of his now captive audience, did they waste time in this way? Makhno chronicled at length the daily horrors of life under the occupation: men and women hung from telephone poles, livestock taken or slaughtered in the fields, and collective punishment. To say nothing of the burning of whole villages, the rapes, and slaughters. He spoke to them with as much fire as he could muster—making the point again and again that this was only occurring because the toilers had not yet armed themselves, had not steeled their hearts and organized against the oppression of the puppet government and the foreigners. In short, he demonstrated the most un-spy-like behavior possible. His speech was interrupted by the young attendees, who accused the old men of being only good at cards and having no guts. The oldsters shot back that the only thing the young could teach them was how to get drunk.

Nestor Makhno retired from the stage, where he was approached by some of the younger members of the audience. "Hey, funny story." One of them said, more or less. "We were all but certain you were a Hetmanate spy! We actually were planning on taking you out back, shooting you in the head, and burying you in an unmarked grave! It'd be like you'd never been here. But now we see you are a great friend to the revolution! Close call, eh? Pretty funny, when you think about it!" Nestor Makhno said nothing. The youth continued, saying in effect: "We have these weapons, old shotguns, bayonets, and rifles from our time in the Red Guards (critical vocab distinction: Red Guards were leftist army volunteers. The Red Army was a "professional" army organized by Leon Trotsky and based on a conscription model). We dug them up to use them on you, originally, but also on the Austro-Hungarians!" Nestor Makhno, unsurprisingly, did not find this especially funny and needed to have a long sit-down. Almost being murdered by the people you're trying to recruit might have that effect.[7]

The Austro-Hungarians and the Ukrainian *varta* (national guards) instituted brutal repressions on the Ukrainian peasantry. Things were rather bleak, as they tend to be when someone can kick down your door in the middle of the night and seize you on the barest pretext. But Makhno and others like him continued organizing peasant guerrilla squadrons in the small villages and farms of southern Ukraine. The field was being set for a counterattack, invisible to the invading armies and the puppet government they supported.

Until it wasn't.

Makhno found himself a celebrity and a leader of a movement nearly overnight. Apparently his comrades around Huliaipole had begun circulating his responses to them in the local broadsheets and pamphlets, as a potent form of anarchist propaganda. People began to organize themselves into bands where Makhno had never set foot and called themselves "Makhnovists." Their specialty was in guerrilla tactics—hitting Austro-Hungarian or varta punitive divisions on the road or assassinating their officers before vanishing back into the steppe or burying their weapons and making their way back to their villages.

It was a legitimate bottom-up social movement based on the key principle of socializing the land back to the peasantry for common use. In this sense, the Makhnovist movement can be seen as an aggressive proponent of *recommoning*: rolling back the spread of private property and private ownership of essential resources. The most direct form of this was expropriations: dividing the lands and wealth of the kulaks among the peasants evenly. Unlike Nikiforova, as we've discussed, Makhno made an allowance for the wealthy classes to join the peasants—by dissolving them as a class and giving them the same resources as their former workers, he offered the chance for integration rather than a complete bloody purge of the upper classes in his territory. Of course, this must be taken with a grain of salt, because the best source we have on this is Makhno himself in his memoirs, and he was sensitive about his revolutionary integrity. It is still fair to say that early in his revolutionary career, Makhno was much more open to nonviolent integration into his movement than he would be later in the long struggles.

None of Makhno and his band's tasks were easy. The peasants had few weapons at hand at any given time, and what they did have were antiques, improvised, or taken from the corpses of their enemies. They were forced to compensate for their lack of formal training through close-range ambushes and surprise attacks.

Recall the motto of Tom Barry of the Irish Republican Army who is purported to have said "There are no bad shots at ten or fifteen yards."[8] Barry was working in similar circumstances to the early Makhnovists: a deeply rural population without much training in formal military matters that was chronically short on weapons and ammunition against professional military forces. But he was very clear that shotguns were almost worse than useless in this context, but a long sight better than nothing and easily gotten in rural environs. However, historian Michael Malet makes the point that even the militarized Red Army in early 1919 handed out shotguns and shortened rifles, they were common in Left Bank Ukraine and could inflict nasty wounds at close range.[9]

All first-person accounts of the Makhnovschina, but especially those of Makhno, Voline, and Arshinov, go out of their way to mention the lack of weapons and ammunition holding back the progress of the movement. They had to turn away eager recruits on more than one occasion simply because there was nothing to arm them with. More popular leftist revolutions have failed due to lack of ammunition than due to lack of a workable strategy.

Makhno, in his memoirs, found time to snark at the anarchist intellectuals he had met in his long travels to Moscow. He wrote: "Without wasting any time, I issued orders (thereby violating a basic tenet of armchair anarchism) to leave the cavalry horses at their feeding troughs, hide their saddles under straw, and then sally forth from the courtyard with only a tachanka mounted with a machine-gun."[10]

Makhno would complain in his memoirs that there simply weren't enough anarchist propagandists and thinkers in the young movement to sufficiently distill and spread anarchist ideology to the peasants. As such, ideologically, the Makhnovist movement was a mixture of anarchists (in the command structure) and peasants who wanted socialized land but didn't make a lot of philosophical distinctions about how they got there. This complaint about a lack of sufficient intellectuals to radicalize the peasantry was also made by the Makhnovist Ossip Tsebry.[11]

It was at the village of Dibrivki that Makhno met Fedir Shchus. Their initial meeting was not an easygoing one, a harbinger for their relationship as a whole. Through the course of their three-year relationship, Makhno would jail Shchus for massacring Mennonite settlers, threaten to have him shot, and imply in his memoirs that Shchus had a cruel streak. Shchus, for his part, would be implicated in at least one scheme to depose Makhno in favor of Ukrainian nationalism under Petliura.[12]

As another charismatic leader with a significant following among the peasants and partisans, Shchus was an undeniable point of tension within Makhno's staff and movement. In short, it was better for Makhno to have Shchus inside the tent of anarchism, pissing out, than outside, pissing in. Had the Makhnovschina lasted longer, it seems likely these two would have come to blows eventually.

Have we mentioned that Shchus seldom took off his sailor's uniform or jaunty hat, making him both the best and worst real-life version of Popeye?[13] Makhno suspected that his first meeting with Shchus was an ambush up to the very last moment. Shchus and his partisans were hiding in a cabin in the woods, and after a protracted and back-and-forth battle with the varta (during which Makhno scolded Shchus via letter, to come out of hiding and join the fray, telling him not to behave "like a scared little boy") joined their group with Makhno's own.[14]

From this, a senior command structure began to emerge—it is the habit of "great man history" to credit all victories to a singular fellow and we shan't make that mistake here. Particularly among Makhno's command staff, despite their lack of formal schooling, Alexei Marchenko and Isidor Liuty stood out for their outstanding generalship and grasp of social realities. In Marchenko's case his keen conscience was used in meetings with Makhno to keep him on the straight and narrow, morally speaking.[15]

Makhno struggled with the difference between justice and vengeance. Sean Patterson quotes from Makhno's account of an incident later in the war, when a disguised Makhno and a few others stumbled across a *Selbstchutz* (Mennonite self-defense squad). Makhno and his friends asked the Mennonites if they had anything to do with the razing and pillaging of a local village, the smoke from which was still visible. The Selbstchutz happily admitted to it, and Makhno stormed off to a nearby hill overlooking the devastated village.

To quote Makhno: "Quite unconsciously I pulled out my revolver and placed it against my forehead."[16] Makhno couldn't reconcile the devastation he was seeing with his vision of equality, even though his forces hadn't been responsible for this incident. The lack of remorse on the part of this particular Selbstchutzen detail doubtless rankled him. This callousness hardened his heart somewhat, and Makhno went back down the hill, ordered his men to arrest the Selbstchutzen, and promptly executed them on the spot. Other, more formally taken Makhnovist captives were lucky—Makhnovist practice was to promptly execute the officers but to let the enlisted men go, sometimes with money but often with a note explaining that they were being spared to tell their comrades back home of the injustices in Ukraine and spread social revolution at home.

Shortly after the Battle of Dibrivki, Makhno's followers started calling him "Batko" Makhno—Father Makhno, a term of leadership and respect.[17] He leaned into this title, signing his letters in this manner (as you may recall from the letter he wrote to Kropotkin in 1919 featured in a previous chapter). To be fair, anyone who can defeat a force of three hundred with a force of twenty in a surprise attack probably deserves some sort of special title, don't you think? That's 15:1 odds, for those who like to gamble.

Makhno's memoirs claim that they defeated an Austro-Hungarian force, but documents from around that time, according to historian Colin Darch, indicate it was more likely that the Makhnovists soundly defeated a smaller varta detachment from a position of disadvantage. No matter who the combatants were, the Battle of Dibrivki was a turning point in Makhno's leadership and popularity. To quote historian Colin Darch: "Its symbolic importance as a personal victory for Makhno—who escaped the encirclement and gained the loyalty of his followers remains undeniable."[18]

The Austro-Hungarians retaliated by burning Dibrivki to the ground and rendering its population homeless. This was a common practice by the Austro-Hungarians, and as Makhno himself noted, one that only drove peasants into the arms of the Makhnovists, since they had nowhere else to go.

The autonomous zone grew rapidly. Among the first to reply to Makhno's call for an uprising were the Greek settlers by the Sea of Azov called Mariupol Greeks or Priazov'ye Greeks (who swiftly organized against the Denikinists).[19] Makhno's movement included a significant numbers of Jews, peasants of all ethnicities, Cossacks, deserters from the other major armies, and even German Mennonites.

Makhno had been busy in more ways than one, raising a partisan peasant movement and falling into a relationship with a local anarchist. Tina Ovcharenko, to be specific, telegraph operator and sometime secret operative for the anarchist movement. She was also on the front lines with Makhno. Makhno could be oddly cavalier about the safety of his partner in his memoirs. When informed that Tina was in a nearby town being captured by enemy forces, Makhno snapped, "Never mind that, it's already too late to save her." Ovcharenko managed to escape on a wagon (and be present when Makhno narrowly avoid capture himself).[20]

Even outside the fairly large extenuating circumstance that is battle, there was strain in their relationship from outside forces. To quote historian Malcolm Archibald: "Their [Makhno and Ovcharenko's] relationship was brought to an end by the Makhnovist commanders who decided Nestor was spending too much time with her and sent Tina back to her home—a striking example of the limits of Makhno's authority. . . . Tina's fate is not currently known to history, but she was still living in the region in 1930."[21]

In late 1918 the Makhnovists captured Huliaipole from the Austro-Hungarians after a bloody, pitched battle.[22] It was at this time that Makhno, as he promised earlier in the chapter, led an investigation into the purges of revolutionary cells in his home city by the Austro-Hungarians and kulaks. In this, he managed to defuse a potential pogrom, exonerate a few members of the purge against anarchists (who, upon examination, had sabotaged the Austro-Hungarian occupation in key ways, like hiding critical bits of artillery from the foreigners or refusing to sell out other revolutionaries), and of course opened the prisons.[23] This focus on revolutionary morality over expedient (and indiscriminate) reprisals was one of the good things about Makhno that was continually tested by stress during the course of the Civil War.

At the end of 1918, the embryonic stage of the Insurgent Army of Ukraine (Makhnovist) was fighting three enemies at once. Makhno viewed the White Army (Denikinists) as the most serious threat to the autonomist zone, followed by the Austro-Hungarians, and the new Ukrainian government, the Directory under Petliura.

Simeon Petliura was a nationalist, a man whose military forces would become a byword for pogroms, at least nominally a socialist, and for a time worked at the periodical *Kievan Thought* as a proofreader.[24] Hey, nobody ever called Petliura a likable guy, and after reading that list it's not hard to see why.

The Makhnovists met the declaration of Petliura's new government (which urged the peasants to respect private property, respect the "socialist" government's wishes, and join with them against their shared enemies, etc.) with ill-concealed scorn. Meet the new boss, same as the old boss. They were inclined to, and could afford to, defy Petliura's government openly.

The Makhnovists correctly believed that the Petliurists had little appeal or reach outside of urban centers, no power to enforce these demands on southern Ukraine without dedicated military action, no legitimate mandate from the people to rule as Petliura had been a collaborator with the Austro-Hungarians for some time prior to this, and furthermore the government worked almost solely in the interests of the landed classes. Thanks, but no thanks, the Makhnovists said.

Besides, the Makhnovists controlled portions of vital rail lines that the Petliurists wanted to move troops along. The Makhnovists allowed the Directory's trains and troops to pass through their territory—with the provision that they could be stopped at any time and that Makhnovist recruiters be allowed to approach these troops with pamphlets to recruit them.[25] Privately, Makhno held that Petliura's Directory was worse than the Austro-Hungarian puppet it had replaced, the Central Rada.

It was around this time that the Austro-Hungarians circulated the rumor that Makhno had been killed (causing many partisans to retreat to their villages or surrender), which was not the case, obviously. Makhno quickly disproved this rumor.

This wouldn't be the last time Makhno's death would be reported due to the uncertain nature of information in the Russian Civil War and his own reckless tendencies. Makhno joined the ranks of historical figures who can use Mark Twain's supposed words: "Reports of my death are greatly exaggerated."

The shaky detente with the Directory didn't last—by the end of the year, the autonomous region of southern Ukraine was at war with the Directory as well.

In less than half a year, Nestor Makhno and the anarchists of Ukraine had managed to shake off the iron hand of the Austro-Hungarians, create an autonomous zone in southern Ukraine, seize major cities, and expropriate millions of acres and rubles of resources from the rich. They had gone from nothing to a major, popular power in Ukraine that others could not simply laugh off.

CHAPTER 10

A Teacher and Terror as Method in Ukraine (1918)

> "Even a small group of people, weak in strength but strong in spirit, inspired by a great idea, can achieve great things."
> —Halyna Kuzmenko

The teacher Halyna Kuzmenko (depending on the transliteration from Ukrainian, the name can also be written as "Galina") was just starting the new school year in 1918 in Huliaipole.[1] As she picked her way across the crowded central square she heard that Makhno himself would be giving a speech. Halyna pushed on.

She reached her classroom, presumably did the few minutes or seconds of tinkering granted to teachers anywhere in all time periods, and then began to take roll call. She'd just finished this task when she was interrupted by a stranger entering the classroom, though quietly, to be sure. The intruder was short, well-dressed

Halyna Kuzmenko, 1917, a year before she met Nestor Makhno. Photograph courtesy of makhno.ru.

in a tailored army uniform, and wore his hair long and combed. His eyes flicked around the classroom, and he settled into a desk by the right side of the door as if it was the most natural thing in the world.

Halyna Kuzmenko and the students just stared at him for a few moments, clearly unsettled. What was a soldier doing in class? In her account of this meeting written in 1973, Kuzmenko doesn't mention what class was interrupted—but I like to imagine it was a math or history class, since Nestor Makhno had a fondness for both subjects. Kuzmenko resumed her lesson. She was starting to get into her stride, two, three minutes into it, shaking off the jitters that only come with having an armed soldier suddenly decide to audit your class without warning.

The stranger was fidgeting—antsy. He stood up and turned to Halyna, saying: "Comrade teacher, take a break and let's leave the class."

Halyna did a quick eyeball of her class. They looked nervous. "Sit quietly," she said. "I shall return right away."

The stranger and the teacher left the classroom and walked down a corridor. The stranger dropped a pistol on the floor, quick as thought. Halyna froze. The stranger kept walking.

"Pick it up." The stranger commanded, turning his head.

"It's yours," Halyna shot back. "You pick it up."

"Do you know who I am?" Asked the stranger, stopping.

"Tell me!"

"I'm Nestor Makhno. And from this moment you will be my wife. We shall go see the principal," Makhno said, scooping the pistol off the floor and continuing down the hallway. (In Voline's recounting of this event, it is a book that is dropped, not a pistol.[2] At least a book can't accidentally go off when it hits the floor.)

And that's how Nestor Makhno met his wife. In a weird twist, he asked the principal, who he apparently went back a ways with, what her name was, rather than asking Halyna herself.

Makhno arranged a dinner date with Halyna for later that night and the two fell to talking. Makhno even started to explain himself. He started with the whole "dropping a loaded gun in the hallway stunt."

"But it's no problem that I don't have a hut [the Germans had burned down Makhno's home and displaced his family earlier] ... and you're not only good looking, you're brave and self-confident. When I dropped the pistol, you weren't afraid to refuse to pick it up. Do you realize how impressed I was?"

Halyna slowly warmed up to Makhno, finally asking what on earth he had been doing at the school that day. Makhno replied that he hadn't intended to get married that day, that he had stopped by the school to see whether anyone with clerical skills was available to serve the Makhnovists (the clerical issue was resolved without Makhno's help later that same day). Instead he found Halyna and asked her to marry him. Halyna burst into laughter. "You weren't in the least bit timid! You issued an order: 'You will be my wife!'" As she said those words, Halyna understood that when Makhno made a pronouncement that seemed to him unsure, others heard it as an order. As they shared a bottle of vodka—helpfully provided by Halyna's landlord—they fell deeper into conversation. The evening ended on a practical note: Makhno passed Halyna a small snub-nosed revolver across the table.

"This is for you."

"What on earth for?"

"From this moment on you will always be with me. The wife of Nestor Makhno cannot be without a weapon. You will be able to defend yourself. Either I or Vanya will teach you how to shoot." The night wrapped up. Makhno and Halyna slept in separate rooms, and Makhno didn't try to hug or kiss Halyna. The next day, Makhno went back to the school with Halyna and informed the principal that she would not be returning but would be working with the Makhnovists from now on.

Halyna Kuzmenko had entered a different world from that of a schoolteacher. She learned to shoot, for one thing, as Makhno promised. Throughout the Civil War she was constantly by Makhno's side. She saw action on the front lines, organized anarchist educational programs based on the work of Ferrer that were well received by the Ukrainian peasantry, and was known to personally execute soldiers caught raping. She was, in other words, a committed anarchist who suffered as much as anyone. Her surviving writings provide a valuable insight into the Makhnovist movement and the human cost of it all. She was absolutely not a bit player and was one of Makhno's closest confidants during this period and through much of their exile.

Despite her title as Makhno's "wife," the two were never formally married.[3] Halyna would claim that they were (to placate her reactionary father, who still insisted on seeing a marriage certificate), but there was never a civil or religious ceremony. Perhaps it is for the best—a marriage party is a fine opportunity for a dustup, and the one time Nestor Makhno and Halyna's father met it ended badly. Mr. Kuzmenko tried to run Nestor off of his land insisting that Makhno was a robber and a murderer, Nestor replied by threatening to have Halyna's father shot as a counterrevolutionary.

Aren't in-laws fun?

All the same, in July 1919 a punitive squad of Bolsheviks (led by one Zatonsky, the Bolshevik who had given Makhno his false papers to reenter Ukraine in 1918) fell upon Halyna Kuzmenko's hometown, where her parents still lived. Mr. Kuzmenko refused to evacuate despite his daughter's warnings and attempts to explain that simply being related to her was enough to warrant immediate torture and execution.

This is what happened: Mr. Kuzmenko, along with several good friends of Halyna (teachers), a local youth who protested, and the mayor of the town were seized, beaten, and shot by the Bolsheviks. Halyna's mother only survived by springing out the window and hiding in the thick cover of the reeds in a nearby river. So well did she hide, that the first reports that reached Halyna also reported her mother dead. It took Halyna herself returning to her old childhood village to discover, to her joy, that her mother was not in fact dead. Makhno sent Fedir Shchus to pursue Zatonsky, and while he succeeded in destroying Zatonsky's detachment, the man himself escaped to die another day.[4]

There were an astonishing number of close calls like this—to be related to a revolutionary, never mind being an actual revolutionary, was something that a frightening amount of people were killed for.

And as if the constant specter of death by treachery or ambush wasn't enough to hang over oneself and one's loved ones, there was the inevitable political infighting at the upper levels of the Makhnovist command. Halyna, as a teacher and as a woman, and now Makhno's wife walked into the hypermasculine world of the Makhnovist high command. Voline, in his account of the Civil War, *The Unknown Revolution*, writes about Makhno's commander's response to their Batko getting married, and to a teacher: "Makhno's friends and collaborators, his commanders of regiments and others, were all good, solid peasants. They would never allow even the slightest presence of any 'intellectual' elements at the heart of their movement … that their mentor was enjoying himself by sleeping with a 'chick' of this type—well, fine! That would still be acceptable … but making her his companion for life, his wife, his confidante … not on your life!"

Voline continues at some length: "The commanders … considered Galina [Halyna] unworthy of being the primary confidante of Makhno.

They believed Makhno's feelings for 'the bitch' were a defect. According to them, he was blinded by his passions for her and didn't notice that she wasn't a true Makhnovist and therefore not a suitable companion for him. And they endeavored, discreetly but persistently, to 'open his eyes', to sow doubt, to put a seed of suspicion in his mind." This passive-aggressive warfare wasn't without consequences. Makhno was a suspicious man by nature and oscillated between favoring his advisors and his wife. His paranoia was at least partly justified—even in 1919, he had survived or avoided multiple assassination attempts.

Paranoia reaches its only point of virtue during the hurly-burly of a civil war—but even then it is not an endearing trait. Makhno would swear his commanders to secrecy on one plan or another, and then tell Halyna, for example, that he had told nobody but her about that same plan.[5] While Makhno was undoubtedly bright in many ways, this particular gambit feels so high school gossip to me. It sounds *absolutely* exhausting.

Navigating the world of the Makhnovist high command was no easy task for Halyna for class reasons as well, according to the anarchist intellectual Voline's account. Voline was close with Halyna later in life and his recollections have proved invaluable. Voline pointed out that large segments of the Makhnovist high command had serious problems with "intellectuals," including teachers, in their movement. Quoting again from Voline's *The Unknown Revolution*: "Among the Ukrainian peasants ... there is a very widespread mixture of distrust, contempt and veiled hostility, sometimes reaching the level of intense hatred, with regard to intellectuals, non-manual workers, and non-peasants. Even in the revolutionary movement, if it is led by the masses themselves, the appearance or intervention of an intellectual ... is very often considered 'undesirable.' An intellectual is still rather considered within the workers' or peasants' movements as an 'alien,' a 'gate-crasher' or almost a 'phony.' This sort of envy, embedded for centuries, will require a long time to eradicate."

While Voline has a point about the latent suspicion of intellectuals in the peasant movements, such attitudes toward teachers weren't universal across the Ukraine, or even in the Makhnovschina. Teachers like Halyna maintained an interesting place in the Makhnovist social movement. Many Makhnovist commanders and rank-and-file soldiers considered teachers to be part of the working class and vital for spreading anarchist ideas and methodology.

Sean Patterson recounts an incident in which Makhnovists boarding with a Mennonite family had the following exchange: "Dietrich Neufeld wrote in his journal with astonishment how a group of Makhnovists billeted in his home wanted him to write a poem as a personal tribute to Makhno. As Neufeld was a teacher, the Makhnovists considered him a part of the working class and assumed Makhno was also his hero."[6]

Halyna was doubtless stressed constantly in her struggle with the Makhnovist commanders for Nestor's trust or favor. She managed to hold her own and navigate that razor-lined strait—though not in comfort—with what Voline calls "extraordinary competence."

Trouble with Makhnovist commanders wasn't isolated to Halyna Kuzmenko. Even for Makhno, balancing the need for his subcommanders against his revolutionary ethics and expediency was difficult. Charismatic leaders of any ideology have to walk a fine line to keep everything from falling apart. Fear and love are the two main ingredients of any charismatic leader—your near peers need to fear at least the possibility of punishment, but you also need to keep them and their troops happy—and obeying your orders in the stress of wartime. Keeping consistent policy balanced between these poles is a ticklish prospect at best.

Makhno, early in his career, offered methods to integrate the rich (Mennonite or otherwise) into the rising anarchist movement by fairly dividing their vast estates—and allowing them to keep the same amount of supplies and lands as their former serfs. They wouldn't be persecuted or treated differently than any other comrade, indeed they were encouraged to do this to preserve the bonds of community and friendship that already existed across class lines, and indeed were hoped to survive this economic leveling.[7] There were some encouraging signs that this was even working as the first communes were set up around Huliaipole. But as the war with the Germans raged and some Mennonite landlords were reinstated to their former properties with the aid of German arms, such a policy became more difficult to implement due to the hunger of the peasants for vengeance, rather than justice. Makhno's urging to not molest or harm colonists who gave up their arms willingly or were unarmed in the first place began to be ignored by his troops.

As historian Sean Patterson notes in his work *Makhno and Memory*: "This process began in fall 1918 when Makhno struggled to formulate what he considered a just policy toward the colonies. After the burning of Velyka Mykhailivka, Makhno was driven to seek vengeance through his raids on estates and colonies. According to Makhno's account, only when he realized that such a policy would descend into indiscriminate terror did he attempt to establish clear rules of engagement. However, it would prove exceedingly difficult to prevent a slip into wanton violence. Unlike Makhno's aggressive policy against anti-Semitism within the movement, any efforts to curb the murder of innocent German and Mennonite colonists were a failure."

The Makhnovist commanders sometimes ignored Makhno's orders against looting or massacre. No better example can be found than the Silbertal massacre in 1918 during the resistance against the Austro-Hungarians.[8] As reported by Patterson and Belash, Fedir Shchus was ordered to levy taxes on the Lutheran colony of Silbertal. He would return to Makhno every day with pairs of boots and no money, which isn't suspicious at all. This was enough to make the notoriously detail-oriented Makhno suspicious. His suspicions were confirmed when a distraught colonist personally confronted Makhno and begged to be allowed to bury her dead family. Makhno blew his stack. He confronted Shchus—telling him that if he kept this sort of wanton slaughter up he'd be executed immediately.

The remaining colonists weren't in a forgiving mood and sent a pair of men to kill Makhno in nearby Huliaipole. The attempt didn't succeed due to Makhno's guards (though an unrelated boy was killed in the crossfire). Shchus took this as an opportunity to return to Silbertal and massacre some more colonists, killing at least thirty more.

Makhno was absolutely livid at this news—both Shchus's defiance and the murder of innocents—and ordered Shchus disarmed and arrested. But here is where the problem of charismatic leadership comes in. If Makhno executed Shchus—as Sean Patterson notes, a commander second in popularity only to himself—who could say what would happen?[9] It might split the entire Makhnovist movement—and armed forces—in half or worse cause armed infighting. It was a huge risk, and Makhno ultimately was unable to roll the dice by executing his subcommander for his crimes. Shchus and others inside the Makhnovist movement weren't prevented from spreading Black Terror, especially among wealthy Mennonite colonies, whether or not they had acquiesced to Makhnovist terms of surrender. Sean Patterson writes in *Makhno and Memory*, speaking of the logic of terror in the context of a civil war:

> Revolutionary terror emerges from a context of extreme reciprocal violence and is ostensibly based on the pursuit of "justice." In a

revolutionary situation, this frequently occurs when the state can no longer maintain its monopoly on violence. Violence becomes decentralized and legitimated through competing local forces. Historian Arno Meyer writes, 'The quantum leap of violence is both cause and effect of the breakup of a state's single sovereignty into multiple and rival power centres, which is accompanied by a radical dislocation of the security and judicial system. As a result, the positive legal standards for judging and circumscribing acts of political violence give way to moral and ethical criteria. In other words, in the calculus of means and ends, the principles of 'law' are superseded by those of 'justice.'" Due to the disappearance of universal law as administered through the state, justice is subjectively applied according to competing power. These competing notions of justice come into conflict, triggering, as is the case of Makhno and the Mennonites, a state of escalating violence in which each group attempts to use force and fear to compel the enemy to accept their regime. In this scenario, the moral line between justice and terror begins to blur.[10]

This was the world that Halyna Kuzmenko had now entered and adapted to. There are no real sidelines in the context of a civil war—neutrality is taken for complicity with the enemy. Being armed is taken as similar endorsement of hostility. There is no good option for a civilian in a civil war—the only safety, such as it is, comes only with picking (or switching allegiances to) a side when the world is crossed by armies. Her fellow intellectual, and later close friend, Voline, wrote:

> Any army of whatever kind, is an evil, and even in a free and popular army composed of volunteers and dedicated to a noble cause, is by its very nature a danger. Once it becomes permanent it inevitably detaches itself from the people and the world of labor. Its members lose the inclination and the ability to lead a healthy working life. With an imperceptible and therefore all the more dangerous gradualness, it becomes a collection of idlers, who acquire anti-social, authoritarian and even dictatorial leanings, who acquire also a taste for violence as a thing in itself, for the use of brute force even in cases where recourse to such means is contrary to the very cause it purports to defend.[11]

The Austro-Hungarians were gone from the battlefield by the summer of 1919, but the increasing militarization of the Makhnovschina continued. Their collaboration with the Red Army against the gathering strength of the White Army under Denikin created unique strains and tensions—tensions that would boil over and bring the Makhnovschina close to its breaking point through the long and horrible summer and fall of 1919.

CHAPTER 11

The Terrible Summer (1919)

> "The annalists of old never failed to chronicle the petty wars and calamities which harassed their contemporaries; but they paid no attention whatever to the life of the masses, although the masses chiefly used to toil peacefully while the few indulged in fighting."
>
> —Pyotr Kropotkin

The year 1919 was a ceaseless battle. The White Army under Denikin had been pushing further and further into Ukraine with only a mix of the Makhnovists, various peasant bands, Petliura's nationalists, and the still unloved Ukrainian government standing in its way. The situation worsened when the Bolsheviks injected themselves into the fray in March of that year.

Makhno had agreed to ally with the Bolsheviks—who came slinking into Ukraine, the same Ukraine that they had unabashedly sold to the kind attentions of the Germans in the Treaty of Brest-Litovsk at Lenin's instruction—out of necessity. Not that this stopped the Bolsheviks—who were indeed still purging anarchists left and right where they thought they could get away with it—from praising Makhno, sight unseen, in the pages of their papers and pamphlets.[1] They praised Makhno with the same vigor that they would later slander him. The Makhnovists had been fighting the White Army for months before the Bolsheviks could be bothered to show their faces.[2] They were hard-bitten by this point and had considerable experience facing White Army units.

This was part of the Bolshevik standard operating procedure—incorporating independent struggles under the wide umbrella of the Red Army (ostensibly in the name of "unity") and using those units as either shock troops or stationing them far from their homelands, leaving the Bolsheviks a free hand to pacify or occupy the lands these units once defended.

This alliance was the death knell for a positive construction of an anarchist polity in Ukraine. From this point on, with the introduction of the Red Army and the intensification of the Civil War, the agenda of the Makhnovschina would, out of necessity, be almost entirely military. As Peter Arshinov writes in *The History of the Makhnovist Movement*: "Consequently, in the summer of 1919 the situation in the insurgent region made large-scale revolutionary construction absolutely impossible. It seemed as though a gigantic grate composed of bayonets shuttled back and forth across the region, from north to south and back again, wiping out all traces of creative social construction."[3] The Makhnovists joined the Red Army with the explicit understanding that they would keep their own internal command structure and remain in their homelands. As Voline writes in *The Unknown Revolution*:

> Here are the essential clauses of the agreement [that was entered into by the two armies]:
> i. The Insurrectionary Army of Ukraine will retain its internal organization intact.
> ii. It will receive political commissars appointed by the Communist authorities.
> iii. It will only be subordinated to the Red supreme military command in strictly military matters.
> iv. It cannot be removed from the front against Denikin.
> v. It will receive munitions and supplies equal to the those of the Red Army.
> vi. It will retain its name of the Revolutionary Insurrectionary Army and its black flags.[4]

Being incorporated into the Red Army was less idyllic than it might sound. Makhno was subordinated to the political oversight of Vladimir Antonov-Ovseyenko, but under the military direction of the erratic and brutish, former sailor Pavel Dybenko whose chief qualification for his role in Ukraine was his Ukrainian last name.[5] Dybenko's full rap sheet of casual brutality, drunkenness, multiple treacheries (he seemed to be waffling between being an independent warlord and a loyal-enough Bolshevik commander, with catastrophic results on successive occasions) is too long

Nestor Makhno (right) and Red Army commander Dybenko (left) during Makhno's first alliance with the Bolsheviks in 1919, Pologi Station.

to get into here. Makhno despised Dybenko, and referred to him only as "that damned sailor" according to Max Chernyak, and took special efforts to avoid the Bolshevik commander.[6]

The Makhnovist disappointments with the Bolsheviks were multi-layered. Instead of the cornucopia of arms and materiel promised, the Bolshevik high command at every turn starved anarchists of promised supplies. Makhno recalls: "It would not take much ferreting through the archives of the 2nd Red Army to unearth my unceasing requests for cartridges and shells (as for rifles, the Bolshevik government never sent us a single one; we had taken ours off the Germans, the supporters of the Hetman and the Denikinists)."[7]

Makhno writes in his memoir with particular vitriol about three thousand Italian rifles that were sent to Makhnovist troops without bullets by the Bolsheviks.[8] What weapons the Bolsheviks did give were often outdated models from the previous century requiring ammunition that was no longer made, making the weapons worse than useless. The Makhnovists were regularly starved of ammunition and cartridges for weeks at a time, in active war zones. To the minds of the Bolshevik high command, it was easier to subdue one-time allies without ammunition than with it. They might as well have sent the Makhnovists brooms and told them to tidy their way across the battlefield.

The obvious intent of the Bolsheviks was to use the non-Bolshevik troops as cannon fodder against their shared enemies, and then betray them once the White Army was defeated. It was a depressingly predictable bit of treachery that marked the Bolshevik attitude toward struggle and revolution: ordinary people couldn't be trusted to manage their own affairs and all who wouldn't kiss the Bolshevik boot would be purged or minimized. The Bolshevik high command made no alliances that it did not intend to betray. Even with joined forces, the fight against the White Army wasn't going well. And that was before the inner conflict boiled to the surface. The trouble truly started when a character named Grigoriev led a mass desertion from the Red front.

Ataman Grigoriev was one of those specimens of nature whose loyalties most resemble a weathervane. That is to say, he went with the prevailing winds. A former czarist officer, he became a Cossack chieftain (ataman). He then switched sides to Petliura's Ukrainian nationalists, and when that became inconvenient promptly fell in line with the Red Army when it seemed they had the upper hand against the White Army. He was also a rabid antisemite who led pogroms wherever he went. His forces were mismatched—peasants (the same base of support the Makhnovists depended on), Cossacks, fellow opportunists (disparagingly called "adventurists"), and whoever else was around.

Ataman Grigoriev's abandonment of the Red Army spread panic through the ranks of the Bolsheviks. He'd left a large amount of their front vulnerable to Denikin and cost them miles upon miles of territory, to say nothing of the human costs. Makhno condemned Grigoriev's opportunism, antisemitism, and lack of revolutionary anything, which didn't stop Grigoriev from sending Makhno several notes urging him to also turn on the Bolsheviks. One note that reached Makhno read as follows: "Batko! Why are you looking toward the Communists? Thrash them!"[9]

This last phrase—"Thrash them" has also been translated as "hit them on the head" or "bop them on the head" in other English accounts. I like "bop them on the head" myself—makes me imagine Grigoriev as the absolute worst version of Little Bunny Foo Foo.

Even when Makhno fought alongside the Red Army, Trotsky repeatedly tried to have him assassinated, viewing him as a grave threat. One of the Red commanders who worked with Makhno in person, Voroshilov (formerly of Tsaritsyn), had standing orders to capture or kill Makhno and attempted to lure him into a planning meeting on his personal armored train.[10] The Bolshevik general was simply waiting for a good time to betray Makhno—a time which never came. Voroshilov's train lure was foiled by a Red intelligence officer warning Makhno in the nick of time—which allowed Makhno to avoid certain death. Getting word that White troops were due to intercept Voroshilov's train, Makhno reluctantly ordered his soldiers to intercept that force—saving his assassin's life in the name of keeping his revolutionary honor. Makhno never would let the White Army do his dirty work for him, yet another thing that set him apart from the Bolsheviks.

Makhno was constantly warned to never answer any official summons from cities that the Bolsheviks presently held—to do so would be to walk into a trap that would certainly end in his death.[11] Trotsky was content to wait until Denikin's forces had captured Huliaipole before proclaiming Makhno an outlaw. To hear him tell it, it was better that the White Army capture all of Ukraine than the Makhnovschina survive.[12] This is a common attitude among authoritarian "'leftists" (Leninists, Stalinists, Trotskyists)— that it would be better for fascists to triumph than their nominal allies the anarchists. It is a theme that has shown the cold cynicism of any possibility of a "united front" that has been repeated in such struggles as the Spanish Civil War, to name but one example.

Trotsky observed in an unedited version of a newspaper article that Denikin's forces had taken over half of the Makhnovist territory—making now an excellent time to betray them. Trotsky issued the order for the Makhnovschina and anarchists in general to be purged and attacked on June 3, 1919—six days before Makhno resigned his commission.

In the face of this ugly decision, Makhno quit the Red Army on June 9. Being ever aware of optics, Makhno risked his life to formally resign from the Red Army properly and hand over all relevant documents and information to the commander appointed to replace him in the small town of Gaichur. Makhno didn't want there to be even a ghost of a chance of being seen as abandoning the ideal of revolution. He sent out a circular saying that he would be more useful to the revolutionary cause as a man in the ranks than a commander, and thus resigned his commission. The Bolsheviks immediately tried to seize Makhno at Gaichur, only to find that he had already left with a small cavalry division for the city of Alexandrovsk.

He left a ticking time bomb behind, though. Before resigning his commission with the Red Army, Makhno had arranged a secret meeting with his captains, commanding Makhnovist troops. They were to abandon their commands as soon as was practicable (and take as many weapons as they could carry) and regroup around Makhno and his small force. Naturally, this small force did not remain small for long—Voline writes that the Bolshevik army feared a widespread mutiny if they tried to stop the Makhnovists from returning to their homes.[13] Within two weeks, every Makhnovist unit had left the Red Army and rejoined Makhno.

Even when involved in espionage, Makhno personally showed far more integrity than his opponents, Red or White, ever did. He didn't simply abandon the front to the White Army, like Grigoriev, to pursue personal advancement—but made sure the troops who had trusted him had a way to return to their homes and continue to the fight in the face formidable odds and treachery. The Makhnovists were joined by swarms of Ukrainian peasants, fleeing the White Army. Denikin's troops were notorious for their brutality and especially their mass rapes of Jewish women, who were numerous in the regions under dispute.

When Winston "I Only Look Good Because Hitler and Stalin Were Also Alive at the Time" Churchill tells you to take the war crimes down a notch, you just might be Anton Denikin. In a letter to Denikin, the man who had no problems with creating concentration camps in Kenya later in the century and already had a lengthy record crushing unions in his own country, wrote: "My task in winning support in Parliament for the Russian Nationalist cause will be infinitely harder if well-authenticated complaints continue to be received from Jews in the zone of the Volunteer Armies [White Army]."[14] Denikin wrote a few perfunctory instructions to his troops to stop their crimes, but they were not listened to and never enforced. We can only conclude that he wrote those instructions to create a paper shield and to help him secure funding from the imperial powers—basically as PR. Better to flee to Makhno than risk staying in White Army territory, went the logic of Ukrainian peasants. Thousands of families loaded what they could onto wagons or set off on foot to join the Makhnovschina.

Makhno at first looked for weaknesses in Denikin's advance hoping for an opportunity to regain the initiative and launch an offensive. But at this point in the war, the White Army was taking no chances—there were few gaps or strategic weaknesses for the Makhnovists to exploit. Makhno reluctantly concluded that a defensive strategy was the only workable option—and that retreat was necessary to survive when a position couldn't be held.[15] Thus began a four-month-long fighting retreat against the White Army. You know, in contrast to the Bolshevik's nonfighting retreat.

Trotsky confidently stated that Denikin's White Army was no kind of threat to the Red Army—before immediately retracting that statement the very next day when it became clear that the White Army was within an ace of capturing Kharkiv.[16] The Red Army turned tail and ran from Denikin when it became clear they had blundered, without even bothering to write a note of apology.

The Bolsheviks abandoned the Ukraine, barely bothering to mount a defense, leaving the weakened Makhnovists to fight the White Army alone. Bolshevik forces in Crimea mutinied in July, the troops taking their commanders hostage and according to Voline, proceeded to force march their way across Ukraine to join Makhno.[17] He received them gladly. Even in retreat, Makhno and the anarchists attracted unlooked for followers.

Adventurers attempted to join the Makhnovschina, now the only real obstacle to White domination over Ukraine. Grigoriev turned up like a bad penny, now that the Bolsheviks had abandoned Ukraine. He joined the Makhnovists, but Makhno hadn't forgotten the Cossack commander's penchant for switching sides, nor his fondness for pogroms. Still, more guns and men wouldn't be despised while he worked to find a way to remove Grigoriev and the pogromists from the ranks of the new arrivals, many of whom were peasants.

This passage from Arshinov's *History of the Makhnovist Movement* (1918–1921) dedicated to Grigoriev's death in July is worth quoting in full:

> On Makhno's initiative, a congress of insurgents from the governments of Ekaterinoslav, Kherson and Tauride was called for July 27, 1919, in the village of Sentovo near Aleksandriya.
>
> The agenda of the congress included the establishment of a program of action for the entire insurrectionary Ukraine which would correspond to the needs of the moment. Nearly 20,000 people came—peasants and insurgents, Grigor'ev's detachments and Makhno's troops. Among the many scheduled orators were Grigor'ev, Makhno, and other representatives of the two movements. Grigor'ev was the first to speak. He invited the peasants and the insurgents to devote all their forces to chasing the Bolsheviks out of the country, without rejecting any allies. Grigor'ev said that for this purpose he was even ready to ally with Denikin. Afterwards, when the yoke of

Bolshevism was broken, the people would themselves see what they had to do. This declaration was fatal to Grigor'ev.

Makhno and his comrade Chubenko spoke immediately after Grigor'ev, and declared that the struggle against the Bolsheviks could be revolutionary only if it were carried out in the name of the social revolution. An alliance with the worst enemies of the people—with generals—could only be a counter-revolutionary and criminal adventure. Grigor'ev invited participation in this counter-revolution, and consequently he was an enemy of the people. Following this, Makhno demanded before the entire congress that Grigor'ev immediately answer for the appalling pogrom of Jews which he had organized in Elisavetgrad in May, 1919, as well as other anti-Semitic actions.

"Scoundrels like Grigor'ev are the shame of all the Ukrainian insurgents; they cannot be tolerated in the ranks of honest revolutionary workers."

Such was Makhno's final indictment of Grigor'ev. Grigor'ev saw that the situation was going badly for him. He reached for weapons. But it was too late. Simon Karetnik—Makhno's comrade—shot him with a Colt revolver, while Makhno himself shouted "Death to the Ataman!" and also shot him.

Grigor'ev's assistants and the members of his staff ran to his help, but they were shot on the spot by a group of Makhnovists who had been placed on guard. All this happened during two or three minutes before the eyes of the entire congress.

After the initial agitation over the events that have just been described, the congress heard the declarations of Makhno, Chubenko and other representatives of the Makhnov'shchina, and approved the act, considering it historically necessary. According to the record of the proceedings of the congress, the Makhnovshchina assumed all responsibility for the events which had just taken place and for their consequences. The assembly also decided that the partisan detachments formerly under Grigor'ev's command would henceforth be part of the general insurrectionary army of the Makhnovists.[18]

However, some sources have the execution of Grigoriev going quite a bit differently. Alexandre Skirda cites sources claiming that it was Alexei Chubenko who shot Grigoriev (with a pistol concealed in his palm) just as Grigoriev, realizing that this was a set-up, turned to draw his own pistol and fire at Makhno.[19] A very cinematic image, if indeed it happened that way. But regardless of who shot the ataman, Grigoriev's movement was integrated into Makhno's own: the pogromists rooted out and executed and, in general, there was much rejoicing. The Makhnovists had perhaps twenty thousand men near the end of the summer, according to Voline's estimate.[20] They were on their own, against overwhelming odds, betrayed twice over. The White Army pushed against them—as it had this entire time—and a four-month fighting retreat against the forces of reaction was in full swing.

CHAPTER 12

The War behind the Lines (1919)

> "But rebellion, in man, is the refusal to be treated as an object and to be reduced to simple historical terms. It is the affirmation to a nature common to all men, which eludes the world of power."
>
> —Albert Camus

Most of 1919 didn't go any better for Maria "Marusya" Nikiforova than it did for Makhno and the Insurgent Army of Ukraine. Her year started off with another show trial, this time in Moscow. The Bolsheviks were even kind enough to recycle charges from her previous trial at Taganrog. Conviction could have net Nikiforova a death sentence. Certainly many other anarchists, Socialist Revolutionaries, or other dissenters had been put to death by the Cheka and the Bolshevik government for far less. For example:

> Among the Chekists' first Moscow victims was the celebrated circus clown Bim-Bom, whose repertoire included jokes about the Communists [Bolsheviks]. Like the KGB, the Cheka was not noted for its sense of humor about ideological subversion. When stern-faced Chekists advanced on Bim-Bom during one of his performances, the circus audience assumed at first that it was all part of the fun. Their mood changed to panic as Bim-Bom fled from the ring with Chekhists firing after him.[1]

Since the Cheka had run out of clowns to shoot at (both clowns, Bim and Bom emerged unscathed from the above incident—the role of "Bom" was passed around the cast and each would take their turn playing the clown on different nights), the Bolsheviks turned their sights on their nominal allies, the anarchists: anarchists like Maria "Marusya" Nikiforova.

Marusya had been in Moscow since at least the tail end of 1918. She even gave a speech in the First All-Russian Congress of Anarchist Communists there. In it, she said, in part: "In their approach to their work, anarchists must not restrict themselves to the big stuff. Any kind of work is useful. To sacrifice oneself is easier than to work constantly, steadily, achieving definite goals. Such work demands staying power and a great deal of energy ... but our work must be based on examples, for example in Moscow itself we should create a whole network of vegetable gardens on a communist basis. This would be the best means of agitation among the people, people who in essence are natural anarchists."[2]

This call for steady organization and on-the-ground solidarity meant a focus not just on the dramatic, but on the necessary daily work of building a new society. Not everyone needed to, or should, pick up a gun or bomb to create a new world. Instead, the work was more difficult: to create solidarity and community with your neighbors, to build something together collectively without coercion. It's quite an admission for one of the more famous champions and practitioners of "propaganda by the deed" in the Russian Civil War.

This sort of talk could hardly go unnoticed by the Bolsheviks, who had been purging anarchists for some time now and had already attempted to convict Nikiforova in one of their show trials at Taganrog. But Marusya still had powerful friends. Bolshevik commander Antonov-Ovseyenko, who had vouched for her at her last trial, and the famous peer of Kropotkin, Apollon "the Beard" Karelin, both guaranteed Maria Nikiforova's good behavior while in Moscow.[3]

Karelin was one of the few examples of a "Soviet/state anarchist"— anarchists who advocated actively participating inside the Bolshevik government instead of opposing it or accepting only temporary alliances— that Makhno seemed to have any regard for. Karelin had nothing but good things to say about Marusya, describing her as someone who completely abstained from drink and was generous to a fault: "All that she had she gave away even to comrades she barely knew. She wouldn't keep a kopeck for herself. She gave away everything."[4]

Marusya was, after some tension, found guilty of some of the lesser charges and given a slap on the wrist by the Bolsheviks. Her sentence was to be off the front lines for six months. Since Maria Nikiforova was a woman of action, we must imagine she chafed at this restriction. Six months? The war might be over then and that would be intolerable. She managed to talk her off-battlefield restriction down to half that time. She left Moscow for Ukraine where she met up with Nestor Makhno in Huliaipole, arriving in spring 1919.[5] Marusya wasn't technically a member of Makhno's command staff and didn't hold an official place in the Black Army but she and her close-knit *druzhina* were accorded a great deal of respect and leeway among both the peasantry and the Black Army.

Not that Marusya was an easy guest for Makhno to accommodate. As Malcolm Archibald notes in his biography of Nikiforova: "An ugly incident occurred at the 2nd Congress of Soviets of Gulyai-Pole raion held in the spring of 1919. Marusya, although not a delegate, asked to speak. When she starting attacking the Bolsheviks, the peasants became upset. They were more concerned about the Whites at that point—the Bolsheviks were their allies. Makhno, always a bit of a demagogue when it came to the peasants, physically dragged her down from the podium."

Not that Makhno's attempts at good faith with the Bolsheviks did much. Trotsky, the head of the Red Army, declared him an outlaw in the summer of 1919. The Bolsheviks had been trying to suss out for some time when it would be safe to betray the anarchists. Even before this decision was made, anarchist divisions and units were constantly given insufficient or defective weapons and ammunition by their Bolshevik allies or stationed far from their native lands so they couldn't melt into the countryside to evade the Bolsheviks. This is to say nothing of the purges of anarchists from major urban centers to the north of Ukraine (which Makhno had delicately navigated) that started in late 1917.

Trotsky outlawing Makhno was not good for the already besieged anarchists of southeastern Ukraine. It deprived the Black Army of badly needed logistical support, weapons, and supplies and left it to face the resurgent White Army under Denikin. Even someone like Makhno, for whom suspicion and contingency were practically a second skin, was taken aback by such a sudden reversal. By 1919 Makhno had managed in the space of two years to transform southeastern Ukraine from occupied territory to its own polity. With enough volunteers and as the struggle lengthened, conscripts recruited by force, he was able to field armies of thousands in a "war of fronts." Makhno had managed to profit from the erratic Ataman Grigoriev's abandonment of the Red Army and executed him, absorbing his forces into the Makhnovist army as we covered in the last chapter.

· MARUSYA NIKIFOROVA AND MAKHNO PART WAYS ·

But under the surface—under the maps and diagrams and footsore, tired troops, lay a more treacherous dimension. It was the domain of intelligence and counterintelligence. Maria Nikiforova was an expert in such means given her long career. Assassination was the cost-effective way to turn the tides of war.

Vladimir "Terror Is the Only Method I Have of Governing" Lenin had already only narrowly escaped death at the hands of Socialist Revolutionary Fanya Kaplan the previous year. His associate, Moisei Uritsky, head of the Petrograd division of the Cheka, wasn't so lucky and was ventilated in public by a Socialist Revolutionary assassin who didn't survive long after.[6] The Bolsheviks responded by having the Cheka conduct a brutal purge of the Left Socialist Revolutionaries and anarchists that left hundreds dead or scattered. This Red Terror was not an isolated event, but rather a continuation and escalation of the Bolsheviks' authoritarian methods as previously mentioned during their purges of anarchists. The Bolsheviks could not rule Russia through any other method but terror. This is a fact, not an opinion. Their idea of consensus was when all the dissenters were freshly made corpses or exiles.

Two of the major powers' intelligence units shared similar recruits: former members of the czarist secret police, the Okhrana. In the case of the White Army, it was a natural fit seeing as they had the most to gain from a restoration of czardom or rule by the aristocracy. In the case of the Cheka, whether by coercion, conviction, or expediency, a fair amount of the people who once stalked and tortured revolutionaries joined the forces of the Bolsheviks and found welcome in the ranks of the Cheka.

The Makhnovist *kontrrazvedka* (counterintelligence), by contrast, was made up of many different types of people. For example, in the city of Berdyansk, the kontrrazvedka section was headed by Max Chernyak, a veteran barber and military commander with experience in expropriations.[7] Some operatives were simple peasants who passed on information about troop movements, supplies, and time tables to the Makhnovist commanders. Then there were the upper staff and active infiltrators, those in charge of recruiting, assassinating, and propagandizing behind enemy lines.

In a desperate case, the Makhnovist kontrrazvedka even coordinated mass purchases of medicine in response to a typhus epidemic, doing so behind enemy lines and shipping it to the afflicted zones. Without the kontrrazvedka—the eyes and ears of the Black Army—the war would have gone very differently.

Max Chernyak, Montevideo, December 1938. Photo courtesy of Anna Voitenko and Sean Patterson. Chernyak was one of the earliest members of Makhno's *kontrrazvedka* (counterintelligence). His activity in the Russian Civil War included volunteering for a mission to Siberia aimed at assassinating the White general Kolchak and surviving time in a horrific Russian prison.
He met Makhno again in Paris (and heartily disapproved of the Platform) before escaping to South America, where he was involved in various union movements.

Marusya had an idea to end the war swiftly, before it could get still worse. She proposed a daring plan that abandoned the idea of a war of fronts, and she would implement it herself. To fund this big idea that would change the anarchists' fortune in the war, Marusya went to the First Bank of Makhno. The First Bank of Makhno was located on an armored train in Huliaipole and had a unique withdrawal system, which Marusya quickly discovered was to point her revolver at Makhno's face and demand the fucking money, please and thank you.

Makhno did not appreciate this in the slightest. He drew his own pistol. Some tension, understandably, followed this moment. Finally, Makhno relented, gave Marusya the money and told her to get out of his hair.[8] We'll get back to him next chapter.

Marusya had decided to cut off the heads of the various snakes threatening the anarchist movement. Never one to stand around, she divided her *druzhina* and any other volunteers into three sections with the following objectives:

The first group would go to Siberia and blow up the headquarters of Alexander Kolchak. They just missed him, and the squad was absorbed into the Siberian anti-White Army partisans. One of the members of this group, Max Chernyak, was a member of Makhno's intelligence apparatus and would actually make it to meet Makhno in Paris during his exile.[9]

The second group set out for Kharkiv to free Makhnovist prisoners and blow up the Cheka headquarters there. Unfortunately, the Bolsheviks had already killed the prisoners and abandoned the city. So the group went on to Moscow. On September 19, 1919, Marusya's Moscow anarchists managed to trigger a bomb in Moscow that killed a number of high-level Bolsheviks and wounded over forty more. The notable Bolshevik Bukharin was giving a speech when the bomb went off—but escaped serious injury. Lenin was unscathed, as he was running late. Mention this fact the next time you are chewed out for being tardy—say you aren't late, but in fact thwarting the timetables of potential assassins. Let me know how it works.

Another, parallel plan to deal with the Bolsheviks by Nikiforova's crew was to screw specificity and simply blow the Kremlin into orbit with a fertilizer bomb. To answer your question, it would take about a ton of fertilizer to achieve the desired effect and it was waiting for this amount to be collected and treated that gave the Cheka time to locate them.[10]

The kontrrazvedka even had infiltrators inside the Cheka themselves, who tipped off the anarchists more than once about raids. Marusya's operatives were hunted down by Chekhists but, rather than surrender, blew themselves up, taking several Chekhists with them.[11] ("What do you call a pile of dead Chekhists?" "A good start.")

The third group, with Nikiforova and her husband, went to Denikin's headquarters in the Crimea with the express goal of blowing him straight out of the planet's atmosphere. The White Army was considered the biggest threat to the anarchist cause at this point at the war—as might be suspected by Maria Nikiforova attempting to see to Denikin personally. Sadly, she was noticed by someone as she was walking down the street. She was caught and executed by the White Army.[12]

Marusya's death was another turd in the water pipe of bad news for the anarchists. While not formally a part of the Makhnovschina, Marusya and her *druzhina* had been a formidable force and a potent vehicle for propaganda as well as military gains. No less than three people claimed the name of Maria Nikiforova after her death in the Russian Civil War.[13] They all perished or vanished, but no less bravely than their namesake.

One of the Marusyas that emerged after Nikiforova's death in Crimea was involved in the hundred-thousand-strong Tambov Rebellion a few hundred miles from Moscow (1920–21). There the peasant guerrillas rose up against the Bolsheviks and dealt them several stinging defeats. The Bolsheviks were flustered by their hit-and-run tactics and so chose to use chemical weapons on the forest where the peasants were hiding rather than continue losing men.[14] And of course, Antonov-Ovseyenko, former sponsor of the real Marusya Nikiforova during both of her show trials, was one of the Bolshevik commanders at this atrocity, being all too happy to murder anarchists and peasants now that they weren't essential to the Bolshevik cause.

CHAPTER 13

Retreating to Victory and Conspiracy (1919)

> "It was not by chance that Makhno, who created uncontaminated sympathy for the anarchist guerrilla throughout almost the whole of this century, was called 'Batko,' i.e. 'Father' by his comrades, a name given to every 'condottiere' in Russia. There, as elsewhere, if one does not want to accept a role (and the people have very schematic ideas on the subject), one should not put oneself in the position of not being able to refuse it."
>
> —Alfredo M. Bonanno

Things weren't going well for Makhno or the Black Army under his command in late September 1919. He was in full retreat from the White Army under their General Slashchev and had been losing men and supplies the whole time across southern Ukraine. September was at the tail end of four months of hell. Nearly everything that could have gone wrong did, and more than a few things he hadn't counted on, as discussed in previous chapters. The Black Army had retreated along railroad tracks, fighting a rearguard action and trying to sting and irritate the pursuing White Army.

Two weeks before, at the village of Pomoshnaya, Grigori Makhno, Nestor's brother, died during a cavalry raid to capture ammunition from the White Army.[1] The Makhnovists would later name a captured Denikinist armored train after Grigori Makhno to honor him.

Ammunition (technically the lack of it) was one of the Makhnovists' largest problems at this point. Throughout his retreat from Slashchev, Makhno had been forced to turn away peasants volunteering to join the

Black Army. The peasants wanted to fight, but he couldn't spare guns, or if he could, the guns were empty. Any chance to gain ammunition from the enemy was taken, but that still wasn't enough to provide for the whole army—to the point that two out of three of their attacks on the White Army were for the express purpose of capturing supplies.[2]

Even if they had enough bullets for their opponents, disease and exhaustion insured that the Black Army left corpses in its wake along with abandoned wagons. The Red Army headquarters—with whom Makhno was temporarily allied against the Whites—repeatedly denied Nestor's frequent requests to fortify the next city they came to, so that they could recover their strength.

On top of all this, Nestor was hurt, which doubtless didn't help his temper any. Makhno hardly thought himself invincible, but he also had a reckless disregard for personal risk, so he was frequently wounded. By the end of the Civil War, he was a patchwork of scars wearing a mustache.

What victories the Black Army under Makhno achieved were delaying actions and daring hit-and-run raids using tachanka and cavalry—not decisive wins, and certainly nothing that seriously dissuaded the pursuing Whites. Makhno was denied credit for the victories he managed to score by his enemies. The White Army, as recorded by General Slashchev, believed that a peasant like Makhno couldn't *possibly* possess the military gifts or training necessary to inconvenience them. Naturally, a rumor sprang up that a German officer had defected to the Black Army, and it was this fictional fellow who was the reason for the Black Army lasting as long as it did.[3] Lieutenant Kleist was the name of this fictional German officer who defected to the Makhnovists, a close relative of Herman von Fakename, John Spurious, and Pyotyr Fictionalcharactervteofvski.

The White Army constantly underestimated the Ukrainian peasantry as a threat or even as human—as was evident from their pogroms, rapes, and burnings. At least the nearby Ukrainian nationalist armies under Petliura—no friends to the Reds or the Whites—had vowed not to interfere in the battle and to shelter the Makhnovist wounded—but neither did he offer any aid to the exhausted Makhnovist army proper, either.[4] General Slashchev summed up Petliura in his later writings, saying: "Petliura was playing it cool and sitting on the fence."[5] Petliura hoped to get concessions for the nationalists from an apparently victorious White Army by simply refusing to commit to battle. Things didn't turn out that way—but it fits Petliura's track record, given that he'd already previously collaborated with the Austro-Hungarians when they had looked to be on the ascent in Ukraine. He had seen what had happened to Ataman Grigoriev and wanted no part of it.

The feelings of distrust and disgust were mutual—in a meeting with a Petliurist general, Nestor Makhno pointedly ignored the commander's hand outstretched in greeting (the general was apparently a big fan of handshakes). Makhno instead theatrically slumped into a chair opposite, glowering at his counterpart.[6]

With his wounded out of harm's way, Makhno drew from his deep well for drama. During this brief pause in the running battle against the White Army, he made the most of it. He called upon his inner theater kid and didn't find it lacking in a moment of need. He rallied his men and women around him. Makhno put a heroic spin on their four months of suffering—all that had been necessary to lure Slashchev into the position in which he now found himself. With this battle, Makhno promised, they would turn everything around.

This was Makhno's St. Crispin's Day speech, in function and essence if not in tone. The most notable fragment of Shakespeare's work wouldn't be out of place in Nestor's mouth at this crucial moment. The most famous lines of said speech from *Henry V* are as follows:

> From this day to the ending of the world,
> But we in it shall be remembered—
> We few, we happy few, we band of brothers;
> For he to-day that sheds his blood with me
> Shall be my brother; be he ne'er so vile,
> This day shall gentle his condition;
> And gentlemen in England now a-bed
> Shall think themselves accurs'd they were not here,
> And hold their manhoods cheap whiles any speaks
> That fought with us upon Saint Crispin's day.

Now would be the turning of the tide against the White Army. The next few days around the town of Perehonivka were consumed by brutal fighting—Slashchev had well-fed and well-armed White cavalry and used them to their fullest effect. Makhno noted in his diaries that the Red cavalry hated to get into melee range unless their foes had been disordered by artillery or gunfire—unlike the White Army cavalry, who positively relished charging directly into combat with sabers and pistols.

The White cavalry kept pushing the Black Army back and back. Slashchev used every trick he had to keep the Makhnovists from gaining the initiative and largely seemed to be succeeding. After three days of fighting, he had them surrounded on three sides, with a forest between the Black Army holding the village of Perehonivka.

But during those three days of battle, Makhno had been getting a better lay of the land than Slashchev—the area around the town was dotted with narrow ravines that were invisible from a distance, along with forests where cavalry could easily conceal themselves.

Makhno vanished the night of September 25, along with his black *sotnia* (his personal bodyguards) all on horseback. The Makhnovists started the fight early on the morning of September 26—bullets flew about like angry bees. It was a mess—Slashchev had the Black Army nearly dead to rights. Chronically low on ammunition, the Black Army made the best of a bad situation. Makhno was still nowhere to be found as the battle worsened for the Black Army. The White Army pushed past the forest, and troops entered Perehonivka where the Black Army administration was headquartered.

Not to put too fine a point on it, but it looked like the end of the Black Army. Makhno's old prison buddy and biographer, Arshinov was an eyewitness to the chaos that unfolded in the town—secretaries, nurses, and other noncombatants picked up what arms they could and fought the White Army in the streets, but it was clear that things were truly desperate. The White soldiers showed no signs of stopping their rampage, until, all of a sudden, they took to their heels, turning back toward the forest. Nestor Makhno's flair for the dramatic had paid off again.

With his personal bodyguards on horseback, they had hidden themselves in the forest outside the town the night before. When the Whites advanced into the town, they had opened themselves up to the worst possible position for a cavalry charge—with their backs to it. Makhno himself is said to have led the sneak attack against the White Army. Things swiftly devolved into "a hacking" as Makhnovists would say, which meant a brutal close quarters battle with sabers, pistols, and bayonets. It is also a fact that swords don't need reloading, so this was a cost-cutting measure as well as utterly frightening.

The White Army fled, and the Black Army, newly energized, gave pursuit. The Black Army chased the Whites to a river and sabered, shot, and stabbed as many of them as they could before they could find a crossing point. A survivor, Almendinger, of the Simferopol division of the White

Army, recalled that barely one hundred men from six whole units survived, with the Makhnovists hurling their few grenades into the retreating Whites to scatter them before closing the gap with sword and bayonet.[7] The only thing that stopped the rout from being worse than it was, was, say it with me now, the lack of ammunition in the Black Army's general ranks.

The Black Army under Makhno had seized victory from the jaws of defeat—and a treasure trove of arms and ammunition from the White Army's supplies. The Black Army could never have enough ammunition. Makhno immediately set to work, capitalizing on his victory: in less than two weeks, the Black Army had recaptured much of the ground they had been forced to cede to the Whites, including the city of Alexandrovsk. On October 8 the Black Army arrived at Berdiansk which was the site of a major White Army ammunition cache at the Varshavskii armory—which exploded mid-battle.

Despite this, the Black Army gained another hoard of technology and ammunition, becoming more formidable rather than less. By October 12, the city was theirs and Denikin was forced to halt his planned advance on Moscow, reeling from this sudden reversal.[8] This turnabout began at Perehonivka, and while Denikin was swift to dismiss Makhno as a threat, that overconfidence came back to bite him in a big way. At any rate, prior to Makhno's victories over the White Army, Denikin's main forces had been within striking range of Moscow and were making the final preparations for the end of the Bolshevik regime. To hear historian Alexandre Skirda tell it, Lenin and Trotsky and the senior Bolshevik commanders were packing comically large suitcases and about to flee to Finland ahead of the White Army.[9] Makhno, in Skirda's estimation, despite loathing the Bolsheviks he was allied with, may have saved them from annihilation.

The rapid undoing of the White Army's gains against Makhno might be explained by two factors—renewed Makhnovist energy and the White Army's policy of horror. The record of the White Army when it comes to human rights scarcely bears repeating, but under Denikin especially they were brutal to the local peasant population—which was also the base of recruitment for the Black and Red armies.

As historian Colin Darch noted, Denikin never understood that the political battle of the Civil War mattered at least as much as the military part and actively refused to discipline or restrain his troops from rape, murder, and theft at a horrifying scale.[10] Even Denikin's own chaplain, a man you might expect to write favorably of his employer if only to earn his paycheck, complained that the White Army was fond of pillage for its own sake, viewed all nonmembers of the army as subhuman, and regularly conducted rapes and pogroms with impunity, and concluded that the White Army was "nothing but a gang of thieves."[11] Such behavior could never win the minds or hearts of the people Denikin intended to rule.

This meant that there were plenty of people who hated the White Army more than the Reds or Blacks or who just wanted revenge. Another theory attributes Makhno's rapid reversal of Denikinist territorial gains to the initiative of the people who saw their White oppressors at a disadvantage and rose up against them ahead of the Batko's troops and then joined the Black Army when they arrived. Whatever the truth of the Battle of Perehonivka and its fallout may be—whether it was simply a smarting (but not decisive) blow to the nose of the overconfident White Army, or the central heroic moment of Makhno's life that turned the tide of the Civil War (as many believe)— scarcely matters. It is undeniable that the cascading defeats at Makhnovist hands could scarcely have helped the White Army, and their margin for error—even with the support of international powers like England, France, and the United States—was too thin to tolerate losses on this level.

The Battle of Perehonivka showed Nestor Makhno at his absolute best militarily when all was against him. I admit this is a mocking reference to the White Army song "Now All Is against Us," which is basically a whiny blog post with a rhythm about how it is not fair that the aristocrats can't oppress the serfs anymore and nobody cares for God or the czar anymore, woe is me.[12]

In contrast to the military glory of the Battle of Perehonivka and Makhno's superb leadership in it, the Polonsky affair (yes, the same Mikhail Polonsky from chapter 8) in December 1919 shows Makhno at his worst.

As the White Army receded, the Bolsheviks redoubled their efforts to discredit, undermine, and assassinate the leadership of the Black Army. Not an "explosives cunningly disguised as red coral" level colorful, as in the CIA's attempt to assassinate Fidel Castro later in the century, but pretty darn close.

This wasn't the first assassination attempt on Makhno's life, but it might have been the most colorful and operatic in character. To put it simply, in the Makhnovist territories, Bolshevik and other nonanarchist groups were allowed to print their own newspapers without censorship—a courtesy that was not extended to anarchists, Mensheviks, or Left Socialist Revolutionaries in Bolshevik lands.

The Bolshevik leadership authorized and encouraged the Bolshevik underground inside the Free Territory to make an attempt to decapitate the Black Army leadership. This task was to be made easier by a typhus epidemic in Nikopol—which laid up a lot of the Makhnovist commanders, impaired their intelligence agency, and partly explains why the Black Army kontrrazvedka initially didn't take this particular conspiracy seriously as a threat. They had out-of-date intelligence. Plagues will do that to you.

The leader of this particular attempt to destroy the Black Army was a Bolshevik named Polonsky.[13] (You may recall that Makhno met Polonsky earlier in his career, in 1918 as he was wandering Ukraine after the German invasion.) The scheme was to place infiltrators in all the major Makhnovist organs and personally poison Makhno and any other high-ranking anarchist leaders who were immobilized or weakened by battle wounds or disease in the hospitals.

The Primary Ingredients of Polonsky's Plan:

- a boatload of poison,
- some well-placed infiltrators in the Black Army,
- his wife, a professional actress, and her birthday party,
- an ornate feast for Nestor Makhno (liberally sprinkled with the above poison),
- and, of course, himself.

The finished dish, if you'll permit me to stretch the food metaphor, was to be the killing of Nestor Makhno and the decapitation of the leadership of the Black Army. In this sense, it can be seen as a mirror of Maria Nikiforova's three-pronged approach to fighting the White and Red armies through assassinations earlier in the year. Except instead of bank robbery and dynamite, Polonsky elected for more traditional methods of assassinating difficult to reach people. The use of poison alone should have been a red flag that Polonsky had a complexity addiction—besides explosives, in assassinations, poisons have the highest rates of failure and complexity inherent in their composition and delivery.

The hook of Polonsky's scheme involved inviting Makhno over to Polonsky's place for some cognac to celebrate his wife's birthday, at which point Makhno would be poisoned. Unfortunately for Polonsky, he was not as good a plotter as he thought he was. The kontrrazvedka got wind of this particular plan six weeks ahead of its scheduled execution and installed its own agents inside the conspiracy, so there was very little they didn't know by the time Polonsky put things into motion.

Things went downhill from there, and on December 2 the attempt on Makhno's life went forward. It didn't get far. Polonsky and the conspirators were allowed to prepare the table and invite Makhno in. One of Makhno's aids tested the food first, but evidently felt something was off and spat it out. Strychnine had been used on the food, but a different poison was used in the cognac meant specifically for Makhno.

The four ringleaders of the conspiracy were arrested along with several other Bolsheviks in the area, and it is here that the picture becomes fuzzy. The official report filed by the kontrrazvedka claimed that the traces of poison were found after testing, then the head suspects (Polonsky, his wife, etc.) were arrested and summarily shot by a riverbank in transit to the kontrrazvedka headquarters.

Naturally, there are some inconsistencies in this story. It isn't like poison testing kits were just lying around in Civil War Ukraine, or that the results would have been available within hours. The timing of all this raised suspicions that the kontrrazvedka killed Polonsky out of hand with Makhno's assurances and the report was drafted later to cover up this impetuous murder.

Not only was the Polonsky conspiracy broken up, but it put Makhno at odds with the local anarchist councils. Makhno didn't have the power to simply sentence people to death—such an exercise smacked of personal feelings clouding his judgment and went counter to basic anarchist precepts of collective decision-making. Simply put, Makhno didn't have the authority to execute people without the local council's approval, which he hadn't sought before having Polonsky and his wife killed. This is something that Denikin, Trotsky, a Chekist, or Lenin might have ordered—a murder without trial and a report covering up the facts of the matter.

Despite his ridiculous mustache, pretentious manner, and constant preening, Lenin had a taste for blood even before the Russian Civil War broke out. Trotsky's notes on the early Bolshevik government record screaming tantrums, multiple times a day, by Lenin on the subject of *not* being able to institute the death penalty more or less at will for crimes. Other Bolsheviks tried to avoid him in the hallways in hopes of avoiding being cornered and lectured by Lenin on "the great terror being unavoidable" with no prompting whatsoever.[14] This push for death penalties cut

RETREATING TO VICTORY AND CONSPIRACY (1919)   **121**

against general Russian trends even under the repression of the czars, which tended to avoid capital punishment except in cases of overt rebellion against the crown. Needless to say, Lenin eventually got his bloodbaths and purges that would make the czars blanch. So you can see why the anarchist councils would be particularly touchy about unsanctioned murders that didn't follow protocol, especially by a military figure like Makhno with a great deal of popular support.

Makhno was called to account for these unsanctioned killings by the anarchist Military Revolutionary Council of Huliaipole, which counted Belash, one of our primary sources for Makhno's activities in this period, among its members. Belash, after the Civil War ended, worked as an informer and provocateur for the Cheka. His main leverage was to try to write himself out of being executed by writing about his role in the Civil War as a member of the Black Army staff. Makhno claimed that things like a trial or due process didn't matter in the Polonsky case, that there were doubtless other Bolshevik conspirators in the Black Army undiscovered, and that the summary execution of traitors was nothing new. He swore at the council and even drew his revolver, threatening the council with it. Voline, who was on the Military Revolutionary Council, called Makhno a "Bonaparte and a drunkard" (I'm saving that insult for my next social interaction).[15] Before there was Hitler, people called self-serving perceived egomaniacs, particularly those with military backgrounds, Bonapartes, with a strong implication that the person so labeled was out for personal power first and principles second, if ever. Makhno was only made to holster his revolver with difficulty and escorted from the room by his companions, crisis narrowly avoided.

By this wrathful tantrum, Makhno was starting to show the strain of constant battle and (justified) fears of assassination that were part and parcel of the Russian Civil War. There weren't any truly safe places or people—betrayal or an artillery shell could come at any time.

The rest of the members of the Polonsky conspiracy were swept up, according to procedure, and given trials. The Bolshevik newspapers and known Bolshevik members were not silenced. The same could not be said for non-Bolsheviks under Bolshevik rule, where repression was in full swing.

Makhno acted like a brute during the Polonsky conspiracy, but the anarchist councils, in this case, lived up to their purpose and prevented a mass purge of Bolsheviks from the civilian and military in territory under their control. Things would only get more difficult from here for Makhno.

CHAPTER 14

Second Alliance with the Bolsheviks against the White Army (1920)

> "The Bolsheviki were no better in this regard than Denikin or any other White element. Anarchists filled Bolshevik prisons; many had been shot and all legal Anarchist activities were suppressed. The Tcheka especially was doing ghastly work, having resurrected the old Tsarist methods, including even torture."
>
> —Emma Goldman

After defeating Denikin's forces in late 1919 and driving back the White Army from much of Ukraine, the Makhnovists understandably let out a collective sigh of relief. They'd come back from the brink of disaster and broken the White Army's advance in the bargain, as well as cooperating with the Bolsheviks. Makhno and the Makhnovists were cautiously optimistic that the Bolsheviks might leave them in peace now that they had demonstrated their worth on the battlefield and held to the terms agreed upon. Perhaps a separate peace or at least an informal understanding had been reached.

That sigh of relief was unfounded. Bolshevik gratitude, never in great supply, proved nonexistent. There was to be no separate peace with the Bolsheviks, only separate wars. Ominous signs of the coming struggle could be detected before the overt hostilities began. In December 1919, Voline was arrested by the Bolsheviks in Ukraine. Voline had known Trotsky back in 1917, in New York. During a conversation in a printshop where Voline expressed worry about the growing power of the embryonic Marxist-Leninists in regard to suppressing anarchists, Trotsky claimed that "like you we are all anarchists in the final analysis." Voline was overreacting to differences of tactics, not goals, Trotsky continued (I imagine in his trademark patronizing tone). Trotsky concluded his soliloquy by saying that he couldn't imagine that his tendency or he personally could ever sanction violence against anarchists, claiming "We are not your enemies."[1] So imagine Voline's surprise—or lack thereof—when back in 1919, Trotsky responded by telegraph to news of the anarchist's capture: "Shoot him immediately—Trotsky."[2]

The Makhnovist historian Arshinov in his *History of the Makhnovist Movement* summarized the situation at the beginning of 1920:

> In the middle of January, 1920, the Bolsheviks declared Makhno and the members of his army outlaws for their refusal to go to the Polish front. This date marked the beginning of a violent struggle between the Makhnovists and the Communist power. We will not go into all the details of this struggle, which lasted nine months. We will only note that it was a merciless struggle on both sides. The Bolsheviks relied on their numerous well-armed and well-supplied divisions. In order to avert fraternization between the soldiers of the Red Army and the Makhnovists, the Bolshevik commander sent against the Makhnovists a division of Lettish sharpshooters and some Chinese detachments, that is to say, *units whose members had not the slightest idea of the true meaning of the Russian revolution and who blindly obeyed the orders of the authorities.*[3]

To condense a bit and put it in plainer English:

Bolsheviks: How's about you take your grassroots army and take it as far as possible from its place of supply and people who support it? Poland is lovely this time of year! We definitely won't use you as suicide troops, or quietly assassinate your leaders, pinky swear!
Makhnovists: How about you go fuck yourselves? We're done here.

There was no other way for the Makhnovists to read Bolshevik intentions except as hostile. The Makhnovists—and Makhno—considered the Bolshevik offer offensive and a blatant attempt to set them up to fail, then be purged the nanosecond they weren't of use. Once pulled far away from their homeland and base of civilian support, they would be sitting ducks for the Bolsheviks—either to be used as suicide troops against the Poles, or to be purged with no hope of melting into the landscape. This was literally the oldest trick in the Bolshevik playbook for liquidating enemies, as well as an insultingly obvious maneuver.

So the brief treaty between the Bolsheviks and Makhnovists ended. Worse, Makhno was still grievously sick in the beginning of 1920—so ill in fact he had to appoint one of his subcommanders, Kalashnikov, to lead the Makhnovists for a time before he fully recovered.[4] That's typhus for you. As the White Army retreated south into Crimea the Makhnovists were forced to fight without respite. But it was more of a contest than the Red Army would have liked.

Troops from Red Army units, mostly peasant conscripts, often deserted to the Makhnovists in large numbers, drawn by the prospect of control over their own lives and land. The barrier between Red and Black armies wasn't always impermeable. In their conflicts with the Bolsheviks, the Makhnovists made a practice of encouraging desertion through dedicated propaganda directed to the rank and file of the Red Army. A Makhnovist leaflet circulated in July 1920 reads, in part:

> Comrade Red Army man! You have been sent by your commis-
> sar and commander to capture the insurgent Makhnovists. On
> orders from your leaders you will destroy peaceful villages, search
> out, arrest and kill folk whom you do not know, folk who they tell
> you are enemies of the people.... We revolutionary insurgents and
> Makhnovists are also peasants and workers, just like our brothers,
> the Red Army men ... our immediate aim is the establishment of a
> free soviet order without the power of the Bolsheviks, without the
> compulsion of any party.... Comrade! Think it over. Whom are you
> with and whom are you against? Don't be a slave—be a man![5]

More heavy-handed methods were used on captured soldiers. It was common practice to execute Bolshevik officers and commissars out of hand but to encourage the foot soldiers—often conscripts forced into service to either return to their homes or join the Makhnovists.

The Makhnovists didn't have the numbers or supplies to compete with the Bolsheviks so soon after their protracted combat with Denikin and the typhus epidemic of the previous year. Almost as long as they'd been in power, the Bolsheviks had the region around Huliaipole, the core of Makhnovist power, under blockade. It was only with great difficulty that basic supplies or weapons could reach that area. This would continue to be true even when they were nominally allied with Makhno, as a way of keeping the Free Territory on a logistical leash.

So the Makhnovists were forced from necessity to rely on their proven tactics of guerrilla warfare. This meant avoiding pitched battles due to their lesser numbers and fewer weapons, striking Bolshevik units on the march, abandoning positions only to conduct lightning raids days later deep in Bolshevik territory, tearing up railroad tracks, cutting telegraph wires between key points—the war equivalent of a full-court press.[6]

On a more personal level of the conflict, the Bolsheviks had always viewed Makhno as a serious enough threat to send multiple assassins after him. The stories of the assassination attempts on Makhno alone would make a sizable—if grim—book. The operatic and byzantine attempt by Polonsky and his coconspirators on Makhno's life had failed in late 1919, but it was far from the only one. Makhno had a thousand lives, it seems—an impression substantiated by his excellent survival instincts, the Makhnovist kontrrazvedka, and informers inside the Bolshevik intelligence services themselves who more than once warned Makhno away from certain doom.

The Bolsheviks under Trotsky and Lenin viewed Makhno as a far greater threat to the stability and legitimacy of their rule, at some time or another, than the counterrevolutionary White Army.[7] A White Army triumph would still result in a Russian state. The triumph—or mere existence of—the Makhnovschina, a stateless and masterless entity, was viewed by the Bolsheviks as a threat to the legitimacy and existence of their entire centralized mode of government.

You know that feeling at the end of a long day, when your muscles begin to loosen and a sigh of relief leaves your lungs? I'm convinced that feeling didn't exist during the Russian Civil War—all sides were as at risk to random variables and treachery as it is possible to be. Makhno didn't have a single relaxing day in the entire Civil War, which doesn't sound so bad until you remember that it went on for four years.

Arshinov mentions that during this period, the Bolsheviks upped their attempts to have Makhno killed using captured anarchists or agents provocateurs. This fact may go some small way toward explaining Makhno's seemingly inexplicable dislike for the anarchist historian Voline in the post–Civil War era. Voline at one point had been captured by the Bolsheviks and held prisoner—anyone who was captured by Bolsheviks was viewed with intense suspicion, though Makhno clearly didn't consider him an assassin. The deal the Cheka often made with captured anarchists was usually something like this: you can die here, or you can be set free to assassinate Makhno. A nontrivial number of anarchists took this deal—Arshinov records one instance of a particular set of anarchist assassins in June 1920.[8] Three former Makhnovist prisoners of the Bolsheviks—Fedya Glushchenko, Kurilenko, and Kostyukhin—were tasked with the assassination of Makhno on the orders of a Cheka handler, Vasiliy Mantsev.

Fedya, a former member of the kontrrazvedka, immediately informed Makhno of the plot against him and revealed his coconspirators, who were quickly arrested and disarmed. This is more remarkable considering that Fedya understood that the Makhnovists would absolutely execute him for cooperating with the Bolsheviks even if he had just saved the batko's life. Fedya considered this a fair trade—he and Kostyukhin were executed by the Makhnovists, and the incident publicized by the Makhnovists to let the Bolsheviks know their attempts had failed spectacularly.

As summer arrived, the White Army regained strength. Denikin resigned from head of the White Army and leadership passed to a forbidding and humorless bald man named General Wrangel. Pyotr Wrangel was likely the most dangerous general on the side of the White Army in the whole war. Denikin had little to no control over his troops and did little prevent their pogroms; Kolchak in Siberia was a prima donna with an alarming tendency to change his mind on major matters at the last moment, with disastrous results.

By contrast, Wrangel tried to at least look and act professional by the standards of the day, and understood that the war was as much political as tactical, a concept that eluded both Denikin and Kolchak. Wrangel notably clashed with Slashchev—the most recent White commander to fight against Makhno. Wrangel called Slashchev "a man in the throes of mental sickness" and an utter "slave to drink and drugs" so it can be assumed they weren't exactly best friends.[9]

General Slashchev was exiled to Constantinople, where he took up gardening. The man who was too antisemitic for Wrangel was eager to take a Bolshevik pardon and teach military classes alongside other former White Army officers in 1921. Here is how Emma Goldman describes Slashchev's reception in Moscow, featuring none other than that snake-among-snakes Trotsky, who finally got his wish to work with the Whites instead of the anarchists after all:

> He was now being received with military honours and feted at the order of the Soviet Government by workers, soldiers, and sailors

singing revolutionary songs for the edification of one of the most implacable foes of the Revolution. We walked over to the Red Square to see the spectacle of Leon Trotsky, the Commissar of the Revolutionary Army of the Socialist Republic, reviewing his forces before the tsarist general Slashchov-Krimsky [Slashchev]. The grandstand was not far from John Reed's grave. Within its shadow Leon Trotsky, the butcher of Kronstadt, was clasping the blood stained hand of his comrade Krimsky. It was a spectacle to make the gods weep with laughter.[10]

Such revolutionary integrity on behalf of the Bolsheviks! Slashchev was killed in his apartment in Moscow by a surviving member of one his pogroms in 1929.[11] Still, there isn't much good to be said of Wrangel, save that he was a more composed specimen of monster than his predecessors and a skilled cavalry commander. He had twenty years of cavalry experience under the czars (based out of Nerchinsk in Siberia), and two of his squad commanders were future famous war criminals: the notoriously unstable and fractious Baron von Ungern-Sternberg who was fond of shooting civilians and his own officers;[12] and Cossack ataman Semyonov who never met a bottle or massacre he didn't like.[13] This says all you need to know about the czarist military, as well as Wrangel. The depths of his morality can be observed by him making some concerned noises about the horrors his troops inflicted, but he certainly didn't make anything more than desultory attempts to stop them.

Under Wrangel's command, the White Army started making serious gains in Ukraine, pushing north from their base in Crimea. Makhno now had to fight both the Reds and the Whites at once. The Bolsheviks, as usual, were far more comfortable helping out the people who longed for a return of the monarchy than the idea of a world without masters, and would frequently interrupt battles between the White Army and the Black Army, as Arshinov documents: "During the summer of 1920, the Makhnovists more than once attempted to engage in battle against Wrangel. On two occasions they had military encounters with his troops, but each time the Red troops struck the Makhnovists from behind, and the Makhnovists had to abandon the firing line and retreat.... The Soviet Authorities did not stop slandering the Makhnovists. Throughout the Ukraine, Soviet newspapers spread the false news of an alliance between Makhno and Wrangel."[14] This obviously was a very bad development for Makhno and the Makhnovist forces. Bad enough they had to fight the Reds, but now they had to deal with the Whites as well. This three-way war in all its horrific brutality went on from summer until fall of 1920.

Wrangel had the advantage of the weakened Black Army, and even the numerically superior Red Army at this stage at the game. Wrangel managed to become an existential threat to both the Red and Black armies. From his base in Crimea, at the southern part of Ukraine on the shores of the Black Sea, he made steady gains against both armies.

Wrangel made repeated entreaties to Nestor Makhno for a possible alliance against the Red Army (or, that failing, the appearance of negotiations that would undercut Makhno's popularity with the peasants and force him to turn to the White Army for help if that base collapsed from under him). Wrangel miscalculated and miscalculated badly with the choice of one of his messengers. The first emissary from the White Army to the Makhnovists was recognized as a commander who had in 1919, executed 120 partisans who he claimed were on the way to join Makhno. This messenger was promptly hanged, and a placard placed around his neck, which read: "No compact between Makhno and the White Guards can or could ever be entered into, and should the White camp send us another emissary, the same fate awaits him."[15]

Wrangel didn't learn and sent another officer to negotiate with the Makhnovists. What do you think happened to him? There was no force on earth that would make the anarchists collaborate with his monarchist forces. The people of the Makhnovschina would rather have died than work with Wrangel. Makhno and the anarchist councils unanimously voted to have any and all messengers from the Whites executed on the spot and did so. That was all the reply that Wrangel would get from the anarchists.

Makhno's rather dramatic refusal of Wrangel's terms got Bolshevik attention, specifically that bloviating scumbag Trotsky of the Red Army. From his personal correspondence we find this record: "A few weeks ago, Wrangel really did try to enter into direct relations with the Makhnovites, and sent two emissaries to Makhno's headquarters to negotiate. As delegates from the Revolutionary War Council of the Southern front were able to assure themselves, the Makhnovists not merely refused to negotiate with Wrangel's emissaries, but hanged them publicly after their arrival at Makhno's headquarters. This very fact—Wrangel's direct attempt to make a deal with the Makhnovites—showed plainly to the latter the full disastrousness of their fight against the Soviet power."[16]

Trotsky, as usual, has his analysis ass-backwards. At this point in the war, the Red Army was losing badly against the Whites—what Wrangel wanted most was to prevent an alliance between the Red and Black armies. This is exactly what happened. The Bolsheviks under Trotsky approached the Makhnovists for an alliance in October and the following terms were agreed to:

1. All anarchist prisoners and dissidents were to be released from Bolshevik custody.
2. Anarchists and Makhnovists would have freedom of expression and assembly in Bolshevik Territory. The Bolsheviks would publish the full text of this agreement across all their territories and not seek to hide Makhnovist involvement in this latest campaign. Until this was done, the Makhnovists wouldn't stir a single soldier.
3. The Makhnovists would lend their forces under the ultimate command of the Red Army but keep their own commanders and internal structure. Any deserters from the Red Army to the Black Army would be returned to the Red Army if the forces recombined. Families and friends of Makhnovists in Bolshevik territory were to have the same rights as in Makhnovist territory.[17]

The Bolsheviks, in a typical act of bad faith tried to publish the agreement piecemeal, and tried to repress the critical fourth clause of the agreement, which reads as follows: "Since one of the essential principles of the Makhnovist movement is the struggle for the self-management of the workers, the Insurrectionary Army (Makhnovist) believes it should insist on the following fourth point of the political agreement: in the region where the Makhnovist Army is operating, the population of workers and peasants will create its own institutions of economic and political self-management; these institutions will be autonomous and joined in federation, by means of agreements, with the governmental organs of the Soviet Republic."[18]

Arshinov elaborates:

Under various pretexts, the Soviet authorities continually put off the publication of this agreement. The Makhnovists understood that this was not a good sign. The full meaning of this delay only became clear some time later, when the Soviet power unleashed a new and brutal assault against the Makhnovists.... Aware of the lack of sincerity of the Soviet authorities, the Makhnovists declared firmly that as long as the agreement was not published, the Insurrectionary Army could not act according to its clauses. It was only after this direct pressure that the Soviet Government finally decided to publish the text of the agreement.[19]

The Bolsheviks eventually buckled and grudgingly published the terms. The agreement was activated—with Commander Frunze signing for the Bolsheviks. With the terms of the agreement published and at least some anarchist prisoners freed, including Voline who had been captured by the Bolsheviks in 1919, Makhno went ahead and lent his military assistance to the Red Army. Makhno sent as many troops as he could afford to help the Red Army push Wrangel out of Crimea. He gave the command to Karetnik and also sent along one of his closest friends and officers, the cavalryman Marchenko, who had been with the Makhnovists from the very beginning.[20] The Makhnovists acquitted themselves well in the Crimean campaign— proving critical in taking an "impregnable" White position and dislodging Wrangel from his fastness. This, combined with the complete collapse of the Bolshevik push on the Polish front, freed up a tremendous amount of manpower to focus on Wrangel.

Historian Serhii Plokhy notes in *The Gates of Europe: A History of Ukraine* that at least one of the reasons the Polish front collapsed (besides Trotsky's insistence on his "military genius") was the overeager pushing of a young officer Iosef Jughashvili (he wasn't Stalin yet), to take the city of Lvov in Ukraine instead of providing reinforcements to the Bolshevik forces.[21] This may account for at least part of the thoroughness of the Stalinist purges on everyone involved in the Crimean or Polish campaign in the late thirties.

The White Army was broken by the combined forces of the Red and Black armies in November 1920, losing half their forces in the battles in Crimea. As many as could fit into boats were evacuated into the Black Sea, including Wrangel himself.[22] Wrangel decided to live on his yacht outside Constantinople—until a boat rammed it at night and sank it. Sadly Wrangel wasn't on it at the time, and the ramming of his yacht was almost certainly one of many assassination attempts on the White general before his final destination of Brussels, where he died in 1928 under mysterious circumstances.

The alliance between the Red Army and Black Army was over the second Wrangel's fleet vanished over the horizon.

CHAPTER 15

The Sudden yet Inevitable Betrayal (1920–21)

> "In the autumn of 1920, the Polish-Petliurist armies fled in blind panic, driven out by rural partisans who thus afforded the Bolsheviks the chance to occupy Kiev, Vinnitsa, Zhmerinka and the entire province of Podolya. A this point Vassili Grigoyyvitch decided to despatch me and a small detachment of men to give the Makhnovists a helping hand. As I took my leave of him. He told me with tears in his eyes that the Makhnovist movement could not hold out, for our men even then had no doubts about what fate the Bolsheviks had in store for them."
>
> —Ossip Tsebry

On November 8, 1920, a meeting was held in Huliaipole between anarchist representatives about what to do about the Bolsheviks' upcoming sudden but inevitable betrayal. Peter Rybin, a member of Makhno's staff, concluded in his diary that the Bolsheviks were doubtless going to betray them at some point.[1] Such was an open secret in the anarchist camp—the agreement to ally with the Bolsheviks had been in the shadow of their previous betrayal. It was just that nobody was quite sure how or when the Bolsheviks would try to backstab the anarchists.

Later that month, the anarchists got their answer to that persistent question. Nine Bolshevik spies were captured in Huliaipole on November 23—members of the Red Army's 42nd Sharpshooter Division. They were sent to provide information on Makhno's whereabouts and prepare the way for a sneak attack on Huliaipole—due around November 24 or 25. Peter

Rybin and the anarchist councils furiously telegraphed local Bolshevik headquarters in Kharkiv, demanding an explanation.

Bolshevik General Frunze (the same one who had signed the truce with the anarchists as you may remember from the previous chapter) telegraphed back, saying of course this was all a misunderstanding and not to worry about this at all.[2] It would all be settled to everyone's satisfaction soon enough. If you're reading that last sentence with an ominous tone, you're not the only one.

Three days later, a Bolshevik army surrounded Huliaipole and began shelling the city. Naturally this treachery had been planned well in advance—Voline and Arshinov agree that this logistics-heavy plan must have taken at least ten or fifteen days to concoct and enact. Red Army soldiers were found with pamphlets reading "Death to the Makhnovschina" on them.

Huliaipole was encircled. Makhno was trapped. The Makhnovists had been comprehensively betrayed. Against this treachery, the Makhnovists didn't collapse, as one might have expect. They had been fighting without pause for nearly four years at this point, enduring constant lies, plagues, and starvation—anyone could have forgiven them for despairing.

The Makhnovists kept their despair off the battlefield and channeled it into reckless bravery. Makhno personally led the cavalry—the only Makhnovist forces in the city at the time and not numbering more than three hundred men—in a breakout attempt. They shattered the Red Cavalry and managed to break free. The Makhnovists were forced to abandon the city and get clear.

In Kharkiv, hours before the attack on Huliaipole, the Cheka arrested or shot any anarchists they could get their hands on. They arrested anyone seen going into anarchist bookstores or meeting places without question. Children as young as fifteen weren't immune from these cruel attentions—and the midnight visits of the Cheka were replicated across the former Russian Empire as a continuation of the Red Terror—Voline himself was arrested in the dead of night at his apartment in Kharkiv.[3]

Anarchists, their families, associates, or friends were tortured, imprisoned, or shot on Lenin's orders and with the Cheka's bloody hands. Thousands of anarchists and labor agitators were put into the same prisons they had languished in under the old empire—the Bolsheviks had merely replicated the system they claimed to wish to overthrow, and stripped it of what formal protestations of humanity it once possessed.

On December 7, eleven days after the fall of Huliaipole, Makhno's army met up with the remains of the forces sent to the Crimea to fight Wrangel alongside the Bolsheviks. They met outside a small town, Kermentchik. According to Peter Rybin's diary, one of Makhno's first worries after managing to get clear of Huliaipole was the fate of the Makhnovists in Crimea—doubtless the Bolsheviks had turned on them as well.

There was a band playing in Kermentchik as the bedraggled Makhnovists awaited the return of their Crimean cavalry. Rumors had already reached Makhno's inner circle that some of their forces in the Crimea had survived—but how many? Late in the afternoon, a small group of horsemen reached the village, led by Marchenko and Taranovsky, members of Makhno's inner circle tasked with the Crimean expedition. The band's triumphant music swelled—but of the 1,500 cavalry that had left for the Crimea, only about 250 had survived.

Marchenko rode up to Makhno. "The Crimean detachment has returned," he said, laconically. "At last we know who the Communists [Bolsheviks] are."[4] Makhno said nothing to this, and tried to keep his emotions off his face and out of his voice. An impromptu public assembly was held in the village—Marchenko and Taranovsky told the story of their escape from the Crimea and the state of affairs there. More Bolshevik treachery. What a shock.

After Wrangel's defeat, the Bolsheviks had called a general meeting with the Makhnovists. Karetnik, the commander of the Crimean expedition, and his staff, had been lured to these meetings and shot. Taranovsky and Marchenko took their troops and fled as best they could. The worst part was that the anarchists had to refuse Bolshevik units that wanted to defect— as many did—for fear that those willing defectors might be feigning this change of heart. The cavalry under Marchenko and Taranovsky met with disaster upon a chance encounter with a Bolshevik regiment—explaining their much diminished numbers now. Even with reduced numbers, the Makhnovists repeatedly escaped encirclements by the Red Army and defeated larger units outright.

A week later, on December 12, the Makhnovists captured Berdiansk, and then mounted a surprise attack on Huliaipole. It completely succeeded and the Bolsheviks fled the city. Makhno was informed that the night before the Makhnovists arrived, the fleeing Bolsheviks executed three hundred suspected Makhnovists or people associated with them. Six hundred Red Army soldiers, mostly peasants, stayed and defected to the Makhnovists.[5]

It was at this time that another general meeting was called. The Makhnovists ultimately decided to split their combined forces into two sections of around 1,500 each—one under the command of Marchenko, the other under the command of Makhno. This was done in response to the Red Army starting to employ more guerrilla tactics against the Makhnovists. This way, a single decisive battle gone wrong couldn't extinguish the Makhnovschina.[6]

This was the last time Makhno saw his old friend Marchenko, who had been with him in the struggle since the first day of the struggle against the Austro-Hungarians in 1918, which must have seemed like a lifetime ago. Marchenko didn't survive the year 1921. Makhno did.

The back and forth of engagements is a wearying list. By now one should be sufficiently convinced of Makhno's military skills to guess at how well he rose to the occasion. I'll let Arshinov's *History of the Makhnovist Movement* capture the mood of the early part of the war:

> For some time, the Makhnovists were encouraged by the thought that victory would be on their side. It appeared to them that it was only necessary to defeat two or three Bolshevik divisions for an important part of the Red Army to join them, and the rest to retreat to the north .... It was increasingly clear that the defeat of two or three Red units was of no importance in view of the enormous mass of troops which was being sent against the Makhnovists. It was no longer a question of achieving victory over the Bolshevik armies, but of avoiding the complete destruction of the insurrectionary army. This army reduced to 3000 soldiers, was obliged to fight daily, each time against an enemy of 10,000 to 15,000 men.[7]

Arshinov's reference to a "grate of bayonets" that scraped over the remains of Ukraine in 1919, continued to slice away at any chance of positive creation of an anarchist polity. Ukraine had been at war for five years straight. Ukraine was a wasteland and made even worse through repeated struggle against the Bolsheviks. The struggle—the taking and losing of cities, the massacre of civilians by the Red Army, the starvation and plagues—should be familiar by now. Even still an overview might be helpful.

General Frunze's overall plan was a triple circle of forces around the Makhnovist territories, tightening the nooses until the partisans ended up

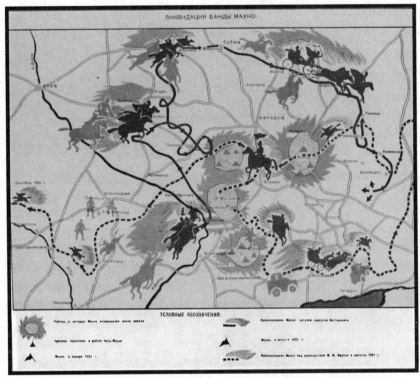

"Liquidation of the Bandit Makhno," inset to map 10 "Banditry and Its Liquidation," in *Triumph and Liquidation: An Essay and Guide to a Series of Ten Pictorial Wall Maps Produced to Illustrate the Military Successes of the Red Army in the Russian Civil War of 1917 to 1922*, compiled and translated by Michael Klein (Library of Congress, Geography and Maps Division, 2017). The legend reads from left, vertically, then to right: (1) Areas to which Makhno returned after the raid. (2) Red garrisons near Makhno's base. (3) Makhno in January 1921. (4) Pursuit of Makhno by the flying corps of Nesterovich. (5) Makhno in August 1921. (6) Pursuit of Makhno under the leadership of M.V. Frunze in August 1921. Note the framing of Makhno as a bandit and counterrevolutionary, and the framing of his movement as antisemitic (in the text of map 10)—while none of this was true, it was a staple of Bolshevik and Soviet sources on Makhno.

with the Sea of Azov at their backs. It was a good plan. It just didn't work the way he wanted it to. Again and again the Makhnovists broke through Red Army lines when surrounded. The Makhnovists almost never, in this terrible year, fought on the defensive or in entrenched positions. Theirs was a war of maneuver, harassment, and guerrilla tactics suited to their advantage in cavalry and tachanki.

Makhno and his army had faced long odds before and won. In the battles that followed, the Makhnovists were almost always outnumbered and outgunned and still triumphed more often than not. Many Red Army troops (and commanders) didn't want to fight their former allies and either refused to march or defected to the Makhnovists in the early stages of this last, hideous war.

Makhnovist victories that would have been backbreaking to the Bolsheviks months earlier were now acceptable casualties. Even Budyenny, a Red Cavalry commander much lauded by Bolshevik historians, wrote in his memoirs: "None of the commanders had any inclination to complete the task of wiping out Makhno, regardless of cost and with all possible speed."[8] Makhno dealt Budyenny a humiliating defeat in which the hero of the Red Army had to beat an ignominious retreat and one of the Bolshevik staff officers took a whole cavalry unit over to the Makhnovists. The life of Budyenny, the pride of the Red Army cavalry, was saved by his keen personal sense of self-preservation and he fled the battlefield, catching a glimpse of Makhno and his commanders observing the rout on a nearby hill as he did so.[9]

Their default move when surrounded was to force a cavalry charge and break through—time and time again the Red Army cavalry had proved it was not a match for the Makhnovist horsemen in that context:

> After routing several units of the Red Army and taking more than 20,000 prisoners, Makhno ... set out first towards the east, though the workers of this mining region had warned him that he was awaited by a solid military barrier; he then turned sharply west following routes only he knew. From this moment, the ordinary roads were completely abandoned. The movement of the army continued for hundreds of miles, across snow-covered fields, guided by a prodigious sense of direction and orientation in this icy desert. This maneuver permitted the Makhnovist army to avoid hundreds of cannon and machine guns, and allowed it to defeat two brigades of the 1st Bolshevik cavalry at Petrovo in the government at [province of] Kherson, believing Makhno to be a hundred miles away, were taken completely by surprise.

The struggle lasted several months with incessant battles day and night.[10] Countless times during this year-long struggle, Makhno's men or peasants who only knew him by reputation if at all would sacrifice themselves in last stands against Red Army troops to buy Makhno time to escape.

General Frunze's long campaign against Makhno and the Makhnovists wasn't precise. Civilian casualties were a major and deliberate part of it, war crimes common. Unable to catch Makhno, he simply ordered his troops to slaughter wholesale any Ukrainian peasants in Makhnovist territory. To quote from Arshinov's account of this final struggle:

> The third campaign of the Bolsheviks against the Makhnovists was at the same time a campaign against the Ukrainian peasantry. The general aim of this campaign was not merely to destroy the Makhnovist army, but to subjugate the dissatisfied peasants and to remove from them all possibility of organizing any type of revolutionary-guerrilla movement. The enormous Red Army, freed from the war against Wrangel, made it fully possible for the Bolsheviks to carry out this plan. The Red Divisions traveled through all the rebel villages in the insurgent region and exterminated masses of peasants on the basis of information provided by local kulaks ... in Novospasovka, the Chekists, thirsting for murder, forced mothers to hold their babes in their arms so as to kill both with one blow ... such cases were quite frequent.[11]

To make a dark picture darker still, in February 1921, Pyotr Kropotkin, anarchist luminary and one of Makhno's inspirations, died in Moscow of pneumonia. His last letters to Lenin were ignored as he argued with the Bolshevik leader that authoritarianism couldn't bring social revolution. Kropotkin witnessed the starving citizens of Moscow firsthand and relayed their desperate plight to a typically indifferent Lenin. All Lenin had done, Kropotkin concluded, bitingly, was show how a revolution was *not* to be conducted, that is, along authoritarian, right-wing lines ("We learn in Russia how Communism cannot be introduced").[12]

The old "saint without a god" of anarchism mourned the lost potential of the revolution in Russia, and would have left for France in the spring of 1920 if he could have (where he was convinced there were more possibilities for social revolution), but this was not to be.

His funeral was the last time the black flag of anarchism was allowed to be openly displayed in Moscow. Anarchist prisoners were released from prison for the day to bid their farewells to their comrade (the Cheka took hostages—if they failed to return, students and random civilians would serve the anarchists' sentences for them). Emma Goldman and Alexander Berkman were present at the old man's funeral, alongside Aron Baron,

Alexei Borovoi and others. Voline was immediately thrown back into Butyrka prison along with other anarchist notables like the anarcho-syndicalist Maximov. They eventually staged an eleven-day hunger strike, that when combined with outside pressure from other anarchists, forced Lenin to release them under pain of exile. They arrived in Berlin in 1922. Many other anarchists weren't so lucky.

The Bolsheviks continued their purge of dissidents, anarchists, and Left Socialist Revolutionaries. They also shamelessly oppressed the peasantry of the former Russian Empire with food requisitions, leaving thousands to either fight their new masters or starve.

In early 1921, in rapid succession, rebellions against the Bolsheviks mushroomed across Russia. We've already discussed the Tambov rebellion (with an estimated twenty to fifty thousand peasants mounting a vicious guerrilla campaign against Bolshevik grain collectors and military units) briefly, but the Kronstadt Rebellion in February–March of that year shook the Bolsheviks.

The Kronstadt sailors had previously been considered the most unquestioningly loyal of the Bolshevik troops—but their demands (actual worker's councils instead of politicized Bolshevik organs answerable to nobody, free speech and expression, unbanning of non-Bolshevik parties, and the dismantling of the Cheka, etc.) were treated as treason and a "White guard plot."[13] In reality, their demands were no less than what the Bolsheviks had promised when they assumed power. Strikes convulsed Petrograd. Consistency of word and deed is not a trait of authoritarians.

The Bolsheviks claimed that the Kronstadt uprising was treason or somehow a White Army "counterrevolutionary" ploy, at least in public. The Kronstadt sailors and strikers were crushed—partly because they refused to attack the Bolsheviks when their guard was down and trusted their enemies to negotiate in good faith, and partly because the Bolsheviks would not tolerate any sort of dissent in their dictatorship. Makhno could have told them that was a wasted avenue, but never mind. For a party allegedly dedicated to creating a workers' paradise, the Bolsheviks sure were fond of gunning down striking workers in the street. How do you know when a Leninist or Trotskyist is lying? Simple. Their mouths are moving. Their entire platform, in the context of the Russian Revolution and Civil War was predicated on saying one thing and doing the exact opposite.

Lenin's response to Kronstadt (and the Siberian uprisings that convulsed the Russian far east) likely saved his hide and his authoritarian government in the bargain.[14] He realized that war communism (forcibly stealing food from the peasants with special detachments of troops and leaving them to starve) was going to spread more rebellions and so adopted the New Economic Policy (NEP): A little bit of land reform, a reinjection of capitalism into the economy, and a pinky promise to never, ever try to starve the people of the former Russian empire into submission ever again.

The NEP was calculated to relieve the absolute minimum of human suffering while keeping the Bolshevik stranglehold on political and military power. Or, as a high-ranking Bolshevik, Bukharin, said of the NEP: "We are making economic concessions to avoid political concessions."[15] The cynical calculation was that the war-weary peasants would take some concessions—any concessions—and stop supporting rebellions against the Bolshevik autocracy. This gambit was largely proven correct, when combined with Cheka repressions of dissent, terror, and the overwhelming numbers of the Red Army. It was just enough to undermine peasant support for popular uprisings to allow the Bolsheviks to solidify power when nearly the whole of Russia rose up against their authoritarianism.

There were significant spontaneous anarchist uprisings in Siberia that were bloodily put down. The whole country shook and for a beautiful moment, it looked as if the whole rotten edifice of Bolshevik power might come whimpering down. Anarchist historian Nick Heath notes that the Makhnovists themselves called this period from 1919 onward the "Third Revolution" against Bolshevik tyranny. That is, mass unconnected (tactically speaking) peasant uprisings against food requisitions, conscriptions, and the specter of Bolshevik fascism, chiefly led by anarchists or Socialist-Revolutionaries.

Sadly, the Bolsheviks survived these uprisings by virtue of crimes against humanity and their own purported ideology. The vastness of Russia conspired against any unification of these efforts, and their spontaneous nature meant that there was a wave of isolated rebellions that were individually squelched, rather than a coordinated push against the new, fragile Bolshevik dictatorship.

It is worth noting that Arshinov makes a reference in his history of the movement to the aftermath of the battle against Budyenny. He writes: "Then I formed a unit of former Siberians, and sent them, armed and equipped with necessities, to Siberia, under the command of comrade Glazunov."[16] This implies some attempted coordination with the Siberian anarchists and the Makhnovists, but given the distances involved and the pressures the Makhnovists were under, it would be simplistic to say that they were allied or coordinating on any meaningful level.

Combined with Frunze's rampant murder of civilians and Makhnovists in the Ukrainian villages, the partisan and guerrilla tactics, the base of Ukrainian peasant resistance was being eroded enough to make Makhnovist guerrilla groups less effective. Exhaustion and war-weariness, combined with lack of armaments, took their toll on the Makhnovists in Ukraine.

Frunze's long fight with the Makhnovists eventually ended with the Bolsheviks in control of Ukraine by mid-1921. The slaughter of peasants, the war-sickness and the numerical superiority of the Red Army were simply too much for the Makhnovists to overcome, no matter how brilliantly they were led or how bravely they fought. Scattered Makhnovist, anarchist, and peasant resistance (called euphemistically "banditry" by the Bolsheviks) would continue in splotches until 1938. It was standard Bolshevik policy to call any struggle against their authoritarianism "banditry," which has only made the work of historians more difficult.

General Frunze didn't live long after his campaign against Makhno. He died under suspicious circumstances during a "routine stomach operation" in 1925, a mere four years later. While nothing can be proved, it fits the pattern of Stalin.[17] Even that early in his career, he was purging any and all generals in the Red Army who had proved popular with the troops or had a great deal of practical experience in war as possible political rivals. It is a case of one monster removing another.

CHAPTER 16

Nestor Makhno En Route to Paris (1921–25)

> "Civilization is mutual aid and self-defense; culture is the judge, the lawbook and the forces of Law & Ordure; Civilization is uprising, insurrection, revolution; culture is the war of state against state, or of machines against people."
>
> —Edward Abbey

Nestor Makhno and his closest comrades escaped Ukraine by the skin of their teeth.

The Bolsheviks tightened the net with border patrols and security in general to try and stop Makhno from escaping. The Makhnovists reacted to the tightening of this Bolshevik net by decentralizing further still and scattering in small units moving rapidly in multiple directions.[1] Some of them went underground inside Ukraine. Victor Belash claims that the underground Makhnovists even received tips on Red Army movements from persecuted Mennonite colonists during this time, so much were they hated.[2]

Makhno and his inner circle—including his wife, Halyna Kuzmenko—fought nonstop to reach the Romanian border to the west, on the other side of the country from their hometown. According to historian Alexandre Skirda, the small party covered one thousand kilometers in three weeks on horseback and tachanki. This is a breakneck pace by any standard. The journey was made worse by the fact that Makhno and his party were constantly fighting, and thusly suffered a wide range of injuries.

Makhno's party had quite a few close calls during this lightning dash for the border. The Makhnovists were in sorry shape, and the tachanki were making an awful din with their un-lubricated wheels. According to Victor Belash, during one stop in a town near the Romanian border to secure fresh horses, the locals took exception to Makhno's demand for horses and wheel oil and a fight broke out. Quite a few Makhnovists died in the ensuing melee, and Makhno's legs were wounded.[3]

Belash goes on to chronicle more misfortune for Makhno: a few days later, he was wounded quite badly in the face during a fight with a Red cavalry unit and fell unconscious—he had to be moved to a tachanka.[4] This final battle may be the source of Makhno's long scar on the left side of his jaw, visible in photographs from his exile.

It is a significant wound—it may have been the work of a cavalry saber or a pistol-shot—the sources differ. There is a grim humor in this— Makhno's scar evokes a similar aesthetic to the popular Germanic tradition of dueling scars worn by aristocrats, also inflicted by being slashed in the face by a heavy saber, as marks of honor (called a "Schmisse" or "bragging scar").

The Roman historian Plutarch chronicled the life of the ancient guerrilla fighter Sertorius, taking time to note that he viewed scars as preferable to other badges of glory. Plutarch writes of Sertorius that he, even as a commander of armies: "performed wonders with his own hands, and never sparing himself, but exposing his body freely in all conflicts, he lost one of his eyes. This he always esteemed an honor to him; observing that others do not continually carry about with them the marks and testimonies of their valor, but must often lay aside their chains of gold, their spears and crowns; whereas his ensigns of honor, and the manifestations of his courage, always remained with him, and those who beheld his misfortune must at the same time recognize his merits." Save for the bit about losing an eye, these words could have just as easily been written about Nestor Makhno, millennia later. By this reckoning, Nestor Makhno was the most personally valorous participant in the Russian Civil War, simply by the amount of wounds he received personally in battle—and more remarkably, survived them.

Fortunately, tricks from earlier in the Civil War still worked to get the determined party over the border, including the old-favorite as dressing up as the enemy. Alexey Nikolaev, in his book *First Among Equals*, quoted by the historian Skirda, tells of an incident where Makhno's chief intelligence officer, Lev Zinkovsky, rode at the head of the party into a Red border guard. The Makhnovists were disguised as fellow Red Army cavalry.

Zinkovsky called the border guards every bad word he could think of in Russian—a language composed of at least 10 percent swear words has a lot of options—excoriating them for having called for cavalry regiment for backup for nothing.[5]

"Don't you know there is a war on?!" Zinkovsky might have fumed at the guards, flushing beet red, "No discipline, no balls!"

"What backup," the confused Red guards might have asked, scratching their heads, "We didn't ask for any backup, you must be mistaken—oh, oh, you have a gun in our face now. Ok. This is a stickup, then."

"Can't get a thing past you, can we?" Zinkovsky might have smirked from horseback.

The rest of the Makhnovists also drew their arms, still in captured uniforms, disarmed the border guards and took stock of their situation. Nikolaev relates that the border guards recommended a particular spot to cross the Dniestr River into Romania. Nestor Makhno rolled in on a tachanka—unconscious and feverish from injury.

That's one account, anyway—others make the claim that the Romanian border guard opened fire on Makhno's group as they crossed the river. They only stopped when the Ukrainians claimed to be Cossacks and not Bolsheviks as their stolen uniforms suggested. Sometimes deceptions can work too well.

Regardless of the details of the escape from Ukraine, the facts remain as follows: On August 28, 1921, an unconscious Nestor Ivanovich Makhno crossed the borders of Ukraine into Romania with a few of his closest friends.[6] Lev Zinkovsky stayed behind in Ukraine. He was killed in a basement in Kiev in 1938 by the Soviet secret police during Stalin's purges.[7]

Once in Romania, the Makhnovists were caught by the Romanian border guard and disarmed. Makhno and his remaining band were transferred to a refugee camp, their request for political asylum rejected. Makhno recovered consciousness in a foreign land, and in only slightly less danger than he had been in previously.

Romania was scarcely a friendly place for the scattered anarchists, but it was better than Ukraine. Most places were better than Ukraine at that time—Poland had pushed out an attempted Bolshevik invasion during the Civil War, and Romania was prickly toward the new Bolshevik government to say the least. The Bolsheviks loudly demanded Makhno's extradition to Russia, where he doubtless would have been executed. The Romanian government stalled these requests, and refused to place a hard "no" to the

Bolshevik howls for Makhno. Neither did they hand over Nestor and his companions. They proudly sat on the fence.

Makhno realized very quickly that the Romanian government would at best be a paper shield. He would need some other force to resist extradition. Even if that force was an old enemy: the Ukrainian nationalists—Petliurists, officially, if not actually, the Ukrainian government in exile, who had taken refuge in Romania and Poland.

Disarmed and isolated, the Makhnovists, headed by Makhno, made advances to the Petliurists for an alliance to retake Ukraine from the Bolsheviks. Both sides in the prospective alliance knew they were kidding themselves—that neither of them, even combined, had the political or military power to retake Ukraine.[8] The anarchists and Petliurists loathed each other, and this partnership (which on paper, at least, subordinated the anarchists to Petliuran oversight and state control) was a dead letter from the start.

During this time, Makhno oscillated between refugee camps and a heavily surveilled private life. The Bolsheviks, frustrated that using legal channels to grab Makhno had failed, even sent an assassination squad into northern Romania in 1922, but they failed to find Makhno.[9] Nestor and Halyna Makhno fled to Poland by April 1922, where trouble began afresh. They lived in a refugee camp for six months under far less than ideal conditions.

The Bolsheviks grew ever more nervous. So naturally they began holding trials of Makhnovists inside Ukraine—including that of Nestor's friend and advisor, Belash.[10] Nestor Makhno was tried and convicted in absentia of as many crimes as the Bolsheviks could think up. This conviction led the Bolsheviks to demand that Makhno—now a convicted and wanted criminal!—be extradited from Poland. Never mind the fact that Poland had no extradition treaty with Ukraine or Russia in the first place. Poland refused, though it kept a very close eye on the Makhnos' activities inside the refugee camp.[11]

They became convinced that the Makhnos were collaborating with the Bolsheviks to send Nestor to the province of Galicia, a place with a large Ukrainian population, to lead an uprising against the Polish government. Makhno at least heard the offer (if an offer was ever made—there is some thought that the maneuver might have been made out of whole cloth by the Bolsheviks as an elaborate mousetrap for Makhno), and Halyna Kuzmenko was said to have been at least once used as a go-between.[12] Makhno is said to have turned down the Bolsheviks' terms, reasoning that they were snakes among snakes. Even if Makhno succeeded in this enterprise, the Bolsheviks would simply turn on him again.

The Bolsheviks, undeterred, simply forged Makhno's signature on a document pledging his support for the Galician uprising, and then allowed one of their runners to be captured, according to historian Alexandre Skirda, thus tipping off the Polish government.[13] Makhno, meanwhile, was desperately petitioning the Polish government to allow him to take himself and his wife to Czechoslovakia or Germany. Anywhere that did not border Russia. These appeals were denied.

It was in this atmosphere thick with mistrust and fear that Nestor and Halyna's daughter, Yelena, was born in October 1923.[14] A year and a month later, the Polish government put Makhno on trial for scheming to foment uprisings in Galicia and/or take the Soviet side if another Polish-Soviet war broke out. Makhno didn't have high hopes for acquittal, grimly predicting that he would get at least an eight year sentence. The Polish press certainly did their best to paint Makhno in as unfavorable a light as possible, portraying him as a butcher.[15]

The world's anarchists (including such noted luminaries as the anarcho-syndicalist Rudolf Rocker, Sebastian Faure, Louis Lecoin, Alexander Berkman, and Emma Goldman) banded together to support Makhno, condemning the trial as hopelessly biased.[16] Some factions even threatened to dynamite Polish assets and government buildings should a guilty verdict be read.

Makhno, for his part, was composed during his trial. He was civil and polite. He only raised his voice once, to correct a prosecutor who asked if he had shot Ataman Grigoriev himself. No, Makhno replied, there was no need because he had "people who unquestioningly carried out every order," and they executed Grigoriev promptly at his direction.[17]

The judge faced a dilemma—by convicting Makhno of the charges, he might start an uprising instead of preventing one. Oh, and the evidence pointed to Makhno's innocence in this case, there was that to consider as well. Makhno was acquitted of all charges. He was visibly stunned by this outcome—this is the only time that any justice system anywhere had done Nestor Ivanovich Makhno a good turn.

The Makhnos moved to the city of Torun at the end of 1923, in a small apartment they shared with two friends. Nestor tried to go into business as a cobbler, but his nerves couldn't take it. The Polish government may have found him innocent in a court of law, but such things mattered little—Nestor Makhno was an anarchist, and so he was under heavy, not particularly subtle, police surveillance. This contributed to the further erosion of his already fraying nerves.

Further speeding this process was the fact that Nestor believed that Halyna Kuzmenko was sleeping with one of their friends and being rather indiscreet about the whole thing.[18] The sources are unclear on this and often contradict each other. Worse still, Halyna had the distressing habit of sharing every bit of information—like which anarchists in America or Sweden Makhno corresponded—with the nice Polish police officers who would visit her from time to time, at least according to historian Colin Darch.[19]

Perhaps, given the stresses upon him, it is not surprising that Nestor Makhno attempted suicide a few months later in April 1924. He attempted to cut his own throat, and was only dragged back from the gates of death by emergency medical treatment.[20]

Shortly thereafter, Makhno was picked up for drunk and disorderly conduct, but managed to escape jail time. From there, he moved to Danzig, where he was hospitalized for tuberculosis. Not comfortable being hospitalized, where anyone might find him in a weakened state, Makhno broke himself out of the hospital.[21]

So as you can imagine, when Bolshevik agents offered to smuggle him into Berlin, Nestor Makhno was feeling just self-destructive enough to say yes. He was, however, shrewd enough to realize this was an obvious trap at the last minute, and to evade it, escaping back to Danzig.[22] In Danzig, Makhno was arrested for not leaving the city by a certain date. This time, Makhno was found guilty and thrown in prison. In prison, he again tried to kill himself—and again, emergency treatment saved his life.[23]

Fortunately for Makhno some comrades, with the help of a financial backer from the United States (with Voline's expert assistance—though he did use some of the money to help his own family, he did have six children after all), orchestrated a jailbreak and Makhno was forced to go into hiding for at least forty days to allay suspicion and avoid arrest—which might have led to his extradition to Russia.[24] During this period, he was supported by the Anarchist Black Cross fund, and was even able to meet the famed anarcho-syndicalist theorist, Rudolf Rocker.[25]

In 1925, things finally began looking up. Lenin's painful death in early 1924—and the infighting it caused among the Bolsheviks—was doubtless an unforeseen bit of good news for Makhno. In 1925, Makhno wrote a short essay on the failings of Lenin and Leninism ("Lenin, His Party and the Misconceptions Concerning Them") was first published in the Russian-American journal, *Dawn*.[26] He had recently escaped from Danzig and was so giddy with excitement to be free that he even signed his true location instead of falsifying one.

Whoops.

It was after this latest fusillade that Makhno finally managed to smuggle himself through Belgium into Paris in July 1925. His wife and daughter had arrived in Paris the previous year. The legendary anarchist May Picqueray provides an account of Makhno's arrival in Paris from her autobiography, *My Eighty-One Years of Anarchy*. This is the same Picqueray, by the way, who during earlier negotiations with Trotsky for the release of anarchist prisoners in Moscow, sang an anarchist fight song at the formal banquet in defiance of her Bolshevik hosts. The same person, who, when Trotsky asked what she had against him, tersely replied: "Makhno and Kronstadt," and refused to shake Trotsky's hand. People had been shot for far less than the bravery shown by May in Bolshevik Russia, so perhaps now one has a sense of how much she admired Makhno—and how stunned she was to see his condition upon his arrival in Paris:

> I lived at #120, two minuscule little rooms, but there was always a good broth simmering on the cooker or coffee ready for serving. Indeed, it was my "privilege" to welcome the waves of immigrant comrades arriving from pretty much all over back then: the Russians fleeing from dictatorship, the Bulgarians likewise, the Italians who managed to dodge Mussolini's castor oil and prison. After being restored, they would be directed by me to the home of this or that comrade who had a room or a bed, or some corner where they might rest, be it in Paris, in the suburbs or out in the countryside.
>
> It is in this way that one morning a couple showed up with their girl, all three worn out and disheveled. Especially the man, whose entire body was covered in wounds. They had some refreshment and stretched out on the only bed where they very quickly dropped off to sleep. I sent for a comrade who knew Russian, whereupon I discovered that my guests were Makhno, his partner Galina, and their daughter. I was greatly moved in the presence of the "great man" whose epic I knew only from hearsay, epic, the word is not

too strong a description of Makhno's exploits. I listened to him talk for nearly an hour, but, realizing he was very weary, I entrusted him and his family to some friends in the suburbs [who] took him in and where a doctor offered him the care he required for his condition.[27]

Nestor Makhno missed Ōsugi Sakae's transcontinental voyage to Paris by a few years. Paris, the home of the one-time Paris Commune and a center of European anarchism and general dissent, was to be Nestor Makhno's final home in the last years of his life.

CHAPTER 17

Enemies and Friends in Parisian Exile (1925–34)

> "Like language, every revolution tends to travel outside its own bounds ... at its finest, the anarchist tradition has always signified 'the revolution within the revolution,' marking out what remains to be done."
>
> —Terry Eagleton

Makhno was a Ukrainian peasant in Paris: his time there was grueling, uncertain, and stressful, a bookend to his formative years. Makhno's experience in Paris was isolated, unsteady. He took any odd job he could— working at various times as a cobbler, a painter, selling his memoirs (what of them he could complete), and as a turner at the Renault car factory.[1]

Aside from work, Makhno couldn't go anywhere alone safely. There was the natural linguistic barrier that surrounds a monolingual person like a transparent but very real bubble in a foreign land, of course. The isolation of that cannot be overstated, especially when stretched over about a decade, in a city that is largely hostile to one's existence.

His old wounds—particularly a bullet lodged above his ankle— wouldn't let Makhno stand for long periods and gave him a rather pronounced limp. It was only through much swearing (swearing in Russian sounds quite terrifying) and insistence on keeping all his limbs that Makhno avoided having his foot lopped off by the doctors.[2]

Where that distinctive scar on Nestor's cheek came from is a matter of some debate. Ida Mett claims that Nestor told her that Halyna had given it to him in a failed murder attempt in Poland. This must be taken with a grain of salt given Makhno's paranoia and bitterness (not to mention Mett's personal dislike of Halyna, who she characterized as a gold digger, a Ukrainian nationalist, and worst of all, one of Makhno's enemies for associating with Voline after Makhno's death). Other sources suggest that Makhno received the scar in the last days of the Civil War, one of the twelve great wounds he suffered, as we've discussed in the previous chapter.

Halyna worked as a maid and house cleaner and was a more reliable source of income for the fractured family than Nestor. He was isolated—not just linguistically but physically. His relationship with his by now ex-wife Halyna was strained to say the least, but they raised their daughter together. At the very least, his relationship with his daughter, Yelena, was good while he lived. He doted on her, all sources agree, though Ida Mett claims that Makhno would grow distraught after giving his child a cuff when she'd misbehaved.[3]

He was often cold or sick or both—donations from comrades around the world, when the Makhnos saw them that is, often kept the wolf from their door. To go into the long list of the indignities and difficulties of Makhno and his family—so reminiscent of Russia under the czars—would only serve to beat a dead horse. Makhno, already generally uncomfortable in cities, broadly speaking, had a bad time in Paris.

Paris was a refuge for revolutionaries and the desperate in the 1920s and into the 1930s. It wasn't necessarily a *safe* refuge. The repression against radicals and foreigners—especially people who were both at once, as we discussed in the prologue with Ōsugi Sakae's misadventures earlier in the 1920s—was intense. Police surveillance was common, infiltration of radical groups—anarchists, socialists—expected, whether from the French state or from their enemies across the borders that they had originally fled from.

Even without the perils of state surveillance or violence, there was the danger of being recognized in the refugee communities. Old wounds and animosities from the Russian Civil War didn't exactly get swept under the rug. Not everyone running from Bolshevik repression was exactly chummy with each other.

To give a high-profile example on the perils of being known, Petliura, one-time head of the Ukrainian nationalist forces with whom Makhno had shared deeply uneasy nonaggression pacts and alliances of convenience, also made it to Paris, living there for two years. Petliura got his—an anarchist, poet, and Jew, Sholem Schwarzbard, tracked him down and emptied a revolver into Petliura on a Paris street in 1926.

Schwarzbard was arrested and put on trial. Legendary lawyer Henri Torrès argued persuasively for Schwarzbard to be found innocent of murder, since under Petliura's orders, fifteen members of his family had been lynched during the pogroms back in Ukraine. This wasn't the first or last time that Henri Torrès defended anarchists in high-profile court cases or public demonstrations either—he previously had represented Ōsugi Sakae and helped lead the successful movement to free Buenaventura Durruti and the Spanish anarchists from French prison. Thanks to Henri Torrès's skillful arguments, Schwarzbard was found innocent of murder and set free.

Speaking of Durruti and the Spanish anarchists, they managed to find a brief window of time to meet with Nestor Makhno in the summer of 1927. According to Abel Paz's exhaustive biography of Durruti, their meeting was a brief thing, though not inconsequential, after their release from French prison.[4] The Spanish anarchists—specifically Durruti and Francisco Ascaso—had a long list of adventures and triumphs behind them: expropriations, particularly targeting banks, most famously and notoriously in South America; and assassinations, chiefly in Spain, netting most famously a corrupt cardinal and a prime minister. They'd been detained in France, after all, after a plot to pick off the Spanish monarch Alphonso XIII was detected and thwarted—the thing that kept the two anarchists alive was that the South American countries, broadly, wanted them extradited back to the New World for trial and execution. The nation-states' inability to agree who got to try the anarchists—and for what—combined with a relentless public pressure campaign involving Louis Lecoin and Henri Torrès, ultimately resulted in their release without charges, with the caveat they couldn't stay in France. Amazingly, Ascaso and Durruti's most famous days were still ahead of them, in the September Days of 1936 and the Spanish Civil War.

I'll be relying on Abel Paz's account of the meeting in his biography of Durruti. Makhno made an exception to see the two Spanish anarchists— he was depressed from feuding with other Russian anarchists over one thing or another, not an uncommon occurrence. Makhno met with the two famous Spanish anarchists, Ascaso and Durruti, in late July 1927. They met at Makhno's hotel room. The two Spaniards paid their respects to Nestor Makhno, and Makhno lit up at the compliment. Paz quotes Ascaso, observing Makhno's reaction: "This very short, thick set man, seemed to come to life again. The look in his slanting eyes became penetrating and forceful, clearly expressing the intense vitality hidden in his sick body."[5]

Nestor Makhno was at his best when he could speak, rather than write. Now the anarchists were off to the races; a wide-ranging conversation covering a lot of different topics ensued. Makhno praised the Spanish anarchist movement's organization and focus, claiming such a thing was missing in the Russian movement. Organization, Makhno said, was the thing that determined the success of revolution, and was hardly anathema to anarchism at all.

Makhno talked at length about his battles and struggles in Ukraine, specifically addressing the often trotted out criticism that the Makhnovschina was primarily an agrarian peasant movement. He rejected this framing firmly, saying that "Our communities were mixed, agricultural-industrial, and even some of them were only industrial. We were all of us fighters and workers. The popular assembly made all the decisions."

It was a difficult talk emotionally, speaking for Makhno—it was not easy for him to revisit his memories. The anarchists only managed to speak for a few hours, with Makhno making a great effort to make himself understood. To speak, to communicate without miscommunication or offense was less and less common in this period in his life, and among the Russian anarchists in general.

Makhno continued speaking, through the help of an interpreter, (Dowinsky, according to Paz) to say that revolutionary conditions were better in Spain than in Russia. Makhno thought this was so important that he endeavored to speak French, with mixed success. And it wouldn't be a Makhno story if he didn't try also to micromanage his translator, telling him not to *dare* alter a single word of what he was saying. According to Paz: "And while the interpreter talked to the Spaniards, Makhno watched carefully to see the effect that his words were having on these young men, interrupting sometimes brusquely to speak passionately himself for fear that his thoughts were being falsified."[6]

While the Ukraine is lost for now—Makhno might have thought— the cause of anarchism lives on. He told Ascaso and Durruti, with what they termed an optimistic smile and slipping into speaking in the third person: "Makhno has never refused to fight. If I am alive when you start your struggle, I will be with you." According to Paz, toward the end of the conversation, Makhno sighed and said to Ascaso and Durruti: "I hope that when the time comes, you will do better than we did." They did.

Durruti and Ascaso were expelled from France two days later to a place beyond its laws: Belgium. One slight problem, Belgium didn't want them and refused to allow Ascaso and Durruti to cross the border. Bizarrely, the problem was solved when the French police helped smuggle the famous Spanish anarchists across the border to Belgium! Ascaso and Durruti would be playing hot potato with national borders for some time before finally returning to Spain. No nation-state wanted anarchists, let alone famous ones that had beat the rap, were good at killing powerful people, and were intensely popular with the working classes.

Not all the visits paid to Nestor Makhno in Paris were so happy. A year earlier, he received a visit from a friend made in Romania and fellow Civil War survivor, Vassili "Zayats" [Rabbit] Zaytsev, who also managed to escape the Bolsheviks. While some scholarship claimed Zaytsev was a Makhnovist, more recent scholarship (as Malcolm Archibald points out) points to Zaytsev fighting in Petliurist units, not Makhnovist ones. Regardless, he and Makhno had established a bond during their stay in Romania, and once Zaytsev arrived in Paris, he looked up Makhno. This was good, for all that it lasted—Makhno could use all the friends he could get. But Zaytsev committed suicide with a revolver—in Makhno's own apartment no less—in October 1926, a year and change after the Makhno's arrived in Paris.[7]

Nestor Makhno was a great one at making friends—and enemies. In the last decade of his life, he definitely grew more skilled in making the former than the latter. His impatience with scholars and ivory-tower anarchists, never great, grew even shorter in the last part of his life. Indeed, his temper seemed on a far shorter fuse in Paris.

American anarchists Alexander Berkman and Emma Goldman befriended Makhno in Paris, even with their strident opposition to Makhno's Platform (which will be discussed later). The pair had experienced Bolshevik terror firsthand and traveled through Ukraine during the later stages of the Civil War, which may have engendered some sympathy for Nestor's plight now. Berkman in particular was close with Makhno (there is a famous picture of them on a day out, Berkman grinning and Makhno doing his best friendly scowl at the camera from inside his swimsuit, with their arms around each other.)

There was something of the man of action to Berkman, which doubtless appealed to Makhno. Berkman had done twelve years in prison for attempting to kill Henry Clay Frick, a Pittsburgh plutocrat who had deployed armed strikebreakers against union members in Pittsburgh, with horrific casualties. Berkman managed to seriously wound Frick with two shots from a revolver in his office. He was prevented from finishing the job

Alexander Berkman (right) and Nestor Makhno (left) in a rare moment of leisure, Paris, 1927. Photograph courtesy of makhno.ru.

by another party and a blow to the head with a hammer. When arrested, a dazed Berkman quipped: "I've lost my glasses."[8] Berkman's arrest was the beginning of a long literary and activist career.

When Makhno knew him in Paris, Berkman worked to raise funds for anarchist political prisoners imprisoned by the Bolsheviks. He met with some success—due to pressure from Berkman and others like him the Bolsheviks released some anarchist prisoners and recategorized some of the worst gulags as "not-for-political prisoners" (like the dreaded Solovki prison) in 1925. These partial victories were definitely something, but not enough to satisfy the demands of those who cried for an end to Bolshevik atrocities.

His lover and long-time anarchist-feminist Emma Goldman wrote in a letter to Berkman in 1928, when they were discussing the trouble of revolutionary violence: "I therefore say that you must set your face sternly against the idea of prisons: the whole revolution would be absolutely futile, if such terrible institutions as prisons, institutions which have proven a failure in the system we want to get rid of, are again established."[9] Goldman clearly shared Makhno's deep hatred of prisons as a concept and believed they had no place in a revolutionary society. Of the trio, only she would live to see the social revolution that started the Spanish Civil War in 1936, and even traveled to Spain to report what she saw.

Makhno himself did his best to stay optimistic but was often forlorn.

One of the people who could be said to have known Makhno well in the last decades of his life was Ida Mett, a Belarussian anarchist. She helped Makhno with the Platform (being one of its original signatories), helped edit his memoirs, and even served as his translator on the rare occasions when he was able to attend parties hosted by Westerners in his honor. But Mett was brutally honest with Makhno (one time telling him: "You're a great soldier but not a writer. Why don't you ask one of your friends to help you write your memoirs? Maria Goldsmit for example.") Makhno didn't care for that at all. He never forgave Mett for such harsh criticism about his writing.[10]

In the end, Makhno's memoirs remained unfinished, terminating before the formation of the Makhnovschina. His habit of interspersing boilerplate anarchist speeches with unique historical facts drove Ida Mett crazy and made the text simply unreadable.[11] Makhno never sat down and outlined or planned how to fit facts into an "integral whole."

If this all seems fairly adversarial for a friendship, that's pretty par for the course for Nestor Makhno in his later years.

In her remembrances of Makhno, Ida Mett drops a reference to Makhno's first wife, Anastasia Vasetskaia. Apparently Makhno would sometimes drop into reveries about life before the Civil War. According to Mett: "Sometimes with sincere regret he recalled his first wife, a peasant girl from his home town who he married shortly after his release from prison in 1917. A child was born of their marriage, but when Makhno had to go into hiding during the German occupation someone told his wife that he had been killed, and she married again. The child died. Makhno never saw his first wife again."[12]

But Mett's observations of Makhno weren't just critical or bittersweet. There were moments of joy, as there always are even in dark times. Despite what she describes as Makhno's stiff and rote writing style, she notes as Ascaso and others have, that when Nestor had the occasion to speak, his transformation was as sudden as it was complete: "Moreover, he was like a great actor who underwent a transformation beyond recognition when in front of a crowd. In a small circle of people he communicated with difficulty. His habit of using grand words seemed absurd and out of place in an intimate environment. But you just needed to put him in front of a large audience and there emerged a brilliant, eloquent, self-confident orator. Once I attended a public meeting in Paris on the question of anti-Semitism and the Makhno movement. I was struck by the incredible powers of transformation which this Ukrainian peasant possessed."[13]

Makhno attended as many anarchist meetings as he could, Platform or otherwise. He was eager to defend both his own honor and that of the Makhnovschina and one has a hard time deciding whether reliving those experiences was cathartic for him or simply opened up old wounds. Nestor Makhno especially hated being second-guessed. Makhno hated armchair generals nearly as much as he hated "armchair anarchists." Any critique of how he had handled troops in the Civil War was likely to be met with a stony stare. Of his old enemies in the military caste (like the "comic opera" Bolshevik cavalry commander Semyon Budyenny) Mett sensed a grudging respect for their technical knowledge and was painfully aware of his lack of formal study in the arts of war.[14]

A person less involved with Makhno's day-to-day life was May Picqueray. Picqueray was an acquaintance and friend of the Makhnos—indeed, when they arrived in Paris, she had been the very person to receive the family in her tiny apartment. She also at times translated for Makhno and smoothed over awkward social situations. Even when he was behaving, Makhno was stressed and harried.

The Parisian police hounded Makhno and would have loved any excuse to see him deported back to Bolshevik-controlled Russia. It took active interference from officials higher up in the French government to prevent this (May Picqueray specifically mentions the anarcho-pacifist Louis Lecoin making special efforts to stop the old anarchist revolutionary from being delivered into the jaws of the Bolsheviks).[15] In the twenties, Lecoin was also key to foiling the extradition of Durruti and his comrades back to Argentina for their string of expropriations. He would later embark on an epic hunger strike after the Second World War, with the support of his friend Albert Camus, to create a law to stop the prosecution of conscientious objectors as criminals and give them a separate legal status. It narrowly succeeded.

That was likely Makhno's ultimate fear—deportation back to Russia. So, cold, tired, often sick, Makhno drank. Mett claims that Makhno was a lightweight during the three years she knew him and that a single glass of wine would make his eyes shine and his voice louder. She says that she never saw him truly out-and-out, fall-down, blackout drunk, and for that period we are forced to take her word for it. What person, constantly on the edge of the despair event horizon, could resist trying to blot it all out? We have mixed reports on whether Makhno depended on alcohol to get through the day or not, but if he did overindulge habitually, it could scarcely have helped his health or his state of mind.

CHAPTER 18

Makhno's Writings outside the Platform in Exile (1926–34)

> "Any state destroys, suppresses, enslaves all the best spiritual values that push for freedom and are based on solidarity."
>
> —Nestor Makhno

Historian and translator Malcolm Archibald gets to the core of Makhno's writing: "Nestor Makhno was not a skilled writer, though he liked to write and had a lot to say."[1] For every penetrating or memorable phrase Makhno penned (and there are more than a few scattered through his works) there are pages of political jargon, run-on sentences, and self-justification that makes him sound a bit more defensive than one might like. There is some justification for his strident—if at times meandering—tone, however.

Nestor Ivanovich Makhno would have profited immensely from a good editor overseeing and paring down his writing. For most of his time in Paris, however, good editors were few and far between. He did publish parts of his memoirs in exile in three parts, though they stop short of the more dramatic parts of the Makhnovschina: the alliances with the Bolsheviks; the repulsion of first Denikin, then Wrangel; and then the desperate final struggle against the Red Army before exile.

Voline called the first volume of Makhno's memoirs "really bad. Poorly written, badly translated, dense, ponderous and monotonous. And it gives scarcely any hints about the personality of the author." Voline does relent on the other two volumes of the memoirs (published after Makhno's death), saying that they were "much more interesting and easy to read."[2]

Makhno, despite his poor health, depression, and poverty, was a prolific writer. He penned many circulars and responses to the histories of the Makhnovschina that popped up like mushrooms after the end of the Russian Civil War. Makhno was concerned with clearing his reputation from the slanderous assaults of the newly solidified power of the Bolsheviks. Chief among these slanders were charges of antisemitism that were repeated ad nauseam and uncritically by Western sources and further amplified by the Bolsheviks.

The Bolsheviks didn't choose to use the documented accounts of massacres under Makhnovist commanders of Mennonites (this not having the same sort of effect they wanted in the international sphere) at places like Silbertal under the command of Fedir Shchus. Makhno was unable to punish his commander and troops responsible for war crimes, as previously discussed. In short, Makhno was party to horrors during the Civil War—just not pogroms.

Things reached such a timbre in 1927 that Makhno replied in writing in a short essay entitled "To the Jews of All Nations" published in *Dyelo Truda*.[3] Makhno keeps it short, and for him, relatively sweet. He takes issue with a fictional portrayal of the Makhnovschina, *Makhno and His Jewess* by Joseph Kessel, a novelette written by a Bolshevik, attributing all sorts of antisemitic crimes to Makhno and his followers. The novelette drew heavily on Bolshevik sources for its "based on a true story" take on the anarchists. Confusingly, the story also cites entirely fictional crimes involving the slaughter and horrific violence against a troop of "performing dwarves."

Makhno's frenemy and anarchist historian/theorist, Voline, writing significantly later in the century, called Kessel an "utterly despicable prostitute of the French bourgeois press" and concluded that Kessel's "novel is abominable not only because it contains not a single word of truth, but especially because it leaves the reader with the impression that this episode is based on real facts."[4] Makhno also makes a point of dismantling photographic evidence said to show Makhnovists at the site of a massacre. He pointed out that the troop in question was on the other side of Ukraine at the time.

Makhno also took pains to clarify that the "death's head" black flag (with the text in Cyrillic reading: "Death to all those who stand in the way of the working class") wasn't associated with the Makhnovist movement, though it did originate during the Russian Civil War (the death's head slogan nonetheless remains a pop culture shorthand for Makhno, to be found on backpacks, shirts, stickers, and flags).

Makhno packed a lot into this short essay (it runs about three and a half pages or so). There was another photo put forward, credited as showing Makhno, but not actually him, by Bolsheviks with the subtitle "Makhno, 'a peaceable' citizen" that Nestor made sure to lambaste in his response.[5] Makhno directly appealed to the international Jewish community to look at his record of revolutionary justice to judge the Makhnovschina. Which leads to our next essay Makhno wrote, a month later: "The Makhnovschina and Anti-Semitism."

In June 1927, Makhno spoke at the Faubourg Club in Paris, the only official institution to reply to his earlier essay, "To the Jews of All Countries." The question of the evening was worded "Was 'General' Makhno the friend of the Jews or did he participate in their slaughter?" Long before the internet, there was pseudo-clickbait, as we can see. Gotta get butts in seats. I'm sure that the quotes around the word 'general' in the title did nothing to improve Makhno's mood either.

Makhno only managed to speak briefly at the end of the night (his speech was shunted to the back of the program). He forcefully laid out evidence of his policies (executing antisemites, that there were Jewish battalions in the Makhnovschina, and that he had explicitly worked against antisemitism even before the Russian Civil War began), and recounted the execution of explicitly pogromist Grigoriev to bolster his case. He ended his brief speech with the following words: "Thus, throughout the entire existence, the Makhnovschina took on an uncompromising stance on the anti-Semitism of pogromists; this was because it was a genuinely revolutionary toilers movement in the Ukraine."[6] Makhno later consolidated his speech into an article in *Dyelo Truda*, published in November 1927.

Nineteen twenty-seven was a busy year for Makhno's writing. During this time, he also penned the strenuous and exhaustive "Reply to Kubanin." Mikhail Kubanin was a Bolshevik writer who analyzed the economic and social policies of the Makhnovschina. Kubanin did his best to be fair, but his Marxist-Leninist worldview led to an overly narrow, ultimately defamatory account of Makhno's anarchist polity. That definitely pissed off Nestor Makhno enough to write a lengthy reply. Bolsheviks were in no circumstances to have the last word on anarchism, even ones that were ultimately sympathetic to aspects of Makhno's movement.

Even when Kubanin tries to give Makhno credit for an action, it doesn't land in the way he intended. For example, Kubanin credits Makhno with shooting a man who posted the antisemitic (and monarchist) sign in a train station outside of Huliaipole reading: "Beat the Jews and Save Russia!" Makhno tears into Kubanin for his inaccuracies in reporting this event.

First, he says, Kubanin deliberately gets the place wrong: the incident took place at Pologi station, not Huliaipole. This was clearly done to "tarnish Huliaipole's revolutionary honor" according to Makhno. He goes on to point out that the executed man—Khizny—and his elder brother were both well-known Bolsheviks and implicitly accuses Kubanin (and his source, Kamenev) of being perfectly willing to hide that inconvenient fact. Makhno concludes that particular section of the text with the line: "Kubanin checks nothing—even when non-Makhnovists could have enlightened him—and makes do with slander."[7]

More inexcusably, from Makhno's point of view, was Kubanin's reliance on the records of Voline's interrogation by the Cheka while he was in custody. It was in this essay that Makhno flirts with calling Voline a spy or Bolshevik collaborator in public. Unsurprisingly, this only worsened their already deteriorating relationship, already strained by their differences over Makhno and Arshinov's Platform anarchism (see the following chapter for more on the Makhno/Arshinov spat with Voline over Platform anarchism).

That is not to say that Nestor wrote no original essays or didn't try to develop his own thoughts on anarchy, power, and the state. "The ABC's of the Revolutionary Anarchist" is Makhno's disquisition on the nature of power and what being an anarchist means in relation to it. The title was a popular formulation in the early twentieth-century anarchist publishing world—for example, Makhno's friend Alexander Berkman wrote *The ABC's of Anarchy*.

Makhno's "ABC's of the Revolutionary Anarchist" is a wandering essay, going from topic to topic like someone shopping at a market but not looking for any one thing in particular. It is the source of his quote that provides this text's title. Makhno makes it clear that to call oneself an anarchist, one must not only refuse to wield power, but also refuse the establishment of any sort of power over others at all.[8]

Makhno further develops his critique of the state in this essay, saying that it is maintained by five forces: the property owner, the soldier, the judge, the priest, and "the one who serves them all, the intellectual … [who] takes it upon himself to demonstrate the 'legitimate' entitlement of his four masters to punish the human race, regulate man's life in its every individual and social aspect."

Here one can see Makhno's long-standing frustrations with "paper anarchists" in the Russian cities (and the intellectuals in those cities) boiling over. Of course, this role of the intellectuals justifying the oppression and murder of the state was not a new anarchist critique of the intelligentsia, but coming from Makhno, and knowing his history of disappointment with intellectuals as a whole (there are notable exceptions, like Kropotkin, Malatesta, and Rocker whom he met in Germany briefly) it rings especially bitter.

One of Makhno's more prescient later writings was his "Letter to the Spanish Anarchists" in 1931. Makhno warns the Spanish anarchists of the National Confederation of Labor–Iberian Anarchist Federation against allying with state socialists (Bolsheviks). Makhno doesn't mince words in this essay, repeatedly calling Bolsheviks "Jesuits" (traitors):

> Obviously they will have to steer clear of unity with the political parties generally and with the Bolshevik-communists in particular, for I imagine that their Spanish counterparts will be worthy imitators of their Russian mentors. They will follow in the footsteps of the Jesuit Lenin or even of Stalin, not hesitating to assert their monopoly over all the gains of the revolution, with an eye to establishing the power of their party in the country, an aim the effects of which are familiar from the shameful example of Russia: the silencing of all free revolutionary tendencies and of all independent toilers organizations. Indeed, they see themselves as holding power alone and being in a position to control all freedoms and rights in the revolution. So they will inevitably betray their allies and the very cause of revolution.[9]

No matter the seeming necessity, Makhno continues, for social revolution to succeed, the Spanish anarchists must at all cost avoid alliances or dealings with Bolsheviks (as a geopolitical polity or their ideological equivalents in the Spanish revolutionary movements). He points to his own experience with the Bolsheviks during the Russian Civil War as evidence, though this was common knowledge by 1931. There could be no united front with such people who only seek to use and discard anarchists for their own ends. Makhno hammers this point again and again.

The problems inherent to the idea of an antifascist united front to the exclusion of all else are numerous from an anarchist perspective and are ably discussed by such luminaries as Peter Gelderloos and Alfredo M. Bonanno in the twenty-first century. The problem becomes, essentially, that every single nonanarchist faction, from reformist-minded liberals to state socialists, all inevitably turn on the anarchists if/when fascism is beaten back, because the anarchist belief in true equality and the abolition of the state threatens the other powers' conception of the world and has broad appeal. Can't have that!

The Bolsheviks had shown that they didn't even really believe their own stated ideology—where Marx prophesied and Lenin promised a "transitory period" of democracy between abolishing the tyrannies of the world and stateless communism—but somehow that transition period never seemed to end and kept the Bolsheviks at the helm of a powerful centralized state. Funny, that, isn't it?

By this time the Soviet Union had discarded the rhetoric of worldwide socialist revolution and had made clear that it was simply another defanged and centralized monstrosity thriving on hierarchy, oppression, and the blood of its imprisoned citizens—in short, a state. One state among many. The final and inevitable betrayal of revolution that lies at the core of Leninism, Trotskyism, and Stalinism is the creation of a state founded and maintained by fear, murder, and the eternal jackboot. As Makhno wrote in "The ABC's of the Revolutionary Anarchist": "There is no such thing as harmless power."

CHAPTER 19

Makhno and the Platform (1925–33)

> "Revolution and war are two different things. For someone who is not only trying to defeat a military opponent but also radically change the society in which he lives, there is no clear-cut front line visibly separating friend from enemy."
>
> —Hans Magnus Enzensberger

Defeat and exile in the Russian Civil War prompted a lot of self-searching in the worldwide anarchist movement. Each major strain of anarchism (individualist, communist, syndicalist, etc.) had its own diagnosis about where the revolution with such promise went wrong.

The Nabat Confederation in Kharkiv had wielded considerable power in the city and in that part of Ukraine in general, but was violently purged by the Bolsheviks in late 1920, scattering, imprisoning, or killing its members. There had been a huge anarcho-syndicalist movement numbering in the tens of thousands that would give Lenin headaches even after the war ended. It was bloodily put down and their work councils absorbed into the political organs of Bolshevik Russia, becoming tools of the state they had tried to overthrow. The Makhnovist Free Territory we have of course covered in detail and was perhaps the most well-armed and organized of the anarchist groups involved in the struggle.

There were multiple well-led, organized bottom-up uprisings against the new iron fist of Bolshevik rule—the most famous of which was the March 1921 uprising of the Kronstadt sailors, formerly the tip of the revolutionary spear, turning against Bolshevik tyranny. As usual, Trotsky and

Lenin couldn't stand to have anyone steal their spotlight or actually force them to *keep* the promises they made to gain power, and so this anarchist-flavored rebellion was bloodily put down.

Why, the question echoed, had these efforts failed when anarchism had demonstrated a broad base of support with the common people when introduced? It was a question that was to haunt the surviving anarchists for years, and they came to a lot of different conclusions.

Makhno and Peter Arshinov, his old prison buddy, along with many other Russian exiles, banded together shortly after Makhno's arrival in Paris in 1925 to form the Group of Russian Anarchists Abroad. This was especially easy for those two in particular, since Arshinov moved into the same building as Makhno and his family shortly after his arrival in Paris. After so many years free from prison, the two men were living in the same location once again. Key members of the group included Arshinov, Makhno, Ida Mett, Henryk Walecki, and Maxime Ranko, and would eventually come to include members from as far away as Spain and China. But that would come later.

In 1926, the Group of Russian Anarchists Abroad published the *Organisational Platform of the General Union of Anarchists (Draft)*. As this ungainly title was commonly shortened to "Arshinov's Platform," or simply, "the Platform," these sobriquets became interchangeable with the name of the organization itself. The Platform argued that the Bolsheviks had out-organized the anarchists and that this self-same organization had been key to their success. Therefore, the only way to save anarchism as a cause was to organize and impose discipline in the same way as the Bolsheviks before the next stage of the struggle began. In the introduction to the *Organisational Platform of the General Union of Anarchists*, Makhno wrote:

> In all countries, the anarchist movement is represented by several local organisations advocating contradictory theories and practices, having no perspectives for the future, nor of a continuity in militant work, and habitually disappearing, hardly leaving the slightest trace behind them.
>
> Taken as a whole, such a state of revolutionary anarchism can only be described as "chronic general disorganisation" ....
>
> Like yellow fever, this disease of disorganisation introduced itself into the organism of the anarchist movement and has shaken it for dozens of years.

It is nevertheless beyond doubt that this disorganisation derives from some defects of theory: notably from a false interpretation of the principle of individuality in anarchism: this theory being too often confused with the absence of all responsibility. The lovers of assertion of "self," solely with a view to personal pleasure. obstinately cling to the chaotic state of the anarchist movement. [A]nd refer in its defense to the immutable principles of anarchism and its teachers.[1]

Furthermore, the introduction to the *Platform* continued, to ensure that anarchist positions were uniform, there would be standard lines for anarchists to use while spreading propaganda, recruiting, and organizing. This diagnosis and prescription was not necessarily met with wild applause by other anarchists. The first edition of the *Platform* was greatly hindered by poor translations. Translations from the Russian (Makhno spoke only Russian fluently and sometimes Bulgarian) to French and other languages were imprecise and burdened the initial thrust of the *Platform* with charges, effectively, of trying to make an anarchist political party. This may not have been entirely fair—given Makhno's expressed admiration for anarcho-syndicalist organizations (like Durruti and Ascaso's National Confederation of Labor–Iberian Anarchist Federation in Spain) and syndicalism being prominently mentioned in the Platform's first International—but once egos and old grudges enter into things, fairness rarely does.

Rebuttals to the perceived centralization (some would call it "Bolshevization") of anarchy weren't slow in appearing. Infighting is nothing new in any struggle, but the personal nature of much of the resistance to the Platform rankled Makhno. And when Makhno got rankled, he would write a great deal whether anyone wanted him to or not. Makhno publicly accused Voline, a former member of the Nabat Confederation and of his general staff, of defecting to the Bolsheviks, or if not that, failing to sufficiently resist being captured by them. Voline heatedly replied in a pamphlet that he was doing his job under Makhno's orders and came down with typhus, like most people did in 1919. It was in this weakened state that he was picked up by the Bolsheviks, who were allies of the Makhnovists at the time, who nursed him back to health, or at least failed to allow him to die.

In early 1927, in response to Makhno and Arshinov's *Platform*, Voline wrote an essay synthesizing the main currents of anarchism mentioned above while "discarding the rest." This attempt, to synthesize or unify the three major strains of anarchism into a single system, or at least a nonaggression pact, would also be undertaken independently and with some success by the Japanese theorist and activist, Hatta Shūzō in 1934.

Voline, always given to intellectual pursuits, was to work on this project with the notable French anarchist Sébastien Faure for quite some time. The crux of "synthesis anarchism," as it would later be called, can be summarized with the following quote: "These three currents—anarcho-syndicalism, libertarian communism and anarchist individualism, distinct currents but not contradictory—have nothing that makes them irreconcilable, nothing that puts them in opposition to each other, nothing that proclaims their incompatibility, nothing that can prevent them from living in harmony, or even coming together for joint propaganda and action."[2]

Faure and Voline proposed their synthesis anarchism be run in a similar manner to the Nabat Confederation during the Russian Civil War. Though, in a bit of colorful fore- and hindsight, the *Anarchist Synthesis* notes: "Each current has spit, drooled and vomited on its neighboring currents in order to smear them and give the impression that it alone was right."[3] The amount of anarchist infighting and counter-infighting that was to proceed from this point onward would make vomit look like ice cream, at least verbally, and result in many ruined friendships.

Even before the *Synthesis* was published, Voline and Makhno had been at each other's throats in a very public manner. It got so bad, in fact, that Alexander Berkman wrote a pamphlet in effect telling Makhno to lay off of Voline. There were bigger problems—like the rise of international fascism, financed in no small part by capitalism and the suppression of anarchists and socialist movements. There wasn't *time* to revisit old grudges and dick-measuring contests from the Civil War. Alexander Berkman wrote:

> We refer here particularly to the case of Comrade Voline. For several years now he has been made the subject of spiteful persecution by N. Makhno, the sole reason for it being personal differences and envy. The matter has been discussed in the Russian anarchist refugee circles in Berlin and Paris for a number of years and has been extremely hurtful for our propaganda. But now that persecution has culminated in a very dangerous defamation of Comrade Voline by Makhno. In a booklet recently published the latter in reply to the Bolshevik Kubanin's charges against the Makhnosoviet, Makhno repeats Kubanin's denunciation of Voline as a renegade. Furthermore, Makhno's own insinuations in this commotion make Voline appear virtually a spy.[4]

Berkman concluded his entreaty on the following note: "[I] earnestly urge our comrades to help put an immediate stop to the vile and grandiose damnation of our best comrades by backbiting and irresponsible individuals. We must unreservedly hold up to execration such practices and free our movement from this malign pest."

Sadly, Berkman would be ignored by both Makhno and Voline and their very public falling out would only get uglier. Part of the tension, outside of the issues of philosophy and organization, undoubtedly, was that Voline was from a more upper-class and intellectual background while Arshinov and Makhno both hailed from working class or peasant circumstances. While Voline was cerebral and precise, Makhno and Arshinov preferred the more hands-on approach to both argumentation and recruitment to the anarchist cause. Makhno's dislike of "armchair anarchists," never subtle at the best of times and evident throughout his writings, often came to the fore when mentioning Voline or others critical of the Platform.

The response from Makhno and Arshinov was hardly complimentary. They basically called Voline a nerd and a Johnny-come-lately to the cause of anarchism (he became an anarchist in 1914). The Makhno-Voline rivalry would persist for years, despite multiple intercessions by mutual friends.

Voline was hardly the only critic of the Platform, however. Notable anarchist and activist Mollie Steimer didn't mince words on what she thought of Makhno and Arshinov's proposal. In 1927 she wrote: "Alas, the entire spirit of the 'platform' is penetrated with the idea that the masses must be POLITICALLY LED during the revolution. There is where the evil starts, all the rest is ... mainly based on this line. It stands for an Anarchist Communist Workers' Party, for an army ... for a system of the revolution that will inevitably lead to the creation of a spying system, investigators, prisons and judges, consequently, a TCHEKA."[5]

The Platform was controversial at the time it was proposed. Errico Malatesta (who had known the first generation of European anarchists like Bakunin) wasn't convinced. Malatesta had been a peer and friend of Kropotkin's—he spent the last years of his life in Rome under house arrest in Mussolini's Italy. The old revolutionary was unable to organize or have a moment to himself. Anyone who spoke to him was arrested—a permanent police post was established on the porch of his home, and his letters were opened.

He and Makhno exchanged several letters over the years. Malatesta was critical of Makhno and Arshinov's proposals, though not of them personally. Their military and prison records, not to mention personal bravery, were beyond reproach (Arshinov having escaped from prison not once but twice, and in daring fashion, before ending up in Butyrka prison and meeting Makhno). But that could have hardly taken the sting out of Malatesta's assessment of the Platform in his second letter to Makhno: "Is this [the Platform] anarchist? This, in my view, is a government and a church. True, there are no police or bayonets, no faithful flock to accept the dictated *ideology*; but this only means that their government would be an impotent and impossible government and their church a nursery for heresies and schisms. The spirit, the tendency remains authoritarian and the educational effect would remain anti-anarchist."[6]

Makhno didn't like that response, and made sure that Malatesta knew it in his final letter in 1930.[7] The intense police surveillance of Malatesta at least partially accounts for the long gaps between Makhno and Malatesta's correspondence—between the censors, geography, and the language barrier, communication was slow and painstaking.

Nor was this a generational disagreement between anarchists. Makhno's peers like Alexander Berkman and Emma Goldman, who had reported on the new Bolshevik government's numerous atrocities from inside Russia, also spoke out against the Platform.

Consider this fragment of a letter Berkman wrote to the anarchist historian Max Nettlau: "[Arshinov's] whole psychology is Bolshevik, for he is [of] a most arbitrary and tyrannical, domineering nature. This throws some light on the program. The trouble with most of our people is that they do not see that Bolshevik methods cannot lead to liberty, that methods and issues are in essence and effects identical."[8]

However, early on, the Platform had many eager adherents, eager to push back against capital and the new Bolshevization of the revolutionary projects. In effect, the Platformists proposed the creation of an Anarchist International (the International Revolutionary Anarchist Communist Federation) with explicit policy positions on all major matters of the day. This was something that could have been quite powerful and an exploratory committee was convened in early 1927 to explore this possibility in Paris with delegates from around the world (particularly notable was the Chinese anarchist Wu Kegang, listed in the minutes as "Chen," Aniela Wolberg of Bulgaria, and Makhno and Arshinov for that matter) Spanish and Polish delegates were also in force. They managed to meet for half a day, and the agenda had the following up for debate:

1. Recognition of the class struggle as the most important factor in the system of anarchism;
2. The recognition of syndicalism as one of the main methods of struggle for anarchism;
3. Recognition of Communist Anarchism as the basis of our movement;
4. The need in each country of a General Union of Anarchists based on the unity of ideology, tactics and on collective responsibility;
5. The need for a creative positive programme for social revolution.[9]

Sadly, these points wouldn't be resolved in that meeting, or any other. The French police burst into the meeting and arrested all the delegates, bringing the First Anarchist International to a crashing halt. The April 1 meeting had almost certainly been compromised by an informer and had resulted in the arrest or mass deportation of a significant amount of the delegates back to their home countries.[10] It should be noted that Makhno was saved from deportation to the Soviet Union in the aftermath of this interrupted meeting by the timely intercession of Louis LeCoin, who according to historian Michael Malet, prevailed upon a friend in Parisian police to destroy the "Makhno dossier."[11]

It is important to note that the Platform in 1926–33 was embryonic and that platformist tendencies in anarchism today tend to borrow or at least expand upon synthesist anarchism's principles. The ground was uniquely poisoned in Makhno's case due to his position as a charismatic military leader—a Bonaparte-in-waiting, according to his critics.

Platformist anarchism in the twenty-first century (with its subcurrents of *especifismo* and other more flexible doctrines) looks very different from its initial form when it was founded in the twentieth century—but that's a topic for another book. While a centralized anarchist political party hasn't come to exist, polities and entities borrowing and expanding on some of the Platform's principles exist in our present world without reverting to a centralized state (such as in Rojava or Chiapas under the Zapatistas).

However, another major weakness of the Platform of Paris during 1926–33 is one twenty-first-century anarchists will be more than a little familiar with, namely infiltrators, snitches, and agents provocateurs. Max Chernyak, a former member of Makhno's kontrrazvedka and one of Maria Nikiforova's volunteers, didn't like the look of Makhno and Arshinov's program. For one thing, despite their best attempts, the Platform anarchists had recurring problems with security and infiltration. The Slavic anarchist community was full of informers and Cheka operators. Chernyak managed to detect and expose one of these informers in the Platform in Paris, before leaving in disgust with his family for Buenos Aires in 1930.[12]

So perhaps the Platform was called Bolshevik by anarchists because it was lousy with Bolshevik infiltrators, and Arshinov eventually repatriated back to the Soviet Union to the tune of a job and a pardon. Arshinov's former prison cell mate, Sergo Ordzhonikidze was now well placed to offer Arshinov a pardon and a job back in Stalinist Russia. The starving Arshinov accepted this offer, and did nearly irreparable damage to the cause of the Platform by doing so, confirming many of its critics' worst fears by defecting.[13]

Makhno, forever desperate in Paris, suffered terribly. The odds against the newborn Platform were almost too much to recover from. Many were at least partly the result of the particular times in which the Platform was founded—in the aftermath of a brutal authoritarian coup, active repression in the country it was formed in by governmental and police forces, the poverty and desperation of its founders—and not inherent to the idea of synthesist anarchism or the Platform itself, necessarily.

To be clear, there is nothing antianarchist about organization. Bakunin had advocated for anarchists to organize themselves (and in secret societies, but that's neither here nor there). In Makhno's written work, he makes it clear that he is drawing on his experience in the Russian Civil War to try to suggest a later course of action. He appeals to lessons learned through bitter experience in his wars against the Bolsheviks and White Army.[14]

But another factor in the Platform's initial failure to thrive has to be Makhno himself, especially his bristly nature and shortness with people whom he might have befriended rather than isolated (like Voline, to name but one of many examples). His brusque nature and tendency towards unilateral action under pressure (and conveniently ignoring organs and councils meant to check him) meant that there was a risk, had the Platform succeeded with Makhno at its head, that the whole enterprise would have become more Bolshevik in character or a cult of personality as its detractors claimed.

Makhno was used to running a military organization first, and social organizations a distant fifth, and his penchant for micromanaging things could easily be read as a potential dictatorial streak to those already skeptical of centralization. Indeed this tendency was viewed with alarm by Fanya and Aron Baron—as well as the Nabat anarchists during the Civil War. The militarization of the anarchist movement—even with the federalism and election of officers by their troops—was seen as playing with fire, as introducing a possibly authoritarian structure onto the greater struggle. Even among the Makhnovschina, sources like Voline and Belash record worries about Makhno's willingness to cut corners around the councils (like in the Polonsky affair) and a lack of accountability that made them nervous that a charismatic leader could turn an ideologically anarchist-led struggle into a cult of personality. That is, a cult of Makhno could not be discounted as a possible problem.

Some anarchists protest this treatment of Nestor Makhno or undercut the very real danger of a Platform built behind a charismatic military leader. Alexandre Skirda in particular seems to dismiss the possibility that a Platformist anarchist party led by Makhno could possibly devolve into Bolshevik-like tyranny. After all, Makhno and Arshinov had fought the Bolsheviks and lost comrades to their purges.

In counterpoint, most of the most strident anti-Platformists like Steimer, Voline, Berkman, and Goldman all knew the people who had gone from revolutionary to tyrant and clearly thought that nobody was immune from that sort of centralized, corrupting power. Because you kill your enemies, or have suffered at their hands, this fact does not prevent you from becoming like them if you aren't careful. History shows us this clearly. Or as noted insurrectionary anarchist and theorist Alfredo M. Bonanno puts it in his introduction to a new edition of Makhno's work:

> Those who allow themselves to be fascinated by efficiency, believing that the only possible solution to the weakness and inefficiency of anarchists is a strong organisation, could not fail to welcome "fronts" that (apparently) favour and increase this efficiency. The outcome is unavoidable. The way to frontist militarism is paved. In fact, the bigger the actions carried out the more significant they will appear to the deformed eye of the militaristic point of view. The more this decision is re-enforced, the further one will move from the practices that make the anarchist generalisation of the struggle possible.[15]

In short, that by measuring success by military rubrics, anarchists are making the mistake of replicating the systems they seeks to demolish. Makhno's creation of the Platform might have been the most important thing he ever did outside of a battlefield—the tragedy of the Platform was the it was introduced in a time and place singularly unsuited to its implementation, limited by the personal weaknesses and feuds of those who proposed it, to lie dormant until almost a century later.

CHAPTER 20

No Gods, No Masters: Nestor Makhno's Death and Legacy (1934)

> "For those escaping
> Incredibly into exile and wandering there.
> For those who live in the small rooms of foreign cities
>
> And who yet think of the country, the long green grass,
>
> The childhood voices, the language, the way wind smelt then,
>
> The shape of rooms, the coffee drunk at the table,
>
> The talk with friends, the loved city, the waiter's face,
> The gravestones, with the name, where they will not lie"
> —Stephen Vincent Benét

Makhno's last written work was a eulogy for his comrade Nikolai "Uncle Vanya" Rogdaev, who died in Tashkent in 1933. In a fitting irony, long-time anarchist and intellectual Rogdaev died on Sacco and Vanzetti Street. Sacco and Vanzetti were a pair of Italian anarchists in America arrested and executed on trumped-up charges in the late 1920s—and this prompted worldwide protest from Russia to Argentina. The trial and sentencing of Sacco and Vanzetti served, for the remaining Russian anarchists under Bolshevik rule (Like Olga Taratuta, Alexi Borovoi, and Rogdaev) as a suitable reason to publicly organize—but they were subject to fresh repression, exile, or executions, nonetheless.

In one of the first paragraphs Makhno said, in words that captured the mood of the last years of his life: "But—I repeat—over the last 12 to 15 years we have been hit by a whole series of terrible physical and moral blows of the same type. It's almost as if some sort of dark cloud hovers over the ranks of the Russian anarchist movement and plucks from our midst our best practical and theoretical human resources. We experience this and we suffer—we suffer much more than any of our comrades of other countries."[1]

It was impossible, it seemed, for Makhno or the exiled anarchists to catch a break. The cofounder of Makhno's Platform anarchism, Peter Arshinov, had run back to Russia once it was promised that he wouldn't be persecuted upon his return. This seemed to legitimate many anarchist's concerns that the Platform was just "Bolshevized anarchism," made worse by Arshinov's chumminess with the Stalinist superstratum of the new Russian state.

Outside of politics, things were hardly any better. Anarchist comrades were dropping like flies—from state repression in Russia (and the world over), from poverty, from exposure, and from suicide. Deaths of despair were distressingly common—in his funeral oration for Rogdaev read at an anarchist meeting, Makhno makes specific mention of the recent suicide of anarchist activist and friend Maria Goldsmit casting a pall over an already bleak day.

She was more commonly known by her alias, Maria Korn. A peer and confidant of Kropotkin (they exchanged more than four hundred letters over their lifetime, and she helped translate his *Memoirs of a Revolutionist*, to name but one of their collaborations). Maria was a committed anarchist thinker and writer. She had worked closely with Makhno along with Ida Mett in preparing and editing Makhno's memoirs until her mother's death in 1933.

The city of Paris ground Makhno down to almost nothing. The great city made him a nub of a man. Paris, one of the major hubs of world anarchism for decades—from the Commune generations prior, to the illegalists and anarcho-communists of the early twentieth century, to the many Slavic and American anarchists hiding there—was barely a refuge, and closer to a prison for Makhno. Paris—with it's pretty lights and long history of starving its citizens to death.

Makhno had been raised in considerable privation and poverty—it's the unkindest cut of all that the last ten years of his life were spent in circumstances that must be considered worse than his rather miserable

THE MAKHNO FAMILY IN EXILE. PARIS

childhood. Makhno and his family lived on the knife's edge, even with the help of others. Earlier, a few Spanish anarchists asked Makhno to lend his considerable military talents to their cause. Makhno expressed enthusiasm in the Spanish anarchist cause and wrote extensively on the subject of revolution there. But his body was definitely not up for travel—he'd rejected offers to live in Bulgaria (a place where he could have spoken freely, without aid of a translator) with comrades, and so he also rejected the possibility of going to revolutionary Spain.[2] His body was simply too weak, the journeys too long and he was a wanted man through most of Europe. In March 1934, Makhno finally collapsed under the strain. Malnutrition worsened Nestor's preexisting lung problems badly enough in early 1934 that he had to be hospitalized with tuberculosis.

Donations poured in from the world in a demonstration of solidarity with the old anarchist—the Makhno Committee was formed once again, soliciting donations to help with the family's financial troubles. Sadly, the Makhno Committee would spend more on Makhno's funeral expenses than they ever did on essentials to help the Makhno family in their time of distress, at one point spending thousands of livres to print and distribute circulars while giving mere hundreds to the people they were fundraising for.[3]

Such is often the way of charity.

Through all this, Nestor Makhno lay in the hospital, weak and feverish. The man who used to sleep mere hours a night on tables, fully dressed for combat, fell into a prolonged sleep inside an oxygen tent in July and never woke up again. His official day of death was July 25, 1934. He was just short of forty-five years old. One can only hope that Makhno's terminal dream was a pleasant one, an escape from the horrors of his life and of Paris in particular.

Makhno's funeral was well attended. Over five hundred people came to his internment in Père Lachaise Cemetery on July 28, 1934, three days after he was pronounced dead and cremated. Even his old friend turned foe turned friend again, Voline, attended.

Eleven years after Makhno's death, Voline, having survived the Second World War, died in 1945, also of tuberculosis. He was buried near his old comrade, in the graveyard that held so many of the old communards, as Paul Avrich rightly notes. In true Voline style, however, he got the last word in his disagreement with Makhno, writing "Makhno: A Contribution to Studies on the Enigma of Personality," an essay essentially about how hard it was to figure out what Makhno was really like even to someone who had known him for decades. This essay also chronicles Halyna Kuzmenko's falling out with the remaining Platformists after her ex-husband's death and the loss of many of Makhno's documents. So in short: Voline and Makhno were friends, foes, friends again, and eventually grave buddies.

Alexander Berkman—who we have discussed in previous chapters, particularly regarding his friendship with Makhno—wrote of Makhno: "A true anarchist, a great revolutionary mass leader was lost to us by the death of Nestor Makhno. He died, alone and almost deserted, far away from the people he so loved and served so faithfully. But his spirit always remained with the great masses of Russia, and with his last breath he confidently hoped that someday the oppressed, much-suffering people will rise in their might to sweep away forever the tyranny and despotism of Bolshevism."[4]

Berkman didn't long outlive his friend—he committed suicide in 1936. His lover and fellow activist and writer Emma Goldman perished in Canada four years later. As for Halyna and Yelena, when the Nazis invaded France, the pair moved to Germany to work and keep from starving. After World War II ended, the Stalinists shipped them first to a gulag and then Kazakhstan where Yelena became an engineer. Halyna was only able to return to Ukraine in the last two years of her life.

Nestor Makhno's face lives in my desk drawer nearly a hundred years after his death. His face is printed on a silver coin, protected by a thin, transparent plastic sheath. The reverse side of the coin features a speeding tachanka. The coin is light for its size, but holding it makes my stomach sink and my heart leaden. The anarchist Nestor Makhno has been literally monetized by the Ukrainian government. The Ukrainian government, for reasons surpassing comprehension, thought that putting Makhno's face on coinage was a good idea—the man who scorned the very idea of the "nation-state" and particularly loathed Ukrainian nationalists. It is difficult to cast an anarcho-communist as an anticommunist crusader, but the Ukrainian government and nationalists appear willing to try—to indulge in "revolutionary tourism" as Denys Gorbach puts it. It takes some serious historical amnesia to put an internationalist anarchist like Makhno on a national currency, as a "patriot." It's like a vegetarian group making a cheeseburger their logo, without a dribble of self-awareness.

As Volodymyr Ischenko said on the subject of modern Ukrainian nationalism: "Ukrainian nationalism now mostly has … right wing connotations ... but when it emerged in the late nineteenth century, Ukrainian nationalism was a predominantly leftist, even socialist movement ... the right has worked to reinterpret figures such as Makhno along nationalist lines—not as an anarchist, but as another Ukrainian who fought against communism. In their eyes, communism is a Russian imposition."[5]

Makhno is idolized without a drop of irony in his native Ukraine by admirers of the Nazi collaborator Stepan Bandera, who appropriated a lot of Makhno's color scheme and populist talking points while committing pogroms. Here is how to tell a Banderite from an anarcho-communist flag: both are red and black without ornamentation—but the Banderites make the division between the colors vertical and the anarcho-communists divide the red and the black diagonally. The direction of the line makes a big difference.[6]

"Anarchism" in the Ukraine has a distinctly Ukrainian chauvinist, nationalist tinge to it today—the anarchist props fly next to nationalist flags, swastikas, and Celtic crosses—a gross bastardization and deliberate misunderstanding of both anarchism and Makhno in particular. This only makes the work of actual anarchists the more difficult.

In short, in some circles, Nestor Makhno has become a brand, in much the same way that other leftist revolutionaries like Emeliano Zapata or Che Guevara passed into the collective consciousness—mutated into a thousand protean shapes. There is something obscene about all this. Nestor Makhno should not be a brand.

Makhno's legacy was dragged through the mud during the Soviet era, when it wasn't quietly being excised from history books. He was called a bandit, a kulak sympathizer, and accused of being secretly in league with the White Army—all charges that are ridiculous on their face and dispelled with even the most cursory look at the evidence. But here lies the trap— while Makhno wasn't the villain the Soviets, the royalists, and nationalists claimed him to be, it doesn't follow that he was a hero.

Makhno wasn't Robin Hood. He did his best in awful situations. He also drank too much, fell off his horse, allowed his temper to run away with him, couldn't enforce uniform discipline when it came to his direct subordinates committing what would now be called war crimes (think Shchus and the Silbertal massacre), often disobeyed or threatened the very anarchist councils put in place to check his power, and was quick to pull the trigger when he was certain someone was guilty of a crime. He also proposed to fight the Bolsheviks in his later years by adopting what some described as a vanguardist, Bolshevized version of anarchism, in what may be, depending on your point of view, a case of attempting to become a monster to fight a monster.

It is tempting to see Makhno as a Stirneresque iron-willed figure or a person of unshakeable heroism. To do so would be to miss the entire point of the anarcho-communist movement for a world without states, exploitation, or borders. Nestor Makhno would reject, I think, the concept of heroism. Heroism places the responsibility for change on a figure made unrecognizable to humanity by myth, constant retellings, and expectations. Hero worship becomes a refuge for inaction, a substitute for the subservient impulse captured and monopolized by God and the modern nation-state. By having heroes—people viewed uncritically, endowed with perceived powers greater than the average person—one becomes passive.

The world Nestor Makhno and countless others fought and died for didn't require heroes—it required people to take action and responsibility into their own hands. It still does require boldness to change the world. That seed must be nurtured and grown—to fight for social justice, for equality, for abolition of prisons and police and the state—one cannot be a coward and do so effectively.

So while the world needs boldness (and empathy, and kindness in equal measure) it does not need heroes. Perhaps that is the lesson that Nestor Ivanovich Makhno's life can teach us.

CHAPTER 21

Anarchists You Should Know: Minibiographies

Ba Jin

Ba Jin (1904–2005) Pen name of a long-lived and farsighted Chinese anarchist from Chengdu. Prolific writer and translator of anarchist works into Chinese, including those of Kropotkin who heavily influenced his own views. Multilingual and a talented Esperantist. Was in Paris writing in 1927 when Makhno and Arshinov's Platform anarchism was introduced and discussed, and eventually penned a pamphlet of his own supporting organization (*Chinese Anarchism and the Question of Organization* published in San Francisco) and may have even met Makhno and other members of the Platform during his time in the city. Became close friends with Alexander Berkman and Emma Goldman and corresponded with the doomed anarchist Bartolomeo Vanzetti before his execution, though not before recommending reading material to him.

His most famous work of fiction was *The Family* completed and published after returning to China from Paris. Ba Jin survived multiple purge attempts and serious pressure from multiple Chinese governments throughout the twentieth century while remaining sharply critical of the government. Speaking in Kyoto in 1980, the old writer and activist said: "I do not write to earn a living or to build a reputation. I write to battle enemies. Who are they? Every outdated traditional notion, every irrational system that stands in the way of social progress and human development, and every instance of cruelty in the face of love. These are my great enemies. My pen is alight and my body aflame. Until both burn down to ash, my love and my hate will remain here in the world."

According to anarchist historian Peter Marshall, Ba Jin was arrested in the aftermath of the Tiananmen Square protests in 1989. He died peacefully in 2005, a free man.

FURTHER READING

Ba Jin. "How Are We to Establish a Truly Free and Egalitarian Society." Revolt Library, accessed March 10, 2023, https://www.revoltlib.com/anarchism/how-are-we-to-establish-a-truly-free-and-egalitarian-society/view.php.

"Ba Jin: "From Rebellion to Endurance." Kate Sharpley Library, accessed March 10, 2023, https://www.katesharpleylibrary.net/4xgxxt.

Marshall, Peter H. *Demanding the Impossible: A History of Anarchism: Be Realistic, Demand the Impossible!* Oakland, CA: PM Press, 2010.

Pino, Angel. "Ba Jin and the 'Arshinov Platform.'" Libcom.org, accessed April 13, 2023, https://libcom.org/article/ba-jin-and-arshinov-platform.

Fanya Baron

Baron, Fanya (1887–1921) Jewish member of the Nabat anarchist collective active in Kharkiv and other Ukrainian cities, with ties to the Makhnovist movement. Specialized in cultural education and delivered messages from Makhno to Alexander Berkman and Emma Goldman during the Russian Civil War. Arrested in late 1920 after the dissolution of Nabat. Undeterred, she broke herself out of a Ryazan prison, snuck to Moscow on foot, and was rearrested in 1921. Her husband, Aron, languished in prison off and on between 1920 and 1925, and then was shuffled around the USSR to various cities and towns before being shot in 1937. Trotsky refused to release Fanya Baron and other anarchists despite significant pressure from anarchist activists in Russia and worldwide. He claimed that Fanya and her peers were bandits who just claimed to be anarchists and thus not legitimate political prisoners. So Fanya Baron was ultimately executed by the Cheka in 1921. Her death was the final straw for many anarchists, including her close friend Alexander Berkman, who fled the country.

FURTHER READING
Avrich, Paul. *The Russian Anarchists.* Princeton, NJ: Princeton University Press, 1967.

Goldman, Emma. *Living My Life.* New York: Penguin Classics, 2006.

Goldman, Emma. *My Further Disillusionment in Russia.* Garden City, NY: Doubleday, 1924. Anarchist Library, accessed March 10, 2023, https://theanarchistlibrary.org/library/emma-goldman-my-further-disillusionment-in-russia.

Alexi Borovoi

Borovoi, Alexi (1875–1935) An instinctive anarchist, Alexi Borovoi survived czarist and Bolshevik Moscow at the crest of the anarchist movement. He wrote and lectured extensively on the topic of anarchism during the Civil War and after. Writing in 1918, Borovoi said: "Anarchism is the doctrine of culture! For it teaches us not merely love for oneself or one's personal freedom, but love for all and freedom for all. It is a call to action, to the great task of making its fruit available not only to our contemporaries but to our brothers of the still distant future." Borovoi was one of the few intellectuals that Makhno admired—having heard him speak about Tolstoy in Moscow before the Civil War began. Widely respected even during the Bolshevik rule of Russia as an anarchist theoretician and a minor celebrity—a fact which shielded him from repression. In 1920, the students of Moscow university petitioned for and won a debate titled "Anarchism vs. Marxism" to be held at the school, with Borovoi representing anarchism and the Bolshevik bigwig Bukharin representing Marxism. The debate was canceled by the local Communist Party at the last minute, presumably so as not to increase Borovoi's popularity. Borovoi later helped distribute and publish Makhno's Platformist periodical *Dyelo Truda* (Cause of labor) inside Russia. Like other anarchists inside the USSR, he was forbidden to live in a major city. He lived in Vyatka, then Vladimir, and worked as a wood-chemical engineer and then as an accountant. Died in 1935 of natural causes.

FURTHER READING

Avrich, Paul. *The Anarchists in the Russian Revolution*. London: Thames and Hudson, 1973.

Dubovik, Anatoly. "Alexei Borovoi (From Individualism to the Platform)." Kate Sharpley Library, accessed, March 10, 2023, https://www.katesharpleylibrary.net/228105.

Makhno, Nestor. *Under the Blows of the Counterrevolution, April–June 1918*. Edmonton, AB: Black Cat Press, 2009.

Maximoff, Gregory Petrovich. *The Guillotine at Work*. Vol.1, *The Leninist Counter-Revolution,*. Hastings, UK: ChristieBooks, 2013.

Max Chernyak

Chernyak, Max (1883–1944) Jewish barber, Makhnovist guerrilla, father, and spymaster. An early member of the Makhnovist movement. He was involved in the taking of Kharkiv from the Austro-Hungarians—he was recognized by a comrade from America, Boris Yelensky, who wrote in his memoirs at his disbelief seeing the heavily armed Chernyak giving orders: "I could scarcely believe my eyes. In Chicago he had not been particularly active in the movement. he was the father of two children and frequently attended our affairs together with his family. None of us could have dreamed that he [Chernyak] possessed the capacity to lead a partisan band and wage battles against well-organized units of the White Army. I asked him how all this had come about and he replied simply that, in revolutionary times all kinds of miracles occur."

He served as the head of Makhno's kontrrazvedka in Berdyansk, which meant his chief occupation was fighting both the Cheka and the White Army intelligence services. Chernyak later joined Maria Nikiforova's hit squad in 1919 to assassinate White Army commander Kolchak in Siberia (thus technically leaving the Makhnovist movement). Kolchak was instead executed by the Bolsheviks before Chernyak and the others could reach him. He returned to the Makhnovists in 1921, but was captured by the Bolsheviks near the end of the war.

Chernyak endured horrifying conditions in prison (being paralyzed temporarily on his left side) and was released through pressure from comrades. Met with Makhno in Paris and opposed Platformist anarchism. He stayed long enough to detect a Cheka infiltrator before leaving for the Americas with his family in disgust at Nestor's prescription for an organized anarchist political party.

In the last years of his life he increasingly favored anarcho-syndicalism, seeing the tilt of revolutionary agitations from peasants to unions of workers. He passed away in Uruguay, in 1944.

FURTHER READING

Archibald, Malcolm. "The Many Lives of Max Chernyak." Kate Sharpley Library, accessed March 10, 2023, https://www.katesharpleylibrary.net/tdz1q9.

Chernyak, Maxim Matveyevich. "A Letter from Max Chernyak." Kate Sharpley Library, accessed March 10, 2023, https://www.katesharpleylibrary.net/bg7bfn.

Maximoff, Gregory Petrovich. *The Guillotine at Work*. Vol.1, *The Leninist Counter-Revolution*. Hastings, UK: ChristieBooks, 2013.

Yelensky, Boris. "Memoirs." Libcom.org, accessed March 10, 2023, http://libcom.org/library/memoirs-russian-revolution-boris-yelensky.

Leah Feldman

Feldman, Leah (1899–1993) Makhnovist nurse and writer. Present in many of the turning points of anarchist history. Attended Kropotkin's funeral in Moscow in 1921 and helped steal flowers for the occasion from a tribute to Lenin with Berkman, Goldman, and other anarchists of note. From there, she went to Ukraine to join the Makhnovists. Served on the Makhnovist trains full of refugees and orphans. Knew Makhno personally. Escaped Ukraine at the end of the Civil War. Later assisted the anarcho-syndicalist National Confederation of Labor–Iberian Anarchist Federation (CNT-FAI) of Barcelona during the Spanish Civil War. Feldman was one of the few Makhnovists to live to old age—her accounts of her time in the Makhnovschina are used as a partial basis for Michael Moorcock's (fictional, deliberately fascist protagonist's) account of Makhno in the *Pyat Quartet* as a wink to the audience that the protagonist is not to be trusted with historical facts.

Always active in the struggle, she worked tirelessly for the anarchist cause raising funds for political prisoners, watching after the armory (despite being blind in one eye from the 1960s onward), and forming associations across national and linguistic boundaries. When asked when and where she became an anarchist, she smiled and said: "I was an anarchist but didn't know. Many people, they are anarchists, but don't know … they cannot give it a name until something gives them a push."

FURTHER READING
"Feldman, Leah, 1899–1993." Libcom.org, accessed March 10, 2023, https://libcom.org/history/articles/1899-1993-leah-feldman.

Feldman, Leah. "Lea Feldman Interview." Kate Sharpley Library, video, 17:14, July 18, 2017, https://archive.org/details/LeahFeldmanInterview.

Meltzer, Albert. "A Rebel Spirit (Obituary of Leah Feldman)." Kate Sharpley Library, accessed March 10, 2023, https://www.katesharpleylibrary.net/dr7tzs.

Jaroslav Hašek

Hašek, Jaroslav (1883–1923) Czech anarchist and author of the most translated (and hilarious) Czech novel, *The Good Soldier Švejk*. Hašek was an inveterate carouser, drinker, satirist, and writer. He held many positions in his short life including that of a newspaper columnist in the zoology section (he was fired after a short time because he got bored and started making up animals without letting the public in on the joke), a bank agent, dogcatcher (and reseller to the credulous and rich, claiming the mutts he collected were in fact rare breeds, a trade the title character of Švejk shares), and a political candidate.

He helped found the Party for Moderate Progress within the Bounds of the Law, a satirical party dedicated to parodying the tentative reforms proposed to right the rotting Austrian empire. These meetings were held in a pub and served as a chance for Jaroslav to tell entertaining stories and stand people drinks—they were popular, and Franz Kafka is said to have attended a few of them as a member of the audience.

When World War I broke out, Hašek was conscripted along with countless others. Despite his countless and ingeniously executed attempts to avoid being at the front lines, he was ultimately sent to the Russian front, where he immediately surrendered. After being captured by the Russians, Hašek took sick passing through Ukraine in 1918, escaped from Russian prison camps with the Czechoslovak Legions, and then immediately defected from them to join the Bolshevik Party, abandoning anarchism. He became a political commissar, got married (never mind his wife back in Czechoslovakia) and was sent to the town of Bugulma in Siberia. He served as mayor there for a time and helped print, edit, and distribute revolutionary literature before ultimately fleeing for the European border in 1920 and returning home to Prague, disillusioned. He died young and in mysterious circumstances.

FURTHER READING

Hašek, Jaroslav. *The Good Soldier Švejk and His Fortunes in the World War.* London: Penguin Classics, 2005.

"Jaroslav Hašek (1883–1923)." Socialist Stories, accessed March 10, 2023, http://www.socialiststories.com/en/writers/Hasek-Jaroslav/.

Hatta Shūzō

Hatta Shūzō (1886–1934) Japanese anarchist, translator, theorist, and writer (and former cleric). Worked hard to create a "pure" anarchism by weaving the three tendencies in it together: individualists (the revolution can only be won by individuals struggling against the state), communists (the revolution can only be won by everyone banding together and federalizing work councils), and syndicalists (the revolution can be won by the workers seizing the means of production and building militant unions to destroy capital and the state). This "pure anarchism" was meant to bring together these divergent strains into a single framework that was somewhat similar to Makhno's conception of the Platform or to Faure and Voline's "synthesis anarchism." Hatta also was a big fan of Makhno, keeping a framed picture of Nestor Ivanovich at his desk. Sadly, he died a death of despair via alcohol—in the same year as the man he admired so.

FURTHER READING

Peter H. Marshall. *Demanding the Impossible: A History of Anarchism: Be Realistic, Demand the Impossible!* Oakland, CA: PM Press, 2010.

Crump, John. "Hatta Shūzō and Pure Anarchism in Interwar Japan." Anarchist Library, accessed March 10, 2023, https://theanarchistlibrary.org/library/john-crump-hatta-shuzo-and-pure-anarchism-in-interwar-japan.

Nestor Kalandarishvili

Kalandarishvili, Nestor (1876–1922) Historian Nick Heath wrote: "One of the odd circumstances of history is that during the Russian Revolution and Civil War, there existed two brilliant anarchist guerrilla leaders both with the first name of Nestor. Whilst Makhno fought in the Ukraine, the other fought at the other end of the Soviet Union."

In short, Nestor Kalandarishvili was the anti-Makhno. He was a Georgian anarcho-communist from a family of minor nobility who served a staggering amount of roles in his life. At one point he was a soldier (before deserting) and seminary student (before being kicked out for distributing revolutionary propaganda among troops) in 1903. Tall, showy, with a crumbcatchingly full beard, he made a name for himself later in the Siberian theater of the Civil War, where he acquired the nickname "Grandpa." Anyone named "Grandpa" who leads cavalry charges in an age with effective artillery is probably bad news. Like Makhno in Ukraine, Kalandarishvili agreed to an alliance with the Bolsheviks to fight the White Army, leading both guerrilla attacks and formal military maneuvers.

Unlike Makhno, Kalandarishvili relished his role in the Red Army, meeting with Lenin in Moscow in 1921 and converting to Bolshevism. Fresh off the high of recognition, he began brutally suppressing anarchist groups in Siberia and the Altai Mountains with new purpose as well as the Whites. He fought against Baron Ungern-Sternberg and the Kolchakite Cossack commander Semyonov with some success before dying in early 1922 in an ambush in unclear circumstances. Awarded the Medal of the Red Banner, and you can still find some streets and monuments dedicated to him in the Russian Far East.

FURTHER READING

Heath, Nick. "Kalandarishvili, Nestor Alexandrevitch, 1876–1922." Libcom.org, accessed March 10, 2023, https://libcom.org/history/anarchists-who-turned-bolsheviks-1.
"Nestor Aleksandrovich Kalandarishvili." Prabook, accessed March 10, 2023, https://prabook.com/web/nestor.kalandarishvili/738395.

Kim Chwa-chin

Kim Chwa-chin (1889–1930) Sometimes transliterated as *Kim Jwa-jin*. Korean anarcho-communist and guerrilla. Born into a noble family, upon turning eighteen he burned the slave registers of his family and freed the families of over fifty slaves. Not only that, he also gave land from his own estate to the freed families. Technically, the first freeing of slaves in modern Korean history—thereafter known as the Gwangbok-dang (Liberation Group) incident—earned Kim Chwa-chin three years in prison. Upon release he continued agitating and organizing for anarchist causes. He later became chief military leader of the Shinmin—a two million strong anarchist polity in Manchuria from 1929 through 1931 formed mainly from Koreans driven from their homeland by the Japanese. Was nicknamed "the Nestor Makhno of Asia/Korea," and the comparison is apt. For two years the Shinmin resisted the Japanese empire, the Chinese Koumintang forces, and Korean Stalinist forces before eventually succumbing to combined attacks from all at the same time. It is unclear if Makhno knew about the existence of the Shinmin—news of it hypothetically could have reached him from Asia.

Kim Chwa-chin was assassinated in 1931 by a Stalinist Korean assassin while repairing a water mill in the Shinmin. These pressures and his death forced the Korean anarchist underground to go underground to continue resistance to empire and dictatorship.

FURTHER READING

"Kim Jwa-jin." Hong Seong, accessed through Wayback Machine, March 10, 2023, https://web.archive.org/web/20151226035222/http://english.hongseong.go.kr/eng/sub01_05_04.do.

Katsiaficas, George. *Asia's Unknown Uprisings.* Vol. 1, *South Korean Social Movements in the 20th Century.* Oakland, CA: PM Press, 2012.

MacSimoin, Alan. "The Korean Anarchist Movement." Anarchist Library, accessed March 10, 2023, https://theanarchistlibrary.org/library/alan-macsimoin-the-korean-anarchist-movement.

Ito Noe

Noe, Ito (1895–1923) Feminist, anarchist, and a prolific writer from Taisho-era Japan. She firmly believed that women's liberation was essential to any successful social revolution and for this, among other things, was routinely harassed by the Japanese police. Wrote and edited for a number of anarchist and feminist periodicals including *Seito* from a young age, with fire and verve. She didn't shy away from taboo topics, either, devoting whole issues to subjects like abortion, chastity, and prostitution, to the shock of her bourgeois peers. One of her more notable quotes was: "If chastity is not necessary for men, neither should it be necessary for women. If chastity is required of women, the same should be required of men." Advocate of free love alongside her partner Ōsugi Sakae, with whom she had four children. Died with him at the hands of the Japanese secret police in the purges that followed the Great Kanto Earthquake of 1923.

FURTHER READING

Stanley, Thomas A. *Ōsugi Sakae, Anarchist in Taishō Japan: The Creativity of the Ego.* Cambridge, MA: Council on East Asian Studies, Harvard University, 1982.

United Anarchists of Tokio. "A Call from Our Japanese Comrades" (1923). Kate Sharpley Library, accessed March 10, 2023, https://www.katesharpleylibrary.net/2fqzm3.

Tina Ovcharenko

Ovcharenko, Tina Makhno's girlfriend during the initial phases of the Civil War. Active on the front lines and did some intelligence work for the anarchists as a double agent and telegraph operator. However, the couple was forced to break up by the anarchist councils, who worried that she was sapping Nestor's concentration on the war effort. Sent back to her home village, where she appeared to survive not only the Civil War but also the waves of Bolshevik repression until at least 1930. What became of her after that date is not known.

FURTHER READING
Makhno, Nestor, and Voldemar Antoni. *Young Rebels against the Empire: The Youth Memoirs of Nestor Makhno and Voldemar Antoni.* Edmonton, AB: Black Cat Press 2021.

May Picqueray

Picqueray, May (1898–1993) French anarchist who was one of the envoys in 1922 to Moscow to negotiate for the release of anarchist and socialist prisoners from Bolshevik prisons. Picqueray was singularly fearless, shook her Cheka handlers, and verified the state of Bolshevik Russia for non-Party members with her own eyes. She was horrified and defiantly sang an anarchist fight song in front of senior Bolshevik apparatchiks at a feast, a bit of defiance that could have easily cost her life. When later granted a meeting with Trotsky, and asked what she had against him, she said: "I am an anarchist and we are divided by Makhno and Kronstadt," and refused to shake his hand. Her audacity succeeded in releasing some of the anarchist prisoners from Bolshevik custody. Improbably, she was also the first person that Makhno encountered upon his arrival in Paris and grew close with Makhno during his time there. Of course, there is more to her life than these two incidents, I heartily recommend her autobiography.

FURTHER READING

Picqueray, May. *My Eighty-One Years of Anarchy: A Memoir*. Translated by Paul Sharkey. Chico, CA: AK Press, 2019.

Batko Pravda

Pravda, Simeon P. (d. 1921) Also known as Batko Pravda. Makhnovist commander and former wandering accordionist. Lost his legs below the knee prior to the revolution due to a misunderstanding with a train (or possibly a mining accident, accounts differ). Sometimes carried around in a wheelbarrow by his men. Said to have murdered his brother in a drunken brawl. Capable of great jollity and affability, but also had a brutal reputation among the Mennonites of Ukraine in particular. Died fighting the Bolsheviks.

FURTHER READING

Birdsell, Sandra. *The Russlander*. Toronto, ON: Penguin Random House, 2002.

Patterson, Sean. *Makhno and Memory: Anarchist and Mennonite Narratives of Ukraine's Civil War, 1917–1921*. Winnipeg: University of Manitoba Press, 2020.

Heath, Nick. "Pravda, Simeon (Batko Pravda), 1877–1921." Libcom.org, accessed March 10, 2023, https://libcom.org/article/pravda-simeon-batko-pravda-1877-1921.

Olga Taratuta

Taratuta, Olga (1876–1938) Founding member of the Black Cross, an anarchist equivalent to the Red Cross, and called the "Granny of Russian Anarchism." Active as a militant in the 1905 uprising against the czarist regime, she fled the country but then returned to continue the struggle, at which point she was thrown into prison. Noted writer and activist, she and Makhno met several times prior to and during the Civil War. Member of the Nabat anarchist group until its overt dissolution in 1920. Survived the Civil War and continued agitating under the Bolshevik regime in Moscow—most notably agitating for the release of the Italian anarchists in America, Sacco and Vanzetti, in 1927 alongside Borovoi and other remaining anarchists—something the Cheka did not appreciate, nor the slogan adopted by the Black Cross: "With the oppressed, against the oppressors, always."

She moved to Odessa to organize anarchist activity among the railroad workers and to help smuggle anarchist literature into the USSR. This last act got her arrested and isolated until 1931, when she was released and moved back to Moscow, where she was rearrested in 1933. Was eventually released in 1937 in the same city, where she worked as a factory driller until she was arrested, tried, and executed on the same day in 1938 by the Cheka.

FURTHER READING

Avrich, Paul. *The Russian Anarchists.* Princeton, NJ: Princeton University Press, 1967.

Goldman, Emma. "Heroic Women of the Russian Revolution." Kate Sharpley Library, accessed March 10, 2023, https://www.katesharpleylibrary.net/3xsk7w.

Heath, Nick. "Taratuta, Olga Ilyinichna 1876–1938 (real name Elka Golda Elievna Ruvinskaia)." Libcom.org, accessed March 10, 2013, https://libcom.org/article/taratuta-olga-ilyinichna-1876–1938-real-name-elka-golda-elievna-ruvinskaia.

Maximoff, Gregory Petrovich. *The Guillotine at Work.* Vol.1, *The Leninist Counter-Revolution.* Hastings, UK: ChristieBooks, 2013.

Ossip Tsebry

Tsebry, Ossip (d. ca. 1958) Committed anarchist and Black Army survivor of the Civil War. Organized his village to fight the White Army and then the Reds. Forced to flee Russia, ended up in Yugoslavia where he successfully introduced anarcho-communism to a village and called it "Makhno" after his idol. The village was burned down by White Army elements, and Tsebry had to flee. Stole back into Ukraine during the Nazi invasion of Russia and formed an anarchist "Green Army" that fought Nazis and Stalinists 1942–43. Captured by the Nazis, but not recognized. Endured a concentration camp before being liberated at the war's end. Finally ended up in America where he died sometime later, though not before contributing numerous articles to *Delo Truda—Probuzhdenie* (Voice of labor—awakening), and writing his memoirs, which are sadly unavailable in English at the time of this writing.

FURTHER READING

Damier, Vadim. "Fate of the Makhnovist: The Story of Osip Tsebry." Anarchist Library, accessed March 10, 2023, https://theanarchistlibrary.org/library/vadim-damier-fate-of-the-makhnovist.

Tsebry, Ossip. *Memoirs of a Makhnovist Partisan*. London: Kate Sharpley Library, 2002.

Acknowledgments

The author's acknowledgments and thanks go to (in roughly chronological order):

The incomparable Matt Stevenson, who approached me after an open mic and said casually: "You know, if you're looking into the Russian Civil War, you might want to look into this Makhno guy I read about . . . ."

Michael Moorcock (whose writings of a fictional Nestor Makhno inspired in large measure my explorations into the real man) for the generous donation of his time and attention to this work.

Sewer Rats Productions (Liz Zimmerman, Kelci Schlierf, Sarah Billings, Spencer Ventresca, and Kiki Ventresca Lawler) for coaching, producing, illustrating, and editing the video series in the hell-year of 2020 that ultimately became the very rough draft of the present volume. Without your combined efforts and encouragement, this work would not exist. Or be even a little entertaining.

My beta-readers: Judy, Jim, and Leslie Allison, Jordan Meyerl, and Alexis Amsden. Thank you for your oceanic patience, kindness, and willingness to take me to task when I wandered far afield, trying to take the express train to Tangentville. That this book follows any sort of logical structure is a testament to their skills.

Dr. Douglas Stiffler, for help with research and sources on Ōsugi Sakae and for generally being a stand-up fellow who helped to imbue me with a healthy skepticism of "heroic biography" through our long association.

The good people of PM Press, in particular Joey who asked me the very good question: "Have you considered adapting your video series into a book?" Thank you for all your words of advice, for shepherding me through the process, and generally offering a helping hand when needed.

N.O. Bonzo for their wonderful illustrations, enthusiasm for details, and continuing support and collaboration throughout this process. And also for fielding my doubtless silly questions during cigarette breaks.

Kevin Matthews, who provided the illustrations of the anarchists that are often overlooked by history (more than most anarchists already are, I mean), and for his extreme tolerance for me turning into a crab at inconvenient times.

Malcolm Archibald for his precise and invaluable translations of Makhno-related documents over the decades, to say nothing of his invaluable assistance in fact-checking the work before you. If errors remain, I assure you they are mine and not his.

Hans Magnus Enzensberger, whose dedicated work, research, and lyrical craft showed that history could use the tools of poetry to build a unique and beautiful house of understanding, particularly around the concepts of anarchy and liberation. Rest in peace.

The Wooden Shoe Collective.

Notes

Preface A Japanese Anarchist in Paris (1923)

1 Thomas A. Stanley, *Ōsugi Sakae, Anarchist in Taishō Japan: The Creativity of the Ego* (Cambridge, MA: Council on East Asian Studies, Harvard University, 1982), 144.

2 Ōsugi Sakae, "Prison Life until Deportation," trans. Michael Shauerte, Marxist Internet Archive, accessed March 10, 2023, https://www.marxists.org/subject/japan/osugi/1923/prison-deportation.htm.

3 Ōsugi, "Prison Life."

4 Stanley, *Ōsugi Sakae*, 145.

5 Peter H. Marshall, *Demanding the Impossible: A History of Anarchism: Be Realistic, Demand the Impossible!* (Oakland, CA: PM Press, 2010), 525.

6 Alan MacSimoin, "1894–1931: Anarchism in Korea," Libcom.org, accessed March 10, 2023, https://libcom.org/history/articles/anarchism-in-korea. Note that Kim's name has sometimes been transliterated as Kim Chwa-jin or Kim Joa-jin.

7 Dongyoun Hwang, *Anarchism in Korea: Independence, Transnationalism, and the Question of National Development, 1919–1984* (Albany: State University of New York Press, 2017), 50–54.

8 Stanley, *Ōsugi Sakae*, 146.

9 Sean Patterson, *Makhno and Memory: Anarchist and Mennonite Narratives of Ukraine's Civil War, 1917–1921* (Winnipeg: University of Manitoba Press, 2020), 55–60.

10 Ōsugi Sakae, "Anarchist General: Nestor Makhno," in *Selected Works of Ōsugi Sakae*, vol. 6, *The Russian Revolution as Viewed by an Anarchist*, trans. Legato Co. (Kate Sharpley Library, 2021), https://www.katesharpleylibrary.net/ncjvr9.

11 Ōsugi, "Anarchist General."

12 Stanley, *Ōsugi Sakae*, 148, 155–57.

13 Ivan I. Morris, *The Nobility of Failure: Tragic Heroes in the History of Japan* (Fukuoka, JP: Kurodahan Press, 2013), 199.

Chapter 1 Pugachev's Uprising and Beyond: Setting the Stage for Makhno's Ukraine (1772–1861)

1   Serhii Plokhy, *The Gates of Europe: A History of* Ukraine (New York: Basic Books, 2015), 134.
2   Will Cuppy, *The Decline and Fall of Practically Everybody* (Stroud, UK: Nonpareil Books, 1984), 128.
3   Paul Avrich, *Russian Rebels 1600–1800* (London: Allen Lane, Penguin Press, 1973), 185.
4   Avrich, *Russian Rebels*, 189–90.
5   Avrich, *Russian Rebels*, 396.
6   Robert K. Massie, *Catherine the Great: Portrait of a Woman* (London: Head of Zeus, 2019), 397.
7   Albert Seaton, *The Horsemen of the Steppes: The Story of the Cossacks* (New York: Hippocrene Books, 1985), 114.
8   Avrich, *Russian Rebels*, 188.
9   Avrich, *Russian Rebels*, 407.
10 Avrich, *Russian Rebels*, 409.
11 "Manifesto of the Empress Catherine II," Wayback Machine–Internet Archive, accessed March 10, 2023, https://web.archive.org/web/20040327234320/http://members.aol.com/jktsn/manifest.htm.

Chapter 2 Makhno's Childhood (1888–1904)

1   Nestor Makhno and Voldemar Antoni, *Young Rebels against the Empire: The Youth Memoirs of Nestor Makhno and Voldemar Antoni* (Edmonton, AB: Black Cat Press 2021), 3.
2   Colin Darch, *Nestor Makhno and Rural Anarchism in Ukraine, 1917–1921* (London: Pluto Press, 2020), 15, 295.
3   Malcolm Archibald, *Atamansha: The Story of Maria Nikiforova, the Anarchist Joan of Arc* (Edmonton, AB: Black Cat Press, 2007), 14.
4   Makhno and Antoni, *Young Rebels*, 3.
5   Makhno and Antoni, *Young Rebels*, 4–5.
6   Alexandre Skirda, *Nestor Makhno, Anarchy's Cossack: The Struggle for Free Soviets in the Ukraine 1917–1921* (Edinburgh: AK Press, 2004), 296.
7   Makhno and Antoni, *Young Rebels*, viii.
8   Makhno and Antoni, *Young Rebels*, 6.
9   Nestor Makhno, *The Russian Revolution in Ukraine*, trans. Malcolm Archibald (Edmonton, AB: Black Cat Press, 2009), 17.
10 Makhno and Antoni, *Young Rebels*, 3.
11 Sean Patterson, *Makhno and Memory: Anarchist and Mennonite Narratives of Ukraine's Civil War, 1917–1921* (Winnipeg: University of Manitoba Press, 2020), 42.
12 Patterson, *Makhno and Memory*, 84–85.
13 Patterson, *Makhno and Memory*, 84.
14 Makhno and Antoni, *Young Rebels*, 9.
15 Patterson, *Makhno and Memory*, 10–12.
16 Patterson, *Makhno and Memory*, viii–ix.
17 Patterson, *Makhno and Memory*, 101–3.
18 Patterson, *Makhno and Memory*, 102.
19 Makhno and Antoni, *Young Rebels*, viii.
20 Makhno and Antoni, *Young Rebels*, 12.

Chapter 3 Makhno's Political Awakening (1905–9)

1   Nestor Makhno and Voldemar Antoni, *Young Rebels against the Empire: The Youth Memoirs of Nestor Makhno and Voldemar Antoni* (Edmonton, AB: Black Cat Press 2021), 14.
2   Paul Avrich, *The Russian Anarchists* (Princeton, NJ: Princeton University Press, 2016), 41.
3   Avrich, *Russian Anarchists*, 44–52.
4   Avrich, *Russian Anarchists*, 69.
5   Avrich, *Russian Anarchists*, 41–42.
6   Roland Elliot Brown, *Godless Utopia: Soviet Anti-Religious Propaganda* (London: Fuel Press, 2019), 182–83.
7   Makhno and Antoni, *Young Rebels*, 104.
8   Makhno and Antoni, *Young Rebels*, 14.
9   Colin Darch, *Nestor Makhno and Rural Anarchism in Ukraine, 1917–1921* (London: Pluto Press, 2020), 21.
10   Darch, *Nestor Makhno*, 105.
11   Yevgenia Albats, *KGB: State within a State: The Secret Police and Its Hold on Russia—Past, Present, and Future* (New York: I.B. Tauris, 1995), 90.
12   Makhno and Antoni, *Young Rebels*, 16
13   Makhno and Antoni, *Young Rebels*, 16–17.
14   Makhno and Antoni, *Young Rebels*, 17.
15   Makhno and Antoni, *Young Rebels*, 17–18.
16   Makhno and Antoni, *Young Rebels*, 18.
17   Makhno and Antoni, *Young Rebels*, 28.
18   Vladimir Danilenko, "The Assassination of Pyotr Stolypin," State Archive of the Kiev Oblast, accessed March 10, 2023, https://www.bsb-muenchen.de/mikro/lit470.pdf.

Chapter 4 Capture and Imprisonment (1908–10)

1   Nestor Makhno and Voldemar Antoni, *Young Rebels against the Empire: The Youth Memoirs of Nestor Makhno and Voldemar Antoni* (Edmonton, AB: Black Cat Press 2021), 19.
2   Makhno and Antoni, *Young Rebels*, 19–20.
3   Makhno and Antoni, *Young Rebels*, 20.
4   Makhno and Antoni, *Young Rebels*.
5   Makhno and Antoni, *Young Rebels*, 21–22.
6   Malcolm Archibald, *Atamansha: The Story of Maria Nikiforova, the Anarchist Joan of Arc* (Edmonton, AB: Black Cat Press, 2007), 3.
7   Archibald, *Atamansha*, 5.
8   Makhno and Antoni, *Young Rebels*, 21–23.
9   Makhno and Antoni, *Young Rebels*, 23–24.
10   Makhno and Antoni, *Young Rebels*, 25–26.
11   Makhno and Antoni, *Young Rebels*, 26.
12   Makhno and Antoni, *Young Rebels*, 28.
13   Makhno and Antoni, *Young Rebels*, 30.
14   Makhno and Antoni, *Young Rebels*, 33.
15   Alexandre Skirda, *Nestor Makhno, Anarchy's Cossack: The Struggle for Free Soviets in the Ukraine 1917–1921* (Edinburgh: AK Press, 2004), 26. Makhno and Antoni, *Young Rebels*, 49

16   Makhno and Antoni, *Young Rebels*, 33–34.
17   Makhno and Antoni, *Young Rebels*, 40–42.
18   Makhno and Antoni, *Young Rebels*, 36–37, 44.
19   Paul Avrich, *The Russian Anarchists* (Princeton, NJ: Princeton University Press, 2016), 66–67; Makhno and Antoni, *Young Rebels*, 53.
20   Makhno and Antoni, *Young Rebels*, 45.
21   Makhno and Antoni, *Young Rebels*, 49.
22   Makhno and Antoni, *Young Rebels*, 52.
23   Makhno and Antoni, *Young Rebels*, 52.
24   Makhno and Antoni, *Young Rebels*, 53.

Chapter 5 The Modest One's Life in Prison (1911–17)

1   Nestor Makhno and Voldemar Antoni, *Young Rebels against the Empire: The Youth Memoirs of Nestor Makhno and Voldemar Antoni* (Edmonton, AB: Black Cat Press 2021), 57.
2   Makhno and Antoni, *Young Rebels*, 59.
3   Makhno and Antoni, *Young Rebels*, 57, 68.
4   Makhno and Antoni, *Young Rebels*, 49.
5   Makhno and Antoni, *Young Rebels*, 61.
6   Colin Darch, *Nestor Makhno and Rural Anarchism in Ukraine, 1917–1921* (London: Pluto Press, 2020), 29.
7   Makhno and Antoni, *Young Rebels*, 61–62.
8   Makhno and Antoni, *Young Rebels*, 60.
9   Makhno and Antoni, *Young Rebels*, 72.
10   Makhno and Antoni, *Young Rebels*, 77.
11   Makhno and Antoni, *Young Rebels*, 79–80.
12   Makhno and Antoni, *Young Rebels*, 63–69.
13   Makhno and Antoni, *Young Rebels*, 68.
14   Makhno and Antoni, *Young Rebels*, 69–70.
15   Makhno and Antoni, *Young Rebels*, 62–63.
16   Makhno and Antoni, *Young Rebels*, 63.
17   Makhno and Antoni, *Young Rebels*, 73.

Chapter 6 Makhno's Education in Prison (1910–17)

1   Nestor Makhno and Voldemar Antoni, *Young Rebels against the Empire: The Youth Memoirs of Nestor Makhno and Voldemar Antoni* (Edmonton, AB: Black Cat Press 2021), 60.
2   Mikhail Lermontov, *A Hero of Our Time*, trans. J.H. Wisdom and Marr Murray (1840; Project Gutenberg, 2016) bk 5., chap. 18, https://www.gutenberg.org/files/913/913-h/913-h.htm.
3   Makhno and Antoni, *Young Rebels*, 60.
4   Metchnikoff quoted in Sho Konishi, *Anarchist Modernity Cooperatism and Japanese-Russian Intellectual Relations in Modern Japan* (Cambridge, MA: Harvard University Asia Center, 2013), 63.
5   Makhno and Antoni, *Young Rebels*, 78, 60.
6   Makhno and Antoni, *Young Rebels*, 73.
7   Makhno and Antoni, *Young Rebels*, 61.
8   Alexandre Skirda, *Nestor Makhno, Anarchy's Cossack: The Struggle for Free Soviets in the Ukraine 1917–1921* (Edinburgh: AK Press, 2004), 257.

Chapter 7 The Kerensky Jailbirds (1917)

1 Nestor Makhno and Voldemar Antoni, *Young Rebels against the Empire: The Youth Memoirs of Nestor Makhno and Voldemar Antoni* (Edmonton, AB: Black Cat Press 2021), 87.
2 Alexandre Skirda, *Nestor Makhno, Anarchy's Cossack: The Struggle for Free Soviets in the Ukraine 1917–1921* (Edinburgh: AK Press, 2004), 42, 46.
3 Makhno and Antoni, *Young Rebels*, 88.
4 Makhno and Antoni, *Young Rebels*, 5.
5 Colin Darch, *Nestor Makhno and Rural Anarchism in Ukraine, 1917–1921* (London: Pluto Press, 2020), 31.
6 I thank Malcolm Archibald for sharing with me his knowledge of this seldom mentioned part of Makhno's life immediately after prison.
7 Nestor Makhno, *The Russian Revolution in Ukraine*, trans. Malcolm Archibald (Edmonton, AB: Black Cat Press, 2009), 17.
8 Makhno, *Russian Revolution*, 17–18.
9 Makhno, *Russian Revolution*, 16–19.
10 Makhno, *Russian Revolution*, 44–46.
11 Makhno, *Russian Revolution*, 62.
12 Makhno, *Russian Revolution*, 20–22.
13 Makhno, *Russian Revolution*, 23–24.
14 Makhno, *Russian Revolution*, 68–72.
15 Makhno, *Russian Revolution*, 69–73.
16 Makhno, *Russian Revolution*, 95.
17 Makhno, *Russian Revolution*, 32.
18 Makhno, *Russian Revolution*, 64.
19 Makhno, *Russian Revolution*, 64–65.
20 Makhno, *Russian Revolution*, 128.
21 Makhno, *Russian Revolution*, 128–29.
22 Makhno, *Russian Revolution*, 135–40.
23 Makhno, *Russian Revolution*, 141–44.
24 Makhno, *Russian Revolution*, 145.
25 Makhno, *Russian Revolution*, 169–80.

Chapter 8 Makhno Returns to Moscow (1918)

1 Nestor Makhno, *Under the Blows of the Counterrevolution*, trans. Malcolm Archibald (Edmonton, AB: Black Cat Press, 2009), 1–6.
2 Makhno, *Under the Blows*, 6.
3 Makhno, *Under the Blows*, 10.
4 Tariq Ali, *Trotsky for Beginners* (Cambridge: Icon Books, 1998), 154–55.
5 Makhno, *Under the Blows*, 21–22.
6 Makhno, *Under the Blows*, 32.
7 Makhno, *Under the Blows*, 57.
8 Makhno, *Under the Blows*, 30.
9 Makhno, *Under the Blows*, 33.
10 Makhno, *Under the Blows*, 61.
11 Makhno, *Under the Blows*, 56, 60.
12 Makhno, *Under the Blows*, 63.
13 Makhno, *Under the Blows*, 98.

14   Anatoly Dubovik, "Alexei Borovoi (from Individualism to the Platform)." Kate Sharpley Library, accessed March 10, 2023, https://www.katesharpleylibrary.net/228105.

15   Makhno, *Under the Blows*, 105.

16   Makhno, *Under the Blows*, 178–79.

17   Robert Payne, *The Life and Death of Lenin* (London: Grafton Books, 1987), 482.

18   "Lenin Orders the Massacre of Sex Workers, 1918," libcom.org., accessed March 10, 2023, https://libcom.org/article/lenin-orders-massacre-sex-workers-1918.

19   Makhno, *Under the Blows*, 137–45.

20   Makhno, *Under the Blows*, 145.

21   Malcolm Archibald, personal correspondence.

22   Payne, *Life*, 488–92.

23   Makhno, *Under the Blows*, 167–69.

24   Nestor Ivanovich Makhno, *The Ukrainian Revolution (July–December 1918)*, trans. Malcolm Archibald and Will Firth (Edmonton, AB: Black Cat Press, 2011), 19.

Chapter 9 Makhno Returns to Huliaipole (1918)

1   Nestor Makhno, *The Ukrainian Revolution*, trans. and ed. Malcolm Archibald (Edmonton, AB: Black Cat Press, 2011), 6–7.

2   Makhno, *Ukrainian Revolution*, 7–9.

3   Makhno, *Ukrainian Revolution*, 19.

4   Makhno, *Ukrainian Revolution*, 24–25.

5   Makhno, *Ukrainian Revolution*, 50.

6   Makhno, *Ukrainian Revolution*, 48.

7   Makhno, *Ukrainian Revolution*, 26–30.

8   Colum Cronin, and Shane Cronin, "Kilmichael Ambush —'A Story of a Century,'" Coppeen Heritage, YouTube video, 42:43, November 26, 2020, https://www.youtube.com/watch?v=FSmgXJh1MLg.

9   Michael Malet, *Nestor Makhno in the Russian Civil War* (London: Macmillan Press, 1982), 89.

10   Makhno, *Ukrainian Revolution*, 63. A *tachanka* is a horse-drawn platform.

11   Ossip Tsebry, *Memories of a Makhnovist Partisan* (London: Kate Sharpley Library, 1993), 7.

12   Vyacheslav Azarov, *Kontrrazvedka: The Story of the Makhnovist Intelligence Service*, trans. Malcolm Archibald (Edmonton, AB: Black Cat Press, 2008), 22.

13   Makhno, *Ukrainian Revolution*, 77.

14   Makhno, *Ukrainian Revolution*, 89.

15   Makhno, *Ukrainian Revolution*, 38.

16   Sean Patterson, *Makhno and Memory: Anarchist and Mennonite Narratives of Ukraine's Civil War, 1917–1921* (Winnipeg: University of Manitoba Press, 2020), 62.

17   Makhno, *Ukrainian Revolution*, 98.

18   Colin Darch, *Nestor Makhno and Rural Anarchism in Ukraine, 1917–1921* (London: Pluto Press, 2020), 32.

19   V.M. Chop, "Participation of Priazov'ye Greek Colonists in the Makhnovist Movement (1918–1921)," trans. Malcolm Archibald, Kate Sharpley Library, accessed March 10, 2023, https://www.katesharpleylibrary.net/nk9b65.

20   Makhno, *Ukrainian Revolution*, 142.

21   Makhno, *Ukrainian Revolution*, 142.

22   Makhno, *Ukrainian Revolution*, 178.

23 Makhno, *Ukrainian Revolution*, 44.

24 Teffi, *Memories: From Moscow to the Black Sea* (New York: New York Review of Books, 2016), 91.

25 Makhno, *Ukrainian Revolution*, 188–91.

Chapter 10 A Teacher and Terror as Method in Ukraine (1918)

1   Malcolm Archibald, *The Makhnovschina and Its Aftermath* (Edmonton, AB: Black Cat Press, 2021), 200–203. I've paraphrased the broad strokes of Halyna Kuzmenko's recollection for concision, humor, and to get at the main point, which is the dynamics between Nestor and Halyna from her perspective.

2   Archibald, *Makhnovschina*, 188–90.

3   Archibald, *Makhnovschina*, 79.

4   Nestor Makhno, *Under the Blows of the Counterrevolution, April–June 1918*, trans. and ed. Malcolm Archibald (Edmonton, AB: Black Cat Press, 2009), 160.

5   Archibald, *Makhnovschina*, 192–93.

6   Sean Patterson, *Makhno and Memory: Anarchist and Mennonite Narratives of Ukraine's Civil War, 1917–1921* (Winnipeg: University of Manitoba Press, 2020), 105.

7   Patterson, *Makhno and Memory*, 54–55, 58–59.

8   Patterson, *Makhno and Memory*, 65–67.

9   Patterson, *Makhno and Memory*, 65.

10 Patterson, *Makhno and Memory*, 142.

11 Patterson, *Makhno and Memory*, 67.

Chapter 11 The Terrible Summer (1919)

1   Voline, *The Unknown Revolution, 1917–1921* (Oakland, CA: PM Press, 2019), 582.

2   Voline, *Unknown*, 582.

3   Peter Arshinov, *History of the Makhnovist Movement: (1918–1921)* (London: Freedom Press, 1987), 171.

4   Voline, *Unknown*, 583.

5   Michael Malet, *Nestor Makhno in the Russian Civil War*, (London: Macmillan Press, 1982), 30.

6   Malcolm Archibald, "The Many Lives of Max Chernyak," Kate Sharpley Library, accessed March 10, 2023, https://www.katesharpleylibrary.net/tdz1q9.

7   Malcolm Archibald, *The Makhnovschina and Its Aftermath* (Edmonton, AB: Black Cat Press, 2021), 26.

8   Archibald, *Makhnovschina*, 26–27.

9   Arshinov, *History*, 122.

10 Voline, *Unknown*, 601–2.

11 Voline, *Unknown*, 593.

12 Voline, *Unknown*, 592.

13 Voline, *Unknown*, 606.

14 Martin Gilbert, *Churchill and the Jews: A Lifelong Friendship*, (New York: Henry Holt, 2008), 24.

15 Voline, *Unknown*, 606.

16 Voline, *Unknown*, 605.

17 Voline, *Unknown*, 610–11.

18 Arshinov, *History*, 147–48.

19 Alexandre Skirda, *Nestor Makhno, Anarchy's Cossack: The Struggle for Free Soviets in the Ukraine 1917–1921* (Edinburgh: AK Press, 2004), 125.

20 Voline, *Unknown*, 611.

Chapter 12 The War behind the Lines (1919)

1 Christopher M. Andrew, and Oleg Gordievskij, *KGB: The Inside Story* (New York: HarperCollins, 1990), 45.

2 Malcolm Archibald, *Atamansha: The Story of Maria Nikiforova, the Anarchist Joan of Arc* (Edmonton, AB: Black Cat Press, 2007), 45–46.

3 Archibald, *Atamansha*, 36–37.

4 Archibald, *Atamansha*, 37.

5 Archibald, *Atamansha*, 38–39.

6 Yevgenia Albats, *KGB: State within a State: The Secret Police and Its Hold on Russia—Past, Present, and Future* (New York: I.B. Tauris, 1995), 97.

7 Vyacheslav Azarov, *Kontrrazvedka: The Story of the Makhnovist Intelligence Service*, trans. Malcolm Archibald (Edmonton, AB: Black Cat Press, 2008), 8.

8 Archibald, *Atamansha*, 40.

9 Archibald, *Atamansha*, 40–41.

10 Vyacheslav Azarov, *Kontrrazvedka: The Story of the Makhnovist Intelligence Service*, trans. Malcolm Archibald (Edmonton, AB: Black Cat Press, 2008), 17.

11 Azarov, *Kontrrazvedka*, 18.

12 Azarov, *Kontrrazvedka*, 41.

13 Archibald, *Atamansha*, 42–43.

14 "Tambov Rebellion," chemeurope.com, https://www.chemeurope.com/en/encyclopedia/Tambov_Rebellion.html.

Chapter 13 Retreating to Victory and Conspiracy (1919)

1 Alexandre Skirda, *Nestor Makhno, Anarchy's Cossack: The Struggle for Free Soviets in the Ukraine 1917–1921* (Edinburgh: AK Press, 2004), 131.

2 Colin Darch, *Nestor Makhno and Rural Anarchism in Ukraine, 1917–1921* (London: Pluto Press, 2020), 140.

3 Skirda, *Nestor Makhno*, 130.

4 Skirda, *Nestor Makhno*, 133.

5 Skirda, *Nestor Makhno*, 129.

6 Skirda, *Nestor Makhno*, 294.

7 Skirda, *Nestor Makhno*, 134–35.

8 Darch, *Nestor Makhno*, 154–55.

9 Skirda, *Nestor Makhno*, 137.

10 Darch, *Nestor Makhno*, 85.

11 Darch, *Nestor Makhno*, 66.

12 Charlie Allison, "The Russian Civil War in 7 Songs," Charlie Allison, August 10, 2020, https://www.charlie-allison.com/the-russian-civil-war-summarized-in-7-songs.

13 Vyacheslav Azarov, *Kontrrazvedka: The Story of the Makhnovist Intelligence Service*, trans. Malcolm Archibald (Edmonton, AB: Black Cat Press, 2008), 35–40. I've drawn heavily from Azarov and Belash's account and synthesized it into a more condensed narrative. Unless otherwise noted, all quotes from this section are from Azarov.

14 Gregory Petrovich Maximoff, *The Guillotine at Work*, vol. 1, *The Leninist Counter-Revolution*, (Hastings, UK: ChristieBooks, 2013), 28–30.

15   Azarov, *Kontrrazvedka*, 39.

Chapter 14 Second Alliance with the Bolsheviks against the White Army (1920)

1   Voline. *The Unknown Revolution, 1917–1921* (Oakland, CA: PM Press, 2019), 713–15.
2   Voline, *Unknown*, 713–15.
3   Peter Arshinov, *History of the Makhnovist Movement: (1918–1921)*(London: Freedom Press, 1987), 174; emphasis added.
4   Colin Darch, *Nestor Makhno and Rural Anarchism in Ukraine, 1917–1921* (London: Pluto Press, 2020), 203.
5   Paul Avrich, *The Anarchists in the Russian Revolution* (London: Thames and Hudson, 1973), 174–75.
6   Voline, *Unknown*, 653; Leon Trotsky, "What Is the Meaning of Makhno's Coming over to the Side of the Soviet Power?" Nestor Makhno Archive, accessed March 10, 2023, http://www.nestormakhno.info/english/trotsky/meaning.htm.
7   Malcolm Archibald, *The Makhnovschina and Its Aftermath* (Edmonton, AB: Black Cat Press, 2021), 70.
8   Arshinov, *History*, 180–82.
9   Darch, *Nestor Makhno*, 167.
10   Emma Goldman, *Living My Life* (New York: Alfred A. Knopf, 1931), 579, https://theanarchistlibrary.org/library/emma-goldman-living-my-life.pdf.
11   Alexandre Skirda, *Nestor Makhno, Anarchy's Cossack: The Struggle for Free Soviets in the Ukraine 1917–1921* (Edinburgh: AK Press, 2004), 359.
12   George Stewart, *The White Armies of Russia: A Chronicle of Counter-Revolution and Allied Intervention*, (East Sussex, UK: Naval and Military Press, 2009), 401.
13   Stewart, *White Armies*, 140.
14   Arshinov, *History*, 174.
15   Skirda, *Nestor Makhno*, 404.
16   People's Commissariat for Military Matters, "Makhno and Wrangel," October 14, 1920, Nestor Makhno Archive, accessed March 10, 2023, http://www.nestormakhno.info/english/trotsky/makhwran.htm.
17   Voline, *Unknown*, 559–60.
18   Voline, *Unknown*, 660.
19   Arshinov, *History*, 192.
20   Arshinov, *History*, 248–49.
21   Serhii Plokhy, *The Gates of Europe: A History of* Ukraine (New York: Basic Books, 2015), 221.
22   Skirda, *Nestor Makhno*, 207–9.

Chapter 15 The Sudden yet Inevitable Betrayal (1920–21)

1   Malcolm Archibald, *The Makhnovschina and Its Aftermath* (Edmonton, AB: Black Cat Press, 2021), 133–34.
2   Voline, *The Unknown Revolution*, 1917–1921 (Oakland, CA: PM Press, 2019), 667–69.
3   Voline, *Unknown*, 670–74.
4   Voline, *Unknown*, 675
5   Archibald, *Makhnovschina*, 134–35.
6   Archibald, *Makhnovschina*, 135–36.

7   Peter Arshinov, *History of the Makhnovist Movement: (1918–1921)* (London: Freedom Press, 1987), 211.

8   Alexandre Skirda, *Nestor Makhno, Anarchy's Cossack: The Struggle for Free Soviets in the Ukraine 1917–1921* (Edinburgh: AK Press, 2004), 253.

9   Skirda, *Nestor Makhno*, 257.

10   Arshinov, *History*, 212.

11   Arshinov, *History*, 224.

12   Paul Avrich, *The Anarchists in the Russian Revolution* (London: Thames and Hudson, 1973), 145, 151.

13   Richard Pipes, *Russia under the Bolshevik Regime 1919–1924* (London: Harvill, 1997), 382.

14   Nick Heath, "The Third Revolution? Peasant Resistance to the Bolshevik Government," libcom.org, accessed March 10, 2023, https://libcom.org/library/third-revolution-nick-heath.

15   Pipes, *Russia*, 374.

16   Arshinov, *History*, 221.

17   Skirda, *Nestor Makhno*, 359.

Chapter 16 Nestor Makhno En Route to Paris (1921–25)

1   Colin Darch, *Nestor Makhno and Rural Anarchism in Ukraine, 1917–1921* (London: Pluto Press, 2020), 129.

2   Darch, *Nestor Makhno*, 129.

3   Darch, *Nestor Makhno*, 129.

4   Darch, *Nestor Makhno*, 129.

5   Alexandre Skirda, *Nestor Makhno, Anarchy's Cossack: The Struggle for Free Soviets in the Ukraine 1917–1921* (Edinburgh: AK Press, 2004), 260.

6   Darch, *Nestor Makhno*, 231.

7   Vyacheslav Azarov, *Kontrrazvedka: The Story of the Makhnovist Intelligence Service*, trans. Malcolm Archibald (Edmonton, AB: Black Cat Press, 2008), 63.

8   Darch, *Nestor Makhno*, 132.

9   Darch, *Nestor Makhno*, 132.

10   Darch, *Nestor Makhno*, 133.

11   Darch, *Nestor Makhno*, 133–34.

12   Darch, *Nestor Makhno*, 134.

13   Skirda, *Nestor Makhno*, 269.

14   Darch, *Nestor Makhno*, 239.

15   Darch, *Nestor Makhno*, 136.

16   Skirda, *Nestor Makhno*, 270.

17   Darch, *Nestor Makhno*, 136.

18   Darch, *Nestor Makhno*, 138.

19   Darch, *Nestor Makhno*, 138.

20   Darch, *Nestor Makhno*, 138.

21   Darch, *Nestor Makhno*, 138.

22   Darch, *Nestor Makhno*, 138.

23   Darch, *Nestor Makhno*, 138.

24   Darch, *Nestor Makhno*, 138.

25   Darch, *Nestor Makhno*, 138.

26   Nestor Makhno, "Makhno's Opinion of Lenin and Leninism," trans. Paul Sharkey, Kate Sharpley Library, accessed March 10, 2023, https://www.katesharpleylibrary.net/ksn1s7.

27 May Picqueray, *My Eighty-One Years of Anarchy: A Memoir*, trans. Paul Sharkey (Chico, CA: AK Press, 2019), 148–49.

Chapter 17 Enemies and Friends in Parisian Exile (1925–34)
1   Colin Darch, *Nestor Makhno and Rural Anarchism in Ukraine, 1917–1921* (London: Pluto Press, 2020), 139.
2   Alexandre Skirda, *Nestor Makhno, Anarchy's Cossack: The Struggle for Free Soviets in the Ukraine 1917–1921* (Edinburgh: AK Press, 2004), 273.
3   Ida Mett, "Makhno in Paris," Nestor Makhno Archive, accessed March 10, 2023, http://www.nestormakhno.info/english/personal/personal5.htm.
4   Abel Paz, *Durruti in the Spanish Revolution*, trans. Chuck Morse (Oakland, CA: AK Press, 2006), 88.
5   Paz, *Durruti*, 88.
6   Paz, *Durruti*, 89.
7   Skirda, *Nestor Makhno*, 274. The information about "Zayats" being a Petliurist was provided by Malcolm Archibald in personal correspondence.
8   Alexander Berkman, *Life of an Anarchist: The Alexander Berkman Reader*, ed. Gene Felner (New York: Seven Stories Press, 2005), 11–13.
9   Berkman, *Life*, 267.
10 Mett, "Makhno in Paris."
11 Mett, "Makhno in Paris."
12 Mett, "Makhno in Paris."
13 Mett, "Makhno in Paris."
14 Mett, "Makhno in Paris."
15 May Picqueray, *My Eighty-One Years of Anarchy: A Memoir*, trans. Paul Sharkey (Chico, CA: AK Press, 2019), 147.

Chapter 18 Makhno's Writings outside the Platform in Exile (1926–34)
1   Malcolm Archibald, *The Makhnovschina and Its Aftermath* (Edmonton, AB: Black Cat Press, 2021), 6.
2   Archibald, *Makhnovschina*, 186.
3   Nestor Makhno, *The Struggle against the State and Other Essays*, ed. Alexandre Skirda (San Francisco, CA: AK Press, 1996), 28–31.
4   Archibald, *Makhnovschina*, 188.
5   Makhno, *Struggle*, 30.
6   Makhno, *Struggle*, 38.
7   Archibald, *Makhnovschina*, 31–32.
8   Makhno, *Struggle*, 81.
9   Makhno, *Struggle*, 89.

Chapter 19 Makhno and the Platform (1925–33)
1   Nestor Makhno, introduction to "Platform, June 1926," Marxists Internet Archive, accessed March 10, 2023, https://www.marxists.org/reference/archive/makhno-nestor/works/1926/platform/ch01.htm.
2   Sébastien Faure, "The Anarchist Synthesis" (1927), Revolt Library, accessed March 10, 2023, https://www.revoltlib.com/anarchism/the-anarchist-synthesis.
3   Faure, *Anarchist Synthesis*.
4   Alexander Berkman, "'To Our Comrades Everywhere!'" (1926) International Institute

of Social History (Amsterdam), accessed March 10, 2023, https://hdl.handle.net/10622/ARCH00040.137.

5   Paul Avrich, *Anarchist Portraits* (Princeton, NJ: Princeton University Press, 1988), 224.

6   Errico Malatesta and Nestor Makhno, "About the Platform," Anarchist Library, accessed April 5, 2023, https://theanarchistlibrary.org/library/errico-malatesta-and-nestor-makhno-about-the-platform.

7   Malatesta and Makhno, "About the Platform."

8   Paul Avrich, *The Russian Anarchists* (Princeton, NJ: Princeton University Press, 2016), 242–43.

9   Angel Pino, "Ba Jin and the 'Arshinov Platform,'" Anarchist Library, accessed March 10, 2023, https://theanarchistlibrary.org/library/angel-pino-ba-jin-and-the-arshinov-platform.

10 Pino, "Ba Jin."

11 Michael Malet, *Nestor Makhno in the Russian Civil War* (London: Macmillan, 1989), 189.

12 Malcolm Archibald, "The Many Lives of Max Chernyak," Kate Sharpley Library, accessed March 10, 2023, https://www.katesharpleylibrary.net/tdz1q9.

13 Alexandre Skirda, *Nestor Makhno, Anarchy's Cossack: The Struggle for Free Soviets in the Ukraine 1917–1921* (Edinburgh: AK Press, 2004), 283.

14 Nestor Makhno, *The Struggle against the State and Other Essays*, ed. Alexandre Skirda (San Francisco, CA: AK Press, 1996), 19–23, 67–70.

15 Alfredo M. Bonanno, introduction to *The Russian Revolution in Ukraine (March 1917–April 1918)* by Nestor Makhno, Anarchist Library, accessed April 12, 2023, https://theanarchistlibrary.org/library/nestor-makhno-the-russian-revolution-in-the-ukraine.

Chapter 20 No Gods, No Masters: Nestor Makhno's Death and Legacy (1934)

1   Nestor Makhno, "Over the Fresh Grave of Comrade N. Rogdaev," trans. Malcolm Archibald, Kate Sharpley Library, accessed March 10, 2023, https://www.katesharpleylibrary.net/547f4n.

2   Alexandre Skirda, *Nestor Makhno, Anarchy's Cossack: The Struggle for Free Soviets in the Ukraine 1917–1921* (Edinburgh: AK Press, 2004), 281, 285.

3   Skirda, *Nestor Makhno*, 281.

4   Alexander Berkman, "Nestor Makhno," 1934. Item 220, Alexander Berkman Papers, International Institute of Social History, https://hdl.handle.net/10622/ARCH00040.220.

5   Colin Darch, *Nestor Makhno and Rural Anarchism in Ukraine, 1917–1921* (London: Pluto Press, 2020), 290–91.

6   Denys Gorbach, "Anarchism in Makhno's Homeland: Adventures of the Red-and-Black Flag," OpenDemocracy, September 30, 2015, https://www.opendemocracy.net/en/odr/anarchism-in-makhnos-homeland-adventures-of-red-and-black-flag.

Selected Bibliography

Albats, Yevgenia. *KGB: State within a State; the Secret Police and Its Hold on Russia—Past, Present, and Future*. New York: I.B. Tauris, 1995.

Archibald, Malcolm. *Atamansha: The Story of Maria Nikiforova, the Anarchist Joan of Arc*. Edmonton, AB: Black Cat Press, 2007.

———. *The Makhnovschina and Its Aftermath*. Edmonton, AB: Black Cat Press, 2021.

Arshinov, Peter. *History of the Makhnovist Movement: (1918–1921)*. London: Freedom Press, 1987.

Avrich, Paul. *Anarchist Portraits*. Princeton, NJ: Princeton University Press, 2009.

———. *The Anarchists in the Russian Revolution*. London: Thames and Hudson, 1973.

———. *The Russian Anarchists*. Princeton, NJ: Princeton University Press, 1967.

———. *Russian Rebels, 1600–1800*. London: Allen Lane, Penguin Press, 1973.

Azarov, Vyacheslav. *Kontrrazvedka: The Story of the Makhnovist Intelligence Service*. Translated by Malcolm Archibald. Edmonton, AB: Black Cat Press, 2008.

Berkman, Alexander. *Life of an Anarchist: The Alexander Berkman Reader*. With a foreword by Howard Zinn. Edited by Gene Felner. New York: Seven Stories Press, 2005.

———. "Nestor Makhno," 1934. Item 220, Alexander Berkman Papers, International Institute of Social History. https://hdl.handle.net/10622/ARCH00040.220.

Camus, Albert. *The Rebel*. Translated by Anthony Bower. New York: Vintage, 1992.

Carr, Edward Hallett. 1961. *Michael Bakunin*. New York: Vintage Books, 1961.

Cohn-Bendit, Daniel, and Gabriel Cohn-Bendit. 1969. *Obsolete Communism; the Left-Wing Alternative*. Translated by Arnold Pomerans. Edinburgh: AK Press, 2001.

Cuppy, Will. *The Decline and Fall of Practically Everybody*. Illustrated by William Steig. Edited by Fred Feldkamp. Stroud, UK: The History Press, 2011.

Darch, Colin. *Nestor Makhno and Rural Anarchism in Ukraine, 1917–21*. London: Pluto Press, 2020.

Dubrovnik, Anatoly, and D.I. Rublev. *After Makhno: The Anarchist Underground in the Ukraine in the 1920s and 1930s: Outlines of History* and *The Story of a Leaflet and the Fate of the Anarchist Varshavskiy*. London: Kate Sharpley Library, 2009.

Everington, Keoni. "Anonymous Hacks into Russian Website, Devices to Retaliate for Ukraine Invasion." *Taiwan News*, February 25, 2022. https://www.taiwannews.com.tw/en/news/4455240.

Frémion, Yves. *Orgasms of History: 3000 Years of Spontaneous Insurrection.* Translated by Paul Sharkey. Oakland, CA: AK Press, 2004.

Gorbach, Denis. "Anarchism in Makhno's Homeland: Adventures of the Red-And-Black Flag." OpenDemocracy, September 30, 2015. https://www.opendemocracy.net/en/odr/anarchism-in-makhnos-homeland-adventures-of-red-and-black-flag.

Hašek, Jaroslav. *The Good Soldier Švejk and His Fortunes in the World War.* Translated by Cecil Parrot. Illustrated by Josef Lada. London: David Campbell Publishers, 2000.

Kropotkin, Peter. "Anarchist Morality." Anarchy Archives, accessed March 10, 2023. http://dwardmac.pitzer.edu/anarchist_Archives/kropotkin/AM/anarchist_moralityI.html.

———. *The Conquest of Bread.* Edited by Paul Avrich. New York: New York University Press, 1972.

Laursen, Eric. *The Operating System: An Anarchist Theory of the Modern State.* Chico, CA: AK Press, 2021.

Makhno, Nestor. *The Struggle against the State and Other Essays.* Edited by Alexandre Skirda. San Francisco, CA: AK Press, 1996.

———. *The Ukrainian Revolution (July–December 1918).* Translated by Malcolm Archibald, and Will Firth. Edmonton, AB: Black Cat Press, 2011.

———. *Under the Blows of the Counterrevolution, April–June 1918.* With a preface and notes by Voline. Translated and edited by Malcolm Archibald. Edmonton, AB: Black Cat Press, 2009.

Makhno, Nestor, and Voldemar Antoni. *Young Rebels against Empire: The Youth Memoirs of Nestor Makhno and Voldemar Antoni.* Translated by Malcolm Archibald. Edmonton, AB: Black Cat Press, 2021.

Malatesta, Errico. *Life and Ideas: The Anarchist Writings of Errico Malatesta.* Edited by Vernon Richards. Oakland, CA: PM Press, 2015.

Marshall, Peter H. *Demanding the Impossible: A History of Anarchism.* Oakland, CA: PM Press, 2010.

Massie, Robert K. *Catherine the Great: Portrait of a Woman.* London: Head of Zeus, 2019.

Maximoff, Gregory Petrovich. *The Guillotine at Work.* Vol.1, *The Leninist Counter-Revolution.* Hastings, UK: ChristieBooks, 2013.

Merriman, John M. *Ballad of the Anarchist Bandits: The Crime Spree That Gripped Belle Époque Paris.* New York: Nation Books, 2017.

Mett, Ida. "Makhno in Paris." The Nestor Makhno Archive, accessed March 10, 2023. http://www.nestormakhno.info/english/personal/personal5.htm.

Moorcock, Michael. *Byzantium Endures.* Oakland, CA: PM Press, 2014.

———. "Starship Stormtroopers." Libcom.org, accessed March 10, 2023. https://libcom.org/article/starship-stormtroopers-michael-moorcock.

———. *The Steel Tsar.* London: Titan, 2013.

Morris, Ivan I. *The Nobility of Failure: Tragic Heroes in the History of Japan.* Fukuoka, JP: Kurodahan Press, 2013.

Ōsugi Sakae. "Anarchist General: Nestor Makhno." Kate Sharpley Library, accessed March 10, 2023, https://www.katesharpleylibrary.net/ncjvr9.

———. *The Autobiography of Ōsugi Sakae.* Translated by Byron K. Marshall. Berkeley: University of California Press, 1992.

———. "Prison Life until Deportation." Translated by Michael Shauerte. Marxist Internet Archive, accessed March 10, 2023. https://www.marxists.org/subject/japan/osugi/1923/prison-deportation.htm.

Patterson, Sean. *Makhno and Memory: Anarchist and Mennonite Narratives of Ukraine's Civil War, 1917–1921*. Winnipeg: University Of Manitoba Press, 2020.

Payne, Robert. *The Life and Death of Lenin*. London: Grafton Books, 1987.

Picqueray, May. *My Eighty-One Years of Anarchy: A Memoir*. Translated by Paul Sharkey. Chico, CA: AK Press, 2019.

Pipes, Richard. 1997. *Russia under the Bolshevik Regime 1919–1924*. London: Harvill, 1997.

Podshivalov, Igor, and Malcolm Archibald. *Siberian Makhnovshchina: Siberian Anarchists in the Russian Civil War (1918–1924)*. Edmonton, AB: Black Cat Press, 2011.

Riha, Thomas, ed. *Readings in Russian Civilization*. Vol. 2, *Imperial Russia, 1700–1917*. Chicago, IL: University of Chicago Press, 1973.

Ruff, Philip. *Towering Flame: The Life and Times of the Elusive Latvian Anarchist Peter the Painter*. London: Breviary Stuff, 2019.

Serge, Victor. *Memoirs of a Revolutionary, 1901–1941*. Translated by Peter Sedgwick. Oxford: Oxford University Press, 1980.

Skirda, Alexandre. *Nestor Makhno, Anarchy's Cossack: The Struggle for Free Soviets in the Ukraine 1917–1921*. Edinburgh: AK Press, 2004.

Stanley, Thomas A. *Ōsugi Sakae: Anarchist in Taisho Japan: The Creativity of the Ego*. Cambridge, MA: Council on East Asian Studies, Harvard University, 1982.

Tolstoy, Leo. *The Cossacks and the Raid*. Translated by Andrew R. MacAndrew. New York: New American Library, 1985.

Tsebry, Ossip. *Memories of a Makhnovist Partisan*. London: Kate Sharpley Library, 1993.

Voline. *The Unknown Revolution, 1917–1921*. Oakland, CA: PM Press, 2019.

Index

Page numbers in *italic* refer to illustrations. "Passim" (literally "scattered") indicates intermittent discussion of a topic over a cluster of pages.

Free Battalion, 68; Makhno childhood in, 18–25; Makhno return, 75–94 passim; Makhnovist retaking (first), 84; Makhnovist retaking (second), 133; Military Revolutionary Council, 121; Nikiforova in, 107; police chief assassination, 38; UPP, 19, 32

infiltrators and informers, 31, 121, 170–71, 189. *See also* shpiks
Ischenko, Volodymyr, 178–79
Ito Noe, 6, 200–201

Japan, 2, 8; Russo-Japanese War, 25
Japanese anarchists, 1–7, 3, 148, 151, 167, 194–95, 200–201, 295
Jews, attacks on. *See* antisemitism; pogroms and pogromists
July Days, 1917, 56

Kalandarishvili, Nestor, *196*, 197
Kalashnikov, Oleksandr, 124
Kamenev, Leo, 161
Kaplan, Fanya, 74, 109
Kapnist, Vasili, 16
Karachentsev (Huliaipole chief of police), 33, 38–39
Karelin, Apollon, 106
Karetnik, Simon, 103, 130, 133
Kerensky, Alexander, 56, 62
Kessel, Joseph: *Makhno and His Jewess*, 159
Kharkiv, 102, 111, 132, 189; Nabat Confederation, 164, 185
Kim Jwa-jin (Chwa-chin), 2, *198*, 199
Klychevsky, Vasily: *History of Russia*, 51
Kolchak, Alexander, 110, 126, 189, 197
Korean anarchists, 2, 198–99
Korn, Maria. *See* Goldsmit, Maria
Kórnilov, Lavr, 62
Kostyukhin, Yakov, 126
Kronstadt Rebellion, 138, 164–65
Kropotkin, Peter, 4, 18, 47–54 passim, 59, 96, 162, 168; Ba Jin and, 183; death and funeral, 137, 191; Goldsmit and, 175; letters to Lenin, 137; Makhno meeting and correspondence, 71–73; *Mutual Aid*, 51

Kubanin, Mikhail, 160–61, 167
Kuban Republic, 69
Kurilenko, Vasily, 126
Kuzmenko, Halyna, 59, 87–92, *87*, 94, 141–50 passim, *176*, 178

Lecoin, Louis, 145, 151, 156, 170
Left Socialist Revolutionaries, 66–70 passim, 119; Bolshevik purge of, 109, 138; in prison, 41
Lenin, Vladimir, 4, 6, 70, 74, 75, 106, 111, 117; death, 146–47; executions, 74, 120–21, 132; hunger strikers and, 138; Kalandarishvili and, 197; Kaplan assassination attempt on, 75; Kronstadt Rebellion and, 138, 164–65; Makhno essay on, 147; Makhno meeting, 72, 74; "transitory period," 163
Lermontov, Mikhail, 49–50
"Letter to the Spanish Anarchists" (Makhno), 162
Liuty, Isidor, 83

Makhno, Grigori, 25, 113
Makhno, Nestor, 3–7 passim, *98*, 179–80; "ABC's of the Revolutionary Anarchist," 161–62, 163; on alleged antisemitism, 159–60; Antoni and, 29–33 passim; assassination attempts on, 75, 93, 99–100, 118–21, 125–26, 144; Battle of Perehonivka, 115–18; Berkman and, 153, 154, *154*; Berkman on, 178; Bolshevik relations, 72, 74, 96–102 passim, 122–30 passim; as brand, 179; capture and early imprisonment (1908–10), 35–42; Chernyak and, 111, 170, 189; childhood, 18–25; death and memorials, 7, 177, *178*; disguises, 19, 35, 77, 78–79, 142–43; *Dyelo Truda*, 187; escape (via Romania, Poland, and Belgium) to Paris, 141–48; Grigoriev and, 99, 102–4; Halyna Kuzmenko and, 87–92, 141–48 passim; health decline, 177; Huliaipole return (1918), 75–94 passim; imprisonment (1911–17), 43–55, 71; Kropotkin meeting and correspondence, 70–72; Lenin and, 72, 74, 147; "Letter to the Spanish Anarchists," 162; military

About the Contributors

Charlie Allison is a writer, researcher, and storyteller based in Philadelphia. Charlie has worked as a gardener, tutor to children with learning disabilities, an English teacher, chess instructor, and as a bureaucrat. He has published short stories in Pickman's Press, PodCastle, and Sea Lion Press. He currently runs his own website at charlie-allison.com, where the genesis for this book was formed as a series of YouTube videos with the help of Sewer Rats Productions. He is active in the Philadelphia storytelling and mutual aid communities. Charlie is frequently bullied by his cat in the small hours of the morning.

N.O. Bonzo is an anarchist illustrator, printmaker, and muralist based in Portland, OR. They are the creator of *Off with Their Heads: An Antifascist Coloring Book* and illustrated *Mutual Aid: An Illuminated Factor of Evolution*.

Kevin Matthews is a computer networking expert and avid gamer. He began digital art during the COVID pandemic to increase his friends' engagement in online tabletop games. It was only later that he proceeded to do professional work.

ABOUT PM PRESS

PM Press is an independent, radical publisher of books and media to educate, entertain, and inspire. Founded in 2007 by a small group of people with decades of publishing, media, and organizing experience, PM Press amplifies the voices of radical authors, artists, and activists. Our aim is to deliver bold political ideas and vital stories to people from all walks of life and arm the dreamers to demand the impossible. We have sold millions of copies of our books, most often one at a time, face to face. We're old enough to know what we're doing and young enough to know what's at stake. Join us to create a better world.

PM Press
PO Box 23912
Oakland, CA 94623
www.pmpress.org

PM Press in Europe
europe@pmpress.org
www.pmpress.org.uk

FRIENDS OF PM PRESS

These are indisputably momentous times—the financial system is melting down globally and the Empire is stumbling. Now more than ever there is a vital need for radical ideas.

In the many years since its founding—and on a mere shoestring—PM Press has risen to the formidable challenge of publishing and distributing knowledge and entertainment for the struggles ahead. With hundreds of releases to date, we have published an impressive and stimulating array of literature, art, music, politics, and culture. Using every available medium, we've succeeded in connecting those hungry for ideas and information to those putting them into practice.

Friends of PM allows you to directly help impact, amplify, and revitalize the discourse and actions of radical writers, filmmakers, and artists. It provides us with a stable foundation from which we can build upon our early successes and provides a much-needed subsidy for the materials that can't necessarily pay their own way. You can help make that happen—and receive every new title automatically delivered to your door once a month—by joining as a Friend of PM Press. And, we'll throw in a free T-shirt when you sign up.

Here are your options:

- **$30 a month** Get all books and pamphlets plus a 50% discount on all webstore purchases

- **$40 a month** Get all PM Press releases (including CDs and DVDs) plus a 50% discount on all webstore purchases

- **$100 a month** Superstar—Everything plus PM merchandise, free downloads, and a 50% discount on all webstore purchases

For those who can't afford $30 or more a month, we have **Sustainer Rates** at $15, $10, and $5. Sustainers get a free PM Press T-shirt and a 50% discount on all purchases from our website.

Your Visa or Mastercard will be billed once a month, until you tell us to stop. Or until our efforts succeed in bringing the revolution around. Or the financial meltdown of Capital makes plastic redundant. Whichever comes first.

The Unknown Revolution: 1917–1921

Voline with an Introduction by Iain McKay and Foreword by Rudolf Rocker

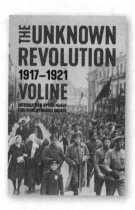

ISBN: 978-1-62963-577-4
$32.95   832 pages

This is the untold story of the Russian Revolution: its antecedents, its far-reaching changes, its betrayal by Bolshevik terror, and the massive resistance of non-Bolshevik revolutionaries. This in-depth, eyewitness history written by Voline, an outspoken activist in the Russian Revolution, is accompanied by a biography of the author by Rudolf Rocker and a contemporary introduction by anarchist historian Iain McKay.

Significant attention is given to what the author describes as "struggles for the real Social Revolution"; that is, the uprising of the sailors and workers of Kronstadt in 1921, and the peasant movement that Nestor Makhno led in Ukraine. These movements, which sought to defend the social revolution from destruction by the politicians, provide important material for a clearer understanding of both the original objectives of the Russian Revolution and the problems with which all revolutions with far-reaching social objectives have to contend.

Drawing on the revolutionary press of the time, Voline reveals the deep cleavage between the objectives of the libertarians and those of the Bolsheviks, differences which the latter "resolved" by ruthlessly eliminating all who stood in their way in the struggle for power.

This edition is a translation of the full text of *La Révolution inconnue*, originally published in French in 1947. It reinstates material omitted from earlier English-language editions and reproduces the complete text of the original volumes.

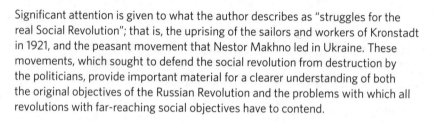

"*A fascinating and valuable book—a combination of history, eyewitness account, and partisan advocacy—about the Russian revolution of 1917–21.*"
—Stephen F. Cohen, author of *Bukharin and the Bolshevik Revolution*

"*In rich detail Voline documents the efforts of workers, peasants, and intellectuals to inaugurate a free society based on local initiative and autonomy. . . . It should be read by every person interested in the anarchist movement and the Russian Revolution.*"
—Paul Avrich, author of *The Russian Anarchists*

Mutual Aid: An Illuminated Factor of Evolution

Peter Kropotkin
Illustrated by N.O. Bonzo with an
Introduction by David Graeber & Andrej
Grubačić, Foreword by Ruth Kinna,
Postscript by GATS, and an Afterword
by Allan Antliff

ISBN: 978-1-62963-874-4 (paperback)
      978-1-62963-875-1 (hardcover)
$30.00/$70.00   336 pages

One hundred years after his death, Peter Kropotkin is still one of the most inspirational figures of the anarchist movement. It is often forgotten that Kropotkin was also a world-renowned geographer whose seminal critique of the hypothesis of competition promoted by social Darwinism helped revolutionize modern evolutionary theory. An admirer of Darwin, he used his observations of life in Siberia as the basis for his 1902 collection of essays *Mutual Aid: A Factor of Evolution*. Kropotkin demonstrated that mutually beneficial cooperation and reciprocity—in both individuals and as a species—plays a far more important role in the animal kingdom and human societies than does individualized competitive struggle. Kropotkin carefully crafted his theory making the science accessible. His account of nature rejected Rousseau's romantic depictions and ethical socialist ideas that cooperation was motivated by the notion of "universal love." His understanding of the dynamics of social evolution shows us the power of cooperation—whether it is bison defending themselves against a predator or workers unionizing against their boss. His message is clear: solidarity is strength!

Every page of this new edition of *Mutual Aid* has been beautifully illustrated by one of anarchism's most celebrated current artists, N.O. Bonzo. The reader will also enjoy original artwork by GATS and insightful commentary by David Graeber, Ruth Kinna, Andrej Grubačić, and Allan Antliff.

"N.O. Bonzo has created a rare document, updating Kropotkin's anarchist classic Mutual Aid, *by intertwining compelling imagery with an updated text. Filled with illustrious examples, their art gives the words and histories, past and present, resonance for new generations to seed flowers of cooperation to push through the concrete of resistance to show liberatory possibilities for collective futures."*
—scott crow, author of *Black Flags and Windmills* and *Setting Sights*

Off with Their Heads: An Antifascist Coloring Book for Adults of All Ages

Illustrated by N.O. Bonzo

ISBN: 978-1-62963-859-1
$10.00   24 pages

A coloring book that brings back the whimsy and delight of the olden days, when more often than not it was the maiden who slayed the dragon, and the heads of tyrants were carried off at the end of a pike.

Beneath the Pavement the Garden: An Anarchist Coloring Book for All Ages

Illustrated by N.O. Bonzo

ISBN: 979-8-88744-003-3
$10.00   24 pages

Beneath the Pavement the Garden is a coloring book featuring the artwork of N.O. Bonzo. Kids and adults of all ages are invited to let their imagination soar with this beautiful celebration of the many forms of anarchism, from direct action and mutual aid to abolition, community gardens, and more.

The Colonel Pyat Quartet

Michael Moorcock
with introductions by Alan Wall

Byzantium Endures
ISBN: 978-1-60486-491-5
$22.00   400 pages

The Laughter of Carthage
ISBN: 978-1-60486-492-2
$22.00   448 pages

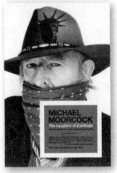

Jerusalem Commands
ISBN: 978-1-60486-493-9
$22.00   448 pages

The Vengeance of Rome
ISBN: 978-1-60486-494-6
$23.00   500 pages

Moorcock's Pyat Quartet has been described as an authentic masterpiece of the 20th and 21st centuries. It's the story of Maxim Arturovitch Pyatnitski, a cocaine addict, sexual adventurer, and obsessive anti-Semite whose epic journey from Leningrad to London connects him with scoundrels and heroes from Trotsky to Makhno, and whose career echoes that of the 20th century's descent into Fascism and total war.

It is Michael Moorcock's extraordinary achievement to convert the life of Maxim Pyatnitski into epic and often hilariously comic adventure. Sustained by his dreams and profligate inventions, his determination to turn his back on the realities of his own origins, Pyat runs from crisis to crisis, every ruse a further link in a vast chain of deceit, suppression, betrayal. Yet, in his deranged self-deception, his monumentally distorted vision, this thoroughly unreliable narrator becomes a lens for focusing, through the dimensions of wild farce and chilling terror, on an uneasy brand of truth.

The Bonnot Gang: The Story of the French Illegalists, 2nd ed.

Richard Parry

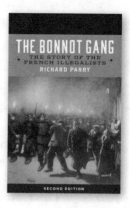

ISBN: 978-1-62963-143-1
$18.95   288 pages

This is the story of the infamous Bonnot Gang: the most notorious French anarchists ever, and as bank expropriators the inventors of the motorized "getaway." It is the story of how the anarchist taste for illegality developed into illegalism—the theory that theft is liberating in itself. And how a number of young anarchists met in Paris in the years before the First World War, determined to live their lives to the full, regardless of the consequences.

Paris in 1911 was a city of riots, strikes, and savage repression of the working class. A stronghold of foreign exiles and homegrown revolutionaries, it was also the base of *L'Anarchie*, the outspoken individualist weekly. *L'Anarchie* drew together people for whom crime and revolution went hand in hand. There was Victor Kibalchich (later known as Victor Serge), whose inflammatory articles would put him on trial with the rest. Then there was the gang itself: Victor's childhood friend Raymond-La-Science, the tuberculous André Soudy, the serious-minded René Valet, Simentoff the southerner, and lastly the prime motivators of the group—the remorseless Octave Garnier and the experienced Jules Bonnot. Their robberies, daring and violent, would give them a lasting notoriety in France. Their deaths, as spectacular as their lives, would make them a legend among revolutionaries the world over.

Extensively researched and fully illustrated with rare period photos, drawings, and maps, this updated edition is the best account of the Bonnot Gang to appear in any language.

"*The first book on the subject in English, and one based on original research in the various libraries and collections in Paris, Amsterdam, and London. . . . Although the book is written as a history, the style is journalistic rather than stuffily academic, and paced so that the narrative gets progressively more exciting. All in all, this is that rare book indeed. It is a good read and action-packed; but also meticulously researched with an impressive attention to detail.*"
—*New Anarchist Review*

"*Although Parry does not try to romanticize the protagonists, the conclusion of the book does try to interpret their story as a political event arising out of the class struggle. . . . It will be widely read; it ought to be widely discussed.*"
—Nicholas Walter in *Freedom*

Words of a Rebel

Peter Kropotkin
Translated and edited by Iain McKay
with a Preface by Elisée Reclus

ISBN: 978-1-62963-877-5
$24.95   320 pages

Peter Kropotkin remains one of the best-known
anarchist thinkers, and *Words of a Rebel* was his first
libertarian book. Published in 1885 while he was in
a French jail for anarchist activism, this collection
of articles from the newspaper *Le Revolté* sees Kropotkin criticise the failings
of capitalism and those who seek to end it by means of its main support, the
state. Instead, he urged the creation of a mass movement from below that would
expropriate property and destroy the state, replacing their centralised hierarchies
with federations of self-governing communities and workplaces.

Kropotkin's instant classic included discussions themes and ideas he returned
to repeatedly during his five decades in the anarchist movement. Unsurprisingly,
Words of a Rebel was soon translated into numerous languages—including Italian,
Spanish, Bulgarian, Russian, and Chinese—and reprinted time and time again.
But despite its influence as Kropotkin's first anarchist work, it was the last to be
completely translated into English.

This is a new translation from the French original by Iain McKay except for a few
chapters previously translated by Nicolas Walter. Both anarchist activists and
writers, they are well placed to understand the assumptions within and influences
on Kropotkin's revolutionary journalism. It includes all the original 1885 text along
with the preface to the 1904 Italian as well as the preface and afterward to the 1919
Russian editions. In addition, it includes many articles on the labour movement
written by Kropotkin for *Le Revolté* which show how he envisioned getting from
criticism to a social revolution. Along with a comprehensive glossary and an
introduction by Iain McKay placing this work within the history of anarchism as
well as indicating its relevance to radicals and revolutionaries today, this is the
definitive edition of an anarchist classic.

*"Peter Kropotkin was a giant of socialist history whose tireless scientific, historical,
and political scholarship and agitational writing united and fueled the transnational
anarchist movement of the turn of the twentieth century. But this aristocrat turned
revolutionary didn't start there.* Words of a Rebel *sheds light on the young Kropotkin's
political transformation in the wake of the destruction of the First International. By
including articles from* Le Revolté, *this volume traces Kropotkin's political journey
farther as he sewed the early seeds of anarchist communism and set an agenda for
anti-authoritarian rebellion for years to come."*
—Mark Bray, author of *Antifa: The Anti-Fascist Handbook* and coeditor of *Anarchist
Education and the Modern School*

The Great French Revolution, 1789–1793

Peter Kropotkin
with an Introduction by David Berry

ISBN: 978-1-62963-876-8
$29.95   448 pages

The Great French Revolution, 1789–1793 is Peter
Kropotkin's most substantial historical work. In it he
presents a people's history of the world-shaking events
of the Revolution and shows the key role the working
men and women of the towns and countryside played in it. Without the constant
pressure of popular organisations and activity, the politicians would never have
created a Republic, nor been able to survive the counterrevolutionary forces
internally or externally.

Focusing on such mass movements—and especially the peasant majority—rather
than on the few great men beloved of bourgeois accounts, this is a groundbreaking
account of the period and a seminal work of "history from below." Later research
may have corrected some factual details and opened new avenues of scholarship,
but Kropotkin's text remains an exemplar of anarchist history-writing, challenging
both bourgeois republican and Marxist interpretations of the Revolution.

Yet it is more than a history: Kropotkin uses the experience of the French Revolution
to aid us in our current struggles and to learn its lessons in order to ensure the
success of future revolutions. This book raises issues which have resurfaced time
and again, as well as offering solutions based on the self-activity of the masses, the
new, decentralised, directly democratic social organisations they forged during the
Revolution, and the need to transform a political revolt into a social revolution which
seeks to secure the well-being of all by transforming the economy from the start.

*"The French Revolution erupted out of the remnants of the old world and set a dynamic
precedent for new centuries of resistance. Multifaceted, contradictory, and compelling,
the French Revolution cast an enormous shadow that influenced every radical faction
of 19th century politics. Peter Kropotkin was perhaps the preeminent anarchist intellect
of his generation, and so his book* The Great French Revolution, 1789–1793 *provides
us with a fascinating exploration into the late 19th century anarchist vision of historical
transformation. This saga of popular upheaval from below provides a fascinating mirror
image of how Kropotkin and many of his comrades envisioned the coming revolution."*
—Mark Bray, author of *Antifa: The Anti-Fascist Handbook* and co-editor of *Anarchist
Education and the Modern School: A Francisco Ferrer Reader*